Describing
Talk

Sage's *Series in Interpersonal Communication* is designed to capture the breadth and depth of knowledge emanating from scientific examinations of face-to-face interaction. As such, the volumes in this series address the cognitive and overt behavior manifested by communicators as they pursue various conversational outcomes. The application of research findings to specific types of interpersonal relationships (e.g., marital, managerial) is also an important dimension of this series.

SAGE SERIES IN
INTERPERSONAL COMMUNICATION
Mark L. Knapp, Series Editor

Describing Talk

A Taxonomy of Verbal Response Modes

William B. Stiles

Sage Series

Interpersonal Communication 12

SAGE Publications
International Educational and Professional Publisher
Newbury Park   London   New Delhi

For information address:

SAGE Publications, Inc.
2455 Teller Road
Newbury Park, California 91320

SAGE Publications Ltd.
6 Bonhill Street
London EC2A 4PU
United Kingdom

SAGE Publications India Pvt. Ltd.
M-32 Market
Greater Kailash I
New Delhi 110 048 India

Printed in the United States of America

Library of Congress Cataloging-in-Publication Data

Stiles, William B., 1944-
    Describing talk: a taxonomy of verbal response modes / William B. Stiles.
        p.   cm.—(Sage series in interpersonal communication; v. 12)
    Includes bibliographical references and indexes.
    ISBN 0-8039-4464-0.—ISBN 0-8039-4465-9 (pbk.)
    1. Interpersonal communication. 2. Verbal behavior—Classification. I. Title. II. Series.
    BF637.C45S76   1992
    306.4′4—dc20   92-7523

92 93 94 95 10 9 8 7 6 5 4 3 2 1

Sage Production Editor: Chiara C. Huddleston

NWST
I ADF0610

Contents

Preface:
How to Use This Book

This book is an introduction to describing talk using a taxonomy of verbal response modes (VRMs). It presents the development of the taxonomy, its conceptual underpinnings, and some of the research that has used it. It also fully describes how to apply the VRM system to the classification of speech acts in any sort of natural discourse. Because this book is a manual for coders as well as an introduction to the approach, some material is repeated, so that coders are more likely to encounter it when they need it.

This book is intended for researchers and students in any discipline who are interested in how talk contributes to relationships between people and for coders—people who are engaged in classifying utterances in discourse. Together with its associated computer disk, it is a self-contained coder training program, appropriate for learning how to apply the VRM system in research or for inclusion as a unit in university courses on any subject that involves language and communication in human relationships.

In overview, Chapters 1 to 4 describe the taxonomy's background and context, while Chapters 5 to 10 comprise a manual for VRM classification, and Chapter 11 offers some suggestions for using the taxonomy in research. Chapter 1 describes the taxonomy's development. Chapter 2 gives a brief overview of the taxonomy and lists its technical features. Chapter 3 compares this coding system with some other approaches to studying verbal interaction. Chapter 4 illustrates the sorts of research in which the VRM system has been used and includes a guide to published VRM studies. Chapter 5 formally presents theoretical concepts involved in construction of the taxonomy, including the principles of classification and levels of meaning. Chapter 6 describes each of the VRM intents, with examples of subtypes of each mode. Chapter 7 presents the VRM form categories and discusses mixed modes—utterances whose form and intent differ. Chapter 8 discusses the VRM unit—the utterance. This includes a theoretical discussion of a psychological unit of communication, a grammatical definition of an utterance, with examples, and a practical discussion of criteria for unitizing natural language. Chapters 9 and 10 present rules (and the conceptual derivation of the rules) for discriminating among codes. These include a variety of "litmus tests"— mental experiments for deciding between certain pairs of codes. Chapter 9 focuses on discriminating among mode intents. Chapter 10 focuses on coding of brief utterances and on decision rules for VRM form codes, with examples from a variety of settings. Chapter 11 discusses the preparation of verbal interaction data for VRM coding, training coders, alternative coding procedures, calculation of VRM reliability, and the aggregation of VRM codes for statistical analysis. It lists some quantitative indexes that can be derived from VRM coding.

In addition to the general index, there is an index of examples organized by their VRM form-intent codes.

This book is designed to be read differently depending on readers' purposes. Readers who just want to learn the coding system can skip the first four chapters and begin with Chapter 5. For them, I recommend also to begin immediately using the computer disk that accompanies this book and to become acquainted with the book's table of contents and indexes. Readers who seek a conceptual background describing talk and the taxonomy can read Chapters 1 to 7 and skip the relatively technical details in Chapters 8 to 11. Readers who want a quick description of the coding system and how to use it can look at Chapters 2 and 11 (readers who are trying to decide whether this particular taxonomy meets their research needs might also look at Chapters 3 and 4). Chapter 1 explains how I came to construct the system in this particular way and is likely to be of interest even though it is not essential for understanding the system itself.

The disk that accompanies this book is a computer-assisted training program in VRM coding. Although the book and the disk are complementary, each can be used independently. The training program is written in PC/Pilot, a proprietary language for educational software (Washington Computer Services, Bellingham, WA), and it can be run on any MS-DOS (IBM-compatible) microcomputer. To run the program, insert the disk in your default drive, type "START," press Enter, and follow directions. For some brief program notes, type "README."

Acknowledgments

Like most intellectual endeavors, the taxonomy of verbal response modes described in this book is the product of many minds. Jerry Goodman's response modes framework was its basis and starting point, as described in Chapter 1, and he has continued to support (and critique) my work on it. Brian Premo was my principal sounding board during the taxonomy's early development, and he made many contributions. In the years that I have worked on extending and refining the taxonomy, I have had extensive and essential help from my students, my teachers, my colleagues, my critics, my collaborators, and especially those who have worked as coders on research projects. I am indebted and grateful to all for the uncounted hours we have spent in discussion of fine and not-so-fine points of grammar, meaning, classification, communication, coder training, and human relationships, and for everyone's comments on the various earlier drafts and versions of descriptions of the taxonomy. Inevitably, I will fail to mention some of the people who have helped, but I won't let that stop me from naming as many as I can. I acknowledge and thank Judith Ahrberg, Cathy Andrews, Laurie Arneke, Melinda Au, Cyndy Baker, Nancy Baker, Margot Barth, Leslie Bartolf, Laine Barton, Nancy Bateman, Rich Bebout, Archie Blanchard, Dana Booe, Michelle Boyd, Pat Brady, Julie Buker, Kim Bullock, Sue Burchill, Kim Burnham, Dean Burnside, Ken Cannon, David Cansler, Isabel Caro, Ed Caropreso, Nicolay Chertkoff, Karen Claus, Kathy Cody, Sharon Cohn, Theresa Colter, Barb Crawford, Laurie Cringle, Elizabeth Cummings, Donna Daeke, Christy Davis, Donna Davis, Randy Davis, Chess Denman, Teri Dill-Standiford, Regina Diulus, Dierdire Donaldson, Mollie Driscol, Debbie Dye, Kevin Edwards, Ruth Egbert, Robin Eisenberg, Robert Elliott, Leslie Estep, Amy Fardella, Chris Farley, Melinda Ferrell, Melissa Ferrell, Laura Finks, Jenny Firth-Cozens, Mary Kate Francis, Zaida Franklin, Bill Freeman, Lisa Furnish, Tracy Gebing,

Terry Gillis, Tina Gnagy, Lori Granchi, Erica Grodhaus, Amy Hamilton, Terry Hamilton, Jim Hannas, Marianne Hansen, Catherine Hanshaw, Monica Hardy, Yvette Harris, Susie Haw, Karen Heil, Elizabeth Held, Sherry Hemphill, Bill Henricks, Lee Anne Herbst, Cliff Hester, Steve Hinkle, Carol Hinshaw, Kathy Holtzman, Jenny Hopkins, Deborah Houchins, Brenda Huddle, Molly Hunter, Sherry Hutchison, Graham Irwin, Jim Jackson, Casey Jacob, Julie Jacobs, Kristen Jacobson, Sherman James, Debra Jamieson, Robin Jarrett, Sheri Johnson, Al Jones, Thomas Jones, Cheryl Joseph, Margaret Joyce, Barbara Kappus, Megan Kelly, Donald Kiesler, Clemmie King, David Knight, Linda Knotts, Elizabeth Knowles, Ellen Kostas, Kelly Kutz, Joyce Labbe, Teri LaJeunesse, Charles Lange, Terry Laquatra, Anne Marie Lasoski, Bob Lawrence, Mark Leary, Camille Leaver, Laura LeBlanc, Mark LeDoux, Linda Lee, Sherri Lee, Scott Lencke, Elizabeth Lewis, Maribeth Lichty, Thomas Lintner, Lauren Loflin, Joe Lowman, Carolyn Lowry, Judy Madigan, Sandy Malek, Jan Markham, Mary Ann Martello, Margaret Martin, Lisa Mason, Jennifer Mattox, Christy Mausser, Bridget McCafferty, Alicia McCallum, Susan McDaniel, Kim McGaughey, Kate McGonagle, Cathy McHugh, Lee McIlwain, Linda McMullen, Lisa Meyer, Nancy Miller, Linda Moline, Leslie Morrison, Gloria Murray, Todd Nahigian, Andy Nocita, Lynda Olsen-Fulero, Jim Orth, Lori Packard, Bruce Palmer, Patsy Peebles, Julia Perlmutter, Vanessa Pittard, George Ploghoft, Sam Putnam, Cathy Read, Julie Rhein, Susana Rosin, Andy Russell, Robert Russell, Larry Scherwitz, Fred Schiir, Carol Schofield, Kim Scola, David Shapiro, Erik Shickedanz, Cecilia Shore, Paul Shuster, Ellen Skurla, Bill Sloan, Richard Smith, Steve Snow, Vicky Sohmer, Susan Sorkin, John Spaulding, Helen Spencer, Natalie Staats, Katie Stack, Lori Steinbrunner, Nancy Stella, Chris Stevens, Beth Storie, Julie Strater, Faye Sultan, Laurie Taylor, Lee Teevan, Phillip Terbay, Alice Thomasson, Victoria Tingen, Jim Troy, Dawn Tucker, Larry Tupler, Carolyn Turbyfill, Helene Ulrich, Suzanne Van Niman, Ally VanOrder, Vicki Vaugn, PJ Violand, Gary Walls, Lisa Walters, Cindy Waszak, Marie Waung, Michelle Whisman, Kathy White, Kim White, Lauren White, Gae Whitener, Dave Wilkerson, Laura Williams, Jane Wilson, Matt Wolf, Milton Wright, Lisa Wurzelbacher, Lee Younts, Kathy Zimmerman, Gail Elkind, Felisa Goldstein, Mary O'Brien, Sarah Turbott, and Sue Stiles.

I also thank Series Editor Mark Knapp for his patient and persistent encouragement over at least 8 years, and the Sage editorial staff, including Ann West, Marie Louise Penchoen, Susan McElroy, Stephanie T. Hoppe, and Chiara C. Huddleston for their responsiveness and help in preparing the manuscript for print.

1

Development of
the Taxonomy

Jerry Goodman introduced me to response modes in the spring of 1969 when I was a graduate student in clinical psychology at UCLA and he was my clinical supervisor. He used the modes to describe my alternatives as I tried to listen and respond helpfully to my psychotherapy clients. He distinguished six categories of "help-intended" communication: (a) Question, for gathering information, (b) Advisement, for guiding another's behavior, (c) Silence, for providing interpersonal space, (d) Interpretation, for explaining or classifying another's behavior, (e) Reflection, for expressing empathy, and (f) Disclosure, for revealing one's personal condition (Goodman & Dooley, 1976; Goodman & Esterly, 1988).

I was attracted to the response modes at first by the therapeutic power of Reflections. I was fascinated by the process-facilitating effects of "simply" repeating a client's communication, in comparison to, say, the process-deflecting effects of Questions. Reflections were followed by deeper exploration; Questions were followed by a change in direction. In the tapes of therapy, in my work as a therapist, and in my own experience of being listened to, response modes seemed to make a dramatic difference.

My encounter with Jerry and response modes occurred in the middle of my graduate training, and its influence on my practice and research was delayed a few years. By late 1973, however, as an assistant professor of psychology at the University of North Carolina, I had begun to study the response modes seriously. I had reread Rogers's (1951) *Client-Centered Therapy* and adopted a very nondirective style of psychotherapy, therapy supervision, and classroom teaching. For me,

Reflections were a core technique. I decided to investigate the effects of response modes in psychotherapy, grinding the axe that Reflections were more therapeutic than other modes. (That's what I thought then, though I no longer think the world is so simple.) I hypothesized that client-perceived "high spots" in therapy sessions would be associated with Reflections more than with other therapist responses. I gathered tape-recorded therapy sessions and postsession questionnaires about clients' in-session experiences. This project eventually foundered on the difficulty of identifying high spots from the client descriptions (but see Elliott & Shapiro, 1988, for a more successful procedure). Nevertheless, it focused my attention on classifying therapists' interventions.

From the outset, the Goodman response mode framework seemed to me to carve nature at the joints. I assumed that each therapist response would fit in one and only one of the six modes. I expected to find "litmus tests"—mental experiments for distinguishing between categories in difficult cases. (I use the term litmus test by analogy with the chemical test in which a strip of litmus paper dipped in a solution turns pink or blue depending on whether the solution is acidic or basic.) For example, I knew that Interpretation and Reflection were distinguished by the viewpoint, or frame of reference, adopted in a therapist's intervention. Responses that take the therapist's viewpoint, such as **"You seem to restrict your choices,"** are Interpretations, whereas responses that take the client's viewpoint, such as **"You wish you could take more risks,"** are Reflections. Confronted with a difficult discrimination between Interpretation and Reflection, I could ask, "Whose frame of reference is being used?" and solve the puzzle. Student coders and I identified a variety of such tests as we tried to improve coding reliability.

In October 1974, Brian Premo (then a first-year graduate student) and I found a litmus test to distinguish between Interpretations and Advisements: Whether the topic of the response was drawn from the experience of the therapist or of the client. Interpretations concerned the client's experience or ideas, whereas Advisements (a directive category that includes commands, suggestions, permission, and prohibition) concerned the therapist's experience or ideas. For example, **"You have only hurt yourself by lying about it"** concerns the client's feelings and is an Interpretation, whereas **"You might as well tell the truth"** concerns the therapist's idea of what to do and is an Advisement.

In a key insight, we realized that the principle underlying this litmus test, which we called *source of experience* (i.e., client's experience as topic versus therapist's experience as topic), applied equally to any therapist response and helped to describe all of the modes. Not only Interpretations, but also therapist Questions and Reflections clearly concerned the client's experience, whereas therapist Disclosures as well as Advisements clearly concerned the therapist's experience. (We used the term "experience" broadly, to include knowledge, ideas, beliefs, feelings, memories, perceptions, intentions, and even voluntary behaviors.) Silence was slightly problematic, because a silence didn't involve anybody's experience explicitly. In the Goodman framework, therapist Silence was considered as providing interpersonal space for the client, so we classified it as concerning the client's experience.

Intrigued, we asked: Are there other principles that, like source of experience, can distinguish between sets of modes? We realized we had been using such a principle already in frame of reference (i.e., client's viewpoint versus therapist's viewpoint), though we so far had applied it only to distinguish Reflections from Interpretations. Not only in Reflections, however, but also in Goodman-conceived Silences, therapists adopted the client's frame of reference, whereas in Advisements, Disclosures, and Questions, as well as in Interpretations, therapists used their own frame of reference.

Cross-classifying the modes by these two *principles of classification,* source of experience and frame of reference, seemed to help characterize the modes. The principles described what therapists were doing in the interventions psychologically. In Reflection (**"You feel proud of your promotion"**), the therapist attempted to express the client's experience as viewed from within the client's own frame of reference—seeing the experience as the client saw it; indeed, Rogers (1951) described Client-Centered Reflections in very similar terms. In Interpretation (**"Perhaps you were overreacting"**), the therapist also talked about the client's experience, but placed it in some external frame of reference—the therapists' own or perhaps some psychological theory—sometimes bringing a new perspective to the client's experience. Therapist Questions (**"How did that make you feel?"**) could be construed as revealing gaps in the therapist's frame of reference and the seeking of information from the client to fill the gaps. Therapist Disclosures (**"I'm finding it hard to listen today"**) expressed the therapist's experience (thoughts or feelings) from the therapist's own viewpoint.

Representing the cross-classification of the six Goodman modes by the two principles as a 2 × 2 matrix (Table 1.1) revealed (to me) a striking incompleteness and asymmetry. There was a blank cell, which reminded me of missing elements in the chemical periodic table. And

TABLE 1.1

Initial Classification of Therapist Response Modes by Source of Experience
and Frame of Reference

| Source of Experience | Frame of Reference | |
	Client	*Therapist*
Client	REFLECTION	INTERPRETATION
	SILENCE	QUESTION
Therapist		ADVISEMENT
		DISCLOSURE

although there were two modes within each cell, the within-cell pairings involved surprisingly dissimilar modes. For example, Interpretation and Question were paired, whereas to me, Interpretation seemed intuitively more similar to Reflection or to Advisement than to Question. Perhaps, we thought, there is some third principle of classification that could distinguish between the modes in each pair. We spent several months identifying and refining our concepts of the third principle and two missing modes.

The third principle, which we identified before the seventh and eighth modes, distinguished Reflection, Interpretation, and Advisement from their Table 1.1 cell mates, Silence, Question, and Disclosure, respectively. The distinguishing feature was whether the therapist had to presume knowledge of the client's experience in order to make the response. In Reflection, Interpretation, and Advisement, the therapist must presume to know what the client's experience is, was, will be, or should be; in the other modes, no such presumption is required. For example, the Interpretation, **"You are exaggerating its importance,"** presumes to know what the client's experience is, whereas the Question, **"How important is this to you?"** requires no such presumption (the speaker may make presumptions privately, but these are not necessary for the Question to have the meaning it has). The Advisement, **"Tell me about your job,"** presumes to know what the client should do (in effect, imposing an experience), whereas the Disclosure, **"I'm glad you told me that,"** does not. The Reflection, **"You were frightened by his threats,"** presumes to understand the client's feelings, whereas a Silence, allowing space, does not.

The name for this presuming principle was problematic. We called it "full versus empty" at first, and we used the name "focus" for several years, but I think it is most informative to call it *presumption about experience*. Three of the modes in Table 1.1 required presumptions about the client's experience (i.e., Reflection, Interpretation, and Advisement); the other three require no such presumption (Silence, Question, Disclosure) and could be said to require the therapist to presume knowledge only of his or her own experience.

The intersection of the three principles pointed us toward the missing modes. Both concerned the therapist's experience and used the client's frame of reference, but they differed in their presumptions—one presuming and one not presuming to know what the client's experience actually was. Although we began with only these characterizations, in the end these two modes seemed as distinct and coherent as the other six.

Therapist *Edifications* concern the therapist's experience but use the client's frame of reference and make no specific presumptions about the client. There is a paradox in using the client's frame of reference without presuming knowledge of the client's experience. The resolution is that the frame of reference is a neutral, general viewpoint shared by *any* other person. Thus, Edifications are representations about objective reality—simple informational statements, such as **"She told me she was going shopping,"** or **"The clinic is on Oak Street."** In retrospect, it seemed surprising that we had not included such a category earlier, as Edifications are common and recognizably distinct. They may have been left out of the Goodman framework because most therapists convey facts relatively rarely, and when they do, they often have some ulterior (e.g., interpretive or directive) purpose.

Naming this category was difficult, and our meaning for "Edification" differs from the common meaning of "edification," referring only to conveying objective information, without necessarily implying that the client is thereby improved. Alternative names such as "Assertion" or "Information" or "Report" seemed too broad.

Therapist *Confirmations* also concern the therapist's experience and use the client's frame of reference, but *do* presume knowledge of the client's experience. These are expressions of agreement, disagreement, or shared experience, such as **"We make a great team," "We disagree about the importance of homework,"** or **"We seem to have reached an impasse."** Such responses convey the therapist's ideas or opinions (therapist's experience), but explicitly compare these to the client's ideas. To make such a comparison, the therapist must presume to understand this particular client's point of view.

The name "Confirmation" does not imply positivity or agreement; **"We disagree"** is just as much a Confirmation as **"We agree."** The name was chosen for its connotation of interpersonal connection: One confirms another person by using his or her viewpoint. Both agreement and disagreement entail presuming to know what the other person thinks.

As a final change in the list of modes, we switched from Silence to *Acknowledgment.* The Silence category had been a continuing problem. Alone among the modes, it was a nonverbal response. Coding pauses in the conversation had presented practical problems: When had a Silence taken place?—How long did the pause need to be? How many Silences should be coded?—Should a long pause be coded as more than one response? Who should receive credit?—When was a pause to count as a therapist Silence and when as a client Silence? After much discussion, and with considerable reluctance, I became convinced that Silence belongs to another realm of phenomena than the other modes, a nonverbal or paralinguistic realm that might encompass interruptions, verbal crowding and allowing, and the management of attention in conversation. This realm is no less important, but it is conceptually separate (see Chapter 3). The verbal response mode category that concerns the other's experience and uses the other's frame of reference but presumes no knowledge of either is better called Acknowledgment.

Acknowledgments are brief, contentless utterances such as **"mm-hm"** and **"oh."** We had had to confront such responses early in our work, because psychotherapists used them very frequently. We had reasoned that **"mm-hm"** and similar utterances were a sort of vocalized Silence, and we coded them as Silences (this now sounds like stretching, but it seemed reasonable at the time). They fit the principles well. The topic of a therapist's **"mm-hm"** was whatever the client had just said (client's experience). The frame of reference adopted was the client's (i.e., the **"mm-hm"** merely signaled receipt of the client's communication). And no specific presumption about the client's experience was entailed; in fact, therapists often said **"mm-hm"** before the client had completed a thought, so no coherent presumption was possible. Thus, when we changed names from Silence to Acknowledgment, we already had in mind a coherent category of verbalizations. The switch made it easier for us to accommodate contentless lexical utterances such as **"yeah,"** **"no,"** and **"hello"** in the category; these fit the principles and seemed appropriately described as Acknowledgments, whereas we had been unable to bring ourselves to call them Silences.

GENERALIZING THE TAXONOMY

I had initially considered the response mode system as a classification of therapist interventions to clients in psychotherapy, or of helpers to help seekers in circumstances analogous to therapy. I had begun by calling the categories *listener response modes* (Stiles, 1975), designed to classify the "help-intended communication" by a "listener" who listened helpfully while a "discloser" revealed a personal concern (see discussion of the Goodman system in Chapter 3). We had called the poles of the three principles "therapist" and "client," or even more confusingly, "listener" and "discloser." It gradually became clear that this construction was far too limited, and that the categories could be used to describe any verbal communication from one person (or collectivity) to another.

In recognition of this far greater generality, we began calling the poles of the principles "speaker" and "other." For example, an Interpretation is described as concerning the other's experience and presuming knowledge of the other's experience, but using the speaker's frame of reference. Both members of a dyad (e.g., client as well as therapist) can be speakers in turn, and the taxonomy applies equally to both. Thus, "speaker" characterizes a momentary role or activity, rather than a fixed role (such as "therapist"). The "other" can be not just another person, but any entity to which talk is directed, including a group or an audience or even a nonhuman, inanimate, or abstract entity.

We also began calling the categories *verbal response modes* (VRMs), in recognition of their applicability to any verbal communication. The categories are theoretically universal, insofar as any verbal communication must be from one center of experience (the speaker) to another (the other). As a general-purpose system, the VRM taxonomy permits direct comparisons across roles (e.g., therapist versus client, doctor versus patient, husband versus wife, parent versus child), as well as across types of relationships or types of discourse. The VRM system has been used to study verbal communication in medicine, law, politics, education, entertainment, advertising, and social and family relations, as well as in psychotherapy (see Chapter 4), and many other applications are possible.

With the addition of Edification and Confirmation and the changes from Silence to Acknowledgment and from "therapist" and "client" to "speaker" and "other," the taxonomy took on a form that has remained stable in its essentials since about 1976. A published manual appeared

TABLE 1.2

Final Classification of Verbal Response Modes

Source of Experience	Presumption About Experience	Frame of Reference	
		Other	*Speaker*
Other	Other	REFLECTION (R)	INTERPRETATION (I)
	Speaker	ACKNOWLEDGMENT (K)	QUESTION (Q)
Speaker	Other	CONFIRMATION (C)	ADVISEMENT (A)
	Speaker	EDIFICATION (E)	DISCLOSURE (D)

in 1978 (Stiles, 1978a). This stable version is summarized in Table 1.2 and is fully elaborated in Chapters 5 to 10.

An important change that emerged gradually while the system was being developed was a shift to *defining* the modes by the principles of classification. The modes began as intuitively recognized classes of utterances, and the principles began as coding aids, or litmus tests, intended to help make distinctions between modes. With the 2 × 2 × 2 taxonomy complete (Table 1.2), however, it became possible to reverse this situation and define the modes by the principles. In effect, the system pulled itself up by its bootstraps. Coders can classify any utterance by answering three questions: Whose experience is the topic? Does the utterance require the speaker to presume knowledge of the other's experience? And whose frame of reference is used? These three forced choices place any utterance in one of the eight VRM categories.

This changeover required surprisingly little alteration in the contents of the categories. The original Goodman modes were built on common intuition, extensive observation, and clinical experience, and they approximated categories that had been widely used in theory, research, and counselor training. The principle-defined categories are essentially identical, still easily recognizable and intuitively distinct.

I think that the principles of classification help to explain why these particular categories seem natural and hence why the principle-defined categories are essentially the same as the intuitively defined ones. Each principle takes the values of "speaker" and "other," reflecting the most obvious line of demarcation in any interpersonal communication (there are no plausible intermediate values). Thus, the distinctness and coherence of the mode categories reflect the separateness of the people who are communicating.

The principles offer a basis for saying that the system is a mutually exclusive and exhaustive classification. By deciding (a) whether the source of experience is the speaker or the other, (b) whether the utterance required presumptions about the other, and (c) whether the speaker's or the other's frame of reference was used, a coder can place every utterance in one and only one category. Of course, "exhaustiveness" in this sense implies only that every utterance can be classified; it does not imply that all of the utterance's meaning is conveyed by the classification. Many distinctions are possible within each mode (see Chapters 3 and 6). Indeed, it would be possible to make the same claim of exhaustiveness about a system that used only one principle. For example, a system that used only the source of experience principle could exhaustively classify utterances into informative (speaker's experience) and attentive (other's experience) categories.

FORMS AND MIXED MODES

It had been clear all along that mixtures of the modes were possible. For example, Goodman and Dooley (1976) acknowledged the existence of "hybrid responses such as Question-in-service-of-Advisement" (p. 106), utterances that are grammatical questions but are intended as directives, for example, **"Can you say that again with more feeling?"** or **"Is it a good idea to be wearing such a heavy sweater?"**

The notion that each mode had a characteristic grammatical form, but that the grammatical form could be used to express other mode intents, was incorporated into the taxonomy systematically.

Very early in my work, I made an assumption that each mode had an associated set of grammatical features and that each utterance could be classified on the basis of these features alone, independently of its classification according to the principles. Thus, each utterance was classified twice, once for form and once for intent. The same eight mode names are used for both form and intent classification. Utterances in which form and intent coincide (e.g., Advisement in service of Advisement) are called *pure modes;* utterances in which form and intent differ (e.g., Disclosure in service of Advisement) are called *mixed modes.* The grammatical criteria for each of the eight form categories are presented and discussed in detail in Chapter 7.

Each of the 64 possible form-intent combinations can be written as a two-letter code. Each mode is abbreviated by its first letter, except for

Acknowledgment, which is abbreviated "K." As a notational convention, the form symbol is written first, and the intent symbol second:

Sit down. AA

Would you sit down? QA

I'd like you to sit down. DA

In earlier publications, the intent symbol was enclosed in parentheses—for example, D(A)—but this now seems unnecessary.

A grammatical form retains some of its force even when it is used to express a different intent. For example, the psychological force of the Question form of **"Would you get me some coffee?"** (QA) attenuates the Advisement intent, making it less presumptuous, more attentive, and hence relatively polite (in comparison to **"Get me some coffee"** [AA]). Such form-intent discrepancies seem often to signal conflicting social pressures. In general, directing someone to do something while minimizing the social imposition yields a realm of form-intent discrepancies that contribute to *politeness* (Brown & Levinson, 1978; Stiles, 1981). These involve using nonpresumptuous forms (Question, Disclosure, Acknowledgment, Edification) to express presumptuous intents (especially Advisement and Interpretation).

Similarly, the Acknowledgment form of yes/no answers contributes to their impact in a conversation. In a yes or no answer, a speaker can, in effect, use the other's words to convey a feeling, impart information, or give directions:

(Are you angry with me?) **No.** KD (conveys feeling)

(Has it stopped raining?) **No.** KE (imparts information)

(Should I slow down?) **No.** KA (gives directions)

Using Acknowledgment forms thus conveys attentiveness and acquiescence at a formal level; the Disclosure, Edification, or Advisement intent conveys information or direction at an intentional level. These mixed modes seemed to me to capture this subtle, relational aspect of question/ answer exchanges.

A few years after the taxonomy had been constructed, I did some reading in linguistics and philosophy (including Austin, 1975; Bach & Harnish, 1979; Grice, 1957, 1969; Searle, 1969) and realized that form and intent can be described as representing distinct levels of an utterance's meaning (Stiles, 1986b). The form codes represent an aspect of the utterance's *literal meaning,* and the intent codes represented an aspect of its *pragmatic meaning,* or, as Grice (1969) described it, its *occasion meaning*—the meaning a speaker intended on a particular occasion. Both levels contribute to the psychological force of the utterance, as do other, off-record levels of meaning (Stiles, 1986b; see Chapter 5). Mixed modes thus represent indirect speech acts—using one literal meaning to convey a different pragmatic meaning.

The long process of identifying which grammatical forms correspond to which intents has drawn on the collective linguistic intuition of the coders and collaborators who have worked on the research. By discussing problematic examples encountered in coding, we have gradually collected a set of grammatical features that characteristically express each of the eight intents. In each instance, we ask, "What is the literal meaning of this grammatical expression when taken out of its context?" Because they are based on linguistic intuition, the form definitions are in one sense less anchored than the intent definitions, even though form is usually coded more reliably than intent. At the same time, the present form specifications (Chapter 7) rest on my discussions with literally hundreds of coders and collaborators who have coded more than 2 million utterances in varied types of discourse, and I have considerable confidence in them.

UNITIZING

Over the first year or two of using the VRM system, the scoring unit shrank from the *speech* (everything a speaker said without being interrupted) to the *sentence* (everything between one initial capital letter and the next on our transcripts) to the *utterance.* As now constituted, an utterance is defined as a simple sentence; an independent clause; a nonrestrictive dependent clause; an element of a compound predicate; or a term of acknowledgment, evaluation, or address. The scoring unit shrank as we found instances of the larger units whose sense demanded two or more different codes. The current definition has been developed to give a grammatical specification of a communicative unit for which there is one and only one VRM code. Details and examples are presented in Chapter 8.

RECENT DEVELOPMENTS

Several hundred coders have now coded several million utterances using the VRM system. Each new application of the system raises new coding issues and requires new adjustments; nevertheless, grounded in the principles of classification, the categories have remained notably stable across time and topics.

Since the publication of the 1978 manual (Stiles, 1978a), I have encountered many examples of utterances that appeared difficult to code at first. Usually coders have brought these to research project staff meetings. Our approach has been to discuss these problematic utterances according to the principles of classification as informed by our understanding of what the speaker meant in context. Almost always we have found a resolution that further articulates the principles without contradicting them. Typically, resolving the coding of one problematic utterance has clarified the coding of many other similar utterances. Thus, extending the taxonomy into new areas has resulted in an elaboration of earlier work rather than a contradiction of it. One product of this work is a body of lore dealing with how to apply the principles to particular linguistic constructions.

The changes that contradict the 1978 manual have been few and relatively minor and technical. An example of one of the largest contradictions will put this in perspective: "**Well**" is now coded as an Acknowledgment form, whereas it was cited as an example of a noncommunicative noise (like "**uhhh**" or throat clearing, which are not coded) in 1978. Psychologically, "**well**" seems to Acknowledge the other's communication while holding the floor for the speaker, whereas other Acknowledgments ("**mm-hm,**" "**yeah**") typically relinquish the floor to the other. But both meet the definition of Acknowledgment (Table 1.2).

A: **Where did you go after you left us last night?** QQ

B: **Well,** KK
   I'm not sure I want to say. DD

In retrospect, this (and the other) contradicting changes appear to correct earlier misconceptions. That is, rather than being arbitrary changes, they seem to represent a better understanding of what expressions mean, and hence of how language mediates interpersonal relationships.

Chapters 5 to 10 of this book reflect the fruits of this process of articulation and elaboration. In comparison with the 1978 manual, the formal characterization of the principles in Chapter 5 is more comprehensive and, I hope, clearer. The unitizing rules in Chapter 8 encompass many grammatical constructions that we had not considered in 1978. And Chapters 9 and 10 in particular represent the lore and examples from coding projects that have been conducted since 1978, the result of time, attention, and thought by many coders.

2

Overview of the Taxonomy

This chapter briefly describes the verbal response mode (VRM) taxonomy and lists its technical features. More detailed descriptions of the principles of classification, the VRM intent categories, and the VRM form categories (and mixed modes) are given in Chapters 5, 6, and 7, respectively.

PRINCIPLES, INTENTS, AND FORMS

Every utterance from one person to another can be considered to concern either the speaker's or the other's experience, with "experience" understood broadly to include thoughts, feelings, perceptions, and intentional actions. For example, in the informative utterance, "**I want to go fishing,**" the *source of experience* is the speaker, whereas in the attentive utterance, "**Do you want to go fishing?**" the source of experience is the other.

Further, in making an utterance, the speaker may or may not make presumptions about the other's experience. That is, the utterance may or may not require the speaker to presume to know what the other person is, was, will be, or should be thinking, feeling, perceiving, or intending. To illustrate, in saying, "**I want to go fishing**" or "**Do you want to go fishing?**" the speaker need not make such a presumption; however, in saying, "**Go fishing**" the speaker presumes to know what the other should do—in effect, he or she seeks to impose an experience (the intention to go fishing) on the other. The former, nonpresumptuous utterances are said to require a *presumption about experience* of the speaker only, whereas the latter, presumptuous utterance requires a presumption about the experience of the other to have the meaning it has.

Finally, in making an utterance, the speaker may represent the experience either from his or her own personal viewpoint or from a viewpoint that is shared or held in common with the other. To illustrate, "**I want to go fishing**," "**Do you want to go fishing?**" and "**Go fishing**" all use the speaker's *frame of reference*—the experience is understood (or, in the case of the question, is to be understood) from the speaker's viewpoint and may be described as directive. By contrast, the more acquiescent utterance, "**You want to go fishing**" takes the other's frame of reference, in effect representing the experience as the other views it.

These three principles of classification—source of experience, presumption about experience, and frame of reference—form the basis of the VRM taxonomy described in this book. The three principles are dichotomous—each can take the value "speaker" or "other"—and they are orthogonal in the sense that all eight ($2 \times 2 \times 2$) combinations of them are possible. Each combination defines one of the modes, as shown in Table 2.1. For example, Questions are defined as utterances that concern the others' experience, presume knowledge of the speaker's experience only (no presumptions about the other's experience required), and use the speaker's frame of reference. The eight VRM categories are Disclosure (D), Edification (E), Advisement (A), Confirmation (C), Question (Q), Acknowledgment (K), Interpretation (I), and Reflection (R). An Uncodable (U) category is used only for utterances that coders cannot understand or hear clearly.

Speaker and other may be individuals, or they may be collectivities, as when a speaker addresses an audience, or they may even be inanimate or imaginary entities, as when a person speaks to the heavens or when one fictional character speaks to another. The VRM codes describe the relationship between the speaker and the other, whoever or whatever they are.

The VRM taxonomy is thus a conceptually based, general-purpose system for coding speech acts. The taxonomic categories are mutually exclusive, and they are exhaustive in the sense that every comprehensible utterance can be classified. The mutual exclusivity and exhaustiveness derive from the modes' basis in the three dichotomous principles of classification (see Chapters 1 and 5 for further discussion of the principles). The abbreviation "VRM" is used in this book to refer to this particular taxonomy of verbal response modes. (See Chapter 3 for references to other classification systems.)

The names of the eight modes are commonly used words; however, in this VRM taxonomy, the modes are defined by the intersection of the three principles and not by the colloquial or the dictionary meanings of

TABLE 2.1
Taxonomy of Verbal Response Modes

Source of Experience	Presumption About Experience	Frame of Reference	Mode
Speaker	Speaker	Speaker	DISCLOSURE (D) Reveals thoughts, feelings, perceptions, or intentions.
		Other	EDIFICATION (E) States objective information.
	Other	Speaker	ADVISEMENT (A) Attempts to guide behavior; suggestions, commands, permission, prohibition.
		Other	CONFIRMATION (C) Compares speaker's experience with other's; agreement, disagreement, shared experience or belief.
Other	Speaker	Speaker	QUESTION (Q) Requests information or guidance.
		Other	ACKNOWLEDGMENT (K) Conveys receipt of or receptiveness to other's communication; simple acceptance; salutations.
	Other	Speaker	INTERPRETATION (I) Explains or labels the other; judgments or evaluations of other's experience or behavior.
		Other	REFLECTION (R) Puts other's experience into words; repetitions, restatements, clarifications.

NOTE: UNCODABLE (U) is used only for incomprehensible utterances.

the names. The descriptions of the modes in the body of Table 2.1 are meant as characterizations of the categories, which are defined by that particular combination of "speaker" and "other" values on the principles. More detailed definitions and examples are given in Chapter 6. In this book, the mode names are capitalized as a way of indicating that the taxonomic meaning may differ from the colloquial meaning in some cases.

In applying the taxonomy, each utterance is coded twice, once with respect to its grammatical form, or literal meaning, and once with respect to its communicative intent, or pragmatic meaning. Thus, the taxonomy includes 64 possible form-intent combinations—8 *pure modes,* in which form and intent coincide, and 56 *mixed modes,* in which they

TABLE 2.2

Summary of Verbal Response Mode Form Criteria

Disclosure	Declarative; first person ("I") or first person plural ("we") where other is not a referent
Edification	Declarative; third person (e.g., "he," "she," "it" or a noun)
Advisement	Imperative, or second person with verb of permission, prohibition, or obligation
Confirmation	First person plural ("we") where referent includes other (i.e., "we" refers to both speaker and other)
Question	Interrogative, with inverted subject-verb order or interrogative words
Acknowledgment	Nonlexical or contentless utterances; terms of address or salutation
Interpretation	Second person ("you"); verb implies an attribute or ability of the other; terms of evaluation
Reflection	Second person ("you"); verb implies internal experience or volitional action

differ. As a notational convention, the form abbreviation is written first and intent second. The relation of form to intent is expressed, "in service of." For example, **"Would you roll up your sleeve?"** is coded QA, which is read as "Question in service of Advisement," that is, Question form (inverted subject-verb order) but Advisement intent (guiding the other's behavior). A brief summary of the forms is given in Table 2.2. Forms and mixed modes are more fully described in Chapter 7.

SO WHAT?

Each VRM category represents a type of *microrelationship*—a way that a speaker can be related to an other for one utterance. Insofar as verbal microrelationships combine with each other and with other attributes to form human relationships, VRM coding is broadly useful for understanding and describing relationships between people (e.g., intimacy, status, social roles) as conveyed in language (see Chapter 3 for a discussion). Qualitatively, VRM concepts link observable response categories (e.g., Question, Disclosure) with general psychological principles (e.g., whose experience or frame of reference is used). Aggregating VRM codes across some stretch of discourse yields numerical indexes that describe relationships (see Chapter 11), permitting quantitative research on topics in which the relationship between people talking to each other figures as important. Chapter 4 illustrates some of the sorts of questions VRM coding can address, but many more uses are possible, and investigators are continually thinking of new ones. As noted in Chapter 4, aggregating utterances according to the VRM principles of classification offers a bridge between the relatively molecular level of coded utterances and the relatively molar level of relationship dimensions (e.g., attentiveness, directiveness, presumptuousness) and of theoretical concepts (e.g., theories of psychotherapy).

TECHNICAL FEATURES OF THE VRM TAXONOMY

Here is a quick sketch of the VRM taxonomy's characteristics.

Applicability

The taxonomy is applicable to any discourse and has already been applied to psychotherapy, medical interviews, informal conversations, letters, family interaction, job interviews, university lectures, political speeches, labor negotiations, courtroom interrogations, radio call-in programs, and television advertisements (see Chapter 4 and References). Coding requires only that there be a "speaker" and an intended audience, or "other." Speaker and other may be collectivities rather than individuals. For example, the opposing sides of a labor-management negotiation (each consisting of several individuals) have been construed as alternating as "speaker" and "other" (Hinkle, Stiles, & Taylor, 1988), and television advertisements have been construed as emanating from a "speaker" addressing the collective television audience (Rak & McMullen, 1987).

Access Strategy

The VRM system uses an observational access strategy, not self-report. The system codes what people *do* in verbal interaction—their speech acts—not what they think.

Communication Channel

The VRM system codes verbal behavior. Other channels, including paralinguistic and kinetic communication, may be useful for identifying the mode of an utterance, but these are not coded directly (see Chapter 3).

Data Format

VRMs can be coded from written documents, transcripts, audiotapes, videotapes, or live interactions. Most utterances in natural interaction can be coded accurately from verbatim transcripts; however, patterns of emphasis, timing, and inflection evident on audiotape can clarify the intent of some utterances. The additional (visual) information available from videotape or live interactions may be needed in some circumstances, for example, (a) in conversations involving several individuals, visual information may be needed to distinguish which person is speaking and which is being addressed; (b) when speech is indistinct, the added redundancy provided by visual information may aid in understanding what was said; or (c) when speech accompanies ongoing activity, such as children playing, the meaning of some utterances draws on the physical activities being performed.

Live coding of complex or rapidly moving interaction is difficult and therefore likely to be inaccurate. Coders working from tapes of such interactions often need to rewind and replay the recordings to catch speakers' meanings.

Coding directly from audiotapes requires more skill than coding from transcripts; good intercoder reliability can be obtained from audiotape coding, however (e.g., McDaniel, Stiles, & McGaughey, 1981; Stiles, Au, Martello, & Perlmutter, 1983; Stiles, Shapiro, & Firth-Cozens, 1988). Coders typically comment that audiotapes make it easier to understand what the speaker meant.

Scoring Unit

A scoring unit is the stretch of text to which individual codes are assigned. The VRM scoring unit is the *utterance,* defined as a simple sentence; an independent clause; a nonrestrictive dependent clause; an element of a compound predicate; or a term of acknowledgment, evaluation, or address. Details and examples are presented in Chapter 8.

Contextual Unit

Contextual unit refers to the amount of text that must be considered by a coder in deciding how to classify an utterance. VRM form codes are based on grammatical features (Chapter 7), so in perfectly grammatical, nonelliptical speech, utterances can be coded in isolation. In natural speech, elliptical, incomplete, and ungrammatical utterances require reference to context, though usually the immediately preceding two or three utterances are sufficient. See Chapters 7 and 10 for discussion and examples.

VRM intent codes classify the speaker's intended meaning on a particular occasion and thus must always be considered in context. For virtually any utterance it is possible to imagine some other context in which its meaning would be different. To illustrate, "**It's starting to rain**" would be EE in most contexts, but it could be ER if it repeated something the other just said, or EA if it was understood that the other was required to close the windows, or EQ if it was spoken with an upward inflection at the end. Many of the examples given later (e.g., Chapters 9 and 10) illustrate the importance of context.

In practice, VRM intent can usually be coded accurately in a context of a few preceding utterances. Some utterances may be understandable only in the context of much earlier events, however, a situation probably most common in long-standing relationships, for example, among family members. Like any outsider, VRM coders may overlook meanings that are clear to participants, but because the VRM system is usually applied only to "on-record" meaning (Chapter 5; Stiles, 1986b, 1987b), coders' ignorance of the more subtle, off-record meanings of some utterances may not impair the validity of VRM codes.

Summarizing Unit

The summarizing unit is the stretch of discourse over which summary indexes are calculated. The VRM system allows any size of summarizing unit, from a single utterance to a whole class of relationships. Most VRM studies have summarized over an encounter or a segment of an encounter (e.g., the medical history-taking segment of a medical interview). Utterances have most often been aggregated separately for each speaker (e.g., the percentage of a client's utterances coded as Disclosure), although it is also possible to aggregate by dyad or by larger groups. See Chapter 11 for a discussion of summary indexes produced by the VRM system.

Level of Measurement

VRM categories are nominal measures, although aggregate VRM indexes used to characterize an episode of communication may be ordinal, interval, or even ratio scales. For example, the frequency of client Disclosures in a psychotherapy session is a ratio measure (e.g.,

80 Disclosures is twice as high as 40 Disclosures). See Chapters 4 and 11 for illustrations and descriptions of VRM aggregate indexes.

Transcribing

The VRM system does not require special transcribing procedures; as indicated above, any discourse, written or spoken, can be coded. Nevertheless, following a few consistent transcribing principles will improve the accuracy and reliability of coding and unitizing. A few rules that I have found useful for transcribing are given in Chapter 11. For more detailed transcribing rules, I recommend those of Auld and White (1956). Fully phonetic transcriptions are not necessary and may be distracting; however, researchers interested in very intensive study of discourse (including other coding in addition to VRMs) may wish to consider the transcription system developed by Jefferson (e.g., Sacks, Schegloff, & Jefferson, 1974).

Coder Qualifications

Applying the VRM system requires high verbal aptitude, interest in interpersonal communication, patience with details, and intensive training and practice. Competence in basic grammar is essential. Psychological-mindedness is helpful, but professional training in psychology is not required. Suggestions for training coders are offered in Chapter 11.

VRM coding is a skill that is acquired gradually, through practice. One cannot become proficient simply by reading descriptions of the system, such as this book. Accuracy of coding—and hence intercoder reliability—can continue to improve for a considerable time. Improvement is facilitated by practice, regular feedback (e.g., comparisons with the work of other coders), and opportunity for discussion of difficult codes.

Computer-Assisted Training Program

A computer-assisted training program for VRM coders (on computer disk) accompanies this book. This program introduces the principles of classification, forms, and intents, and it offers practice to train new coders in the basic skills needed to code unitized transcripts. As described in Chapter 11, additional practice is required for coders to become proficient in unitizing (following rules described in Chapter 8) or in direct coding of untranscribed material (audiotapes, videotapes, or live interactions).

USE OF EXAMPLES IN THIS BOOK

Conventions for Examples

This book contains many examples of utterances, particularly in Chapters 6 through 10. The following are some conventions I have used for presenting them.

If more than one line is taken from a conversation—even if only one party's utterances are taken—then a speaker indication is given using a colon.

   A: **Hello. KK**
      This is a recording. EE
      I can't come to the phone right now, DD
      but if you'll leave your name and number, I'll return your call as soon as I can. DD

Fragments taken from different conversations are separated by "###."

   Th: **You are an obsessive-compulsive neurotic. II**

###

   Th: **You feel that your hands are always dirty. RR**

If no speaker indications are present, then each line is an independent utterance—not part of the same conversation or stretch of discourse.

   Hello. KK

   This is a separate utterance. EE

Context and Caution in Interpreting Examples

The examples used in this book are taken out of context and may be subject to multiple interpretations. Insofar as VRM coding (particularly VRM intent coding) always depends on context, it is necessary to imagine a context for each of the examples. In most cases, I think the context you imagine will be sufficiently similar to the one I imagine for the VRM code to be the same, but in some cases, you may imagine a context that would lead to a different code, and in such cases, the code given here will be wrong from your perspective.

I don't know any complete solution for this problem. I recommend caution. Be aware that differences between your code and mine may reflect our different interpretations of what the speaker meant rather than differences in how we think a particular meaning should be coded.

An additional possibility is that we understand the context similarly, but that I have coded the utterance incorrectly. This could be a result of a typographical error, or it could be a result of a misconception on my part. In this taxonomy, ultimate recourse is to the principles of classification and not to the private opinion of this book's author.

I would very much like to hear from you if you believe that examples in this book are coded incorrectly for any reason.

3

Comparisons With
Other Approaches

How does the VRM taxonomy compare with other approaches to studying verbal interaction? With which other systems of analysis is it complementary and with which does it compete? How can the VRM system be modified to accommodate additional categories or conceptual distinctions?

This chapter is intended to locate the VRM system in the context of other research on verbal interaction. The number of different approaches that have been used is very large, however, and I can cite only a few representatives here.

CLASSIFICATION OF THE VRM CLASSIFICATION

Coding and Qualitative Analysis

To begin with, the VRM taxonomy is a coding system. *Coding* verbal behavior refers to classifying and counting utterances. Coding is only one of several ways of studying verbal behavior.

Coding should be distinguished from such primarily linguistic approaches as discourse analysis (e.g., Labov & Fanshel, 1977; Potter & Wetherell, 1987) or conversational analysis (e.g., Frankel, 1984; Schegloff, 1987) or narrative, phenomenological, or hermeneutic methods of studying texts (e.g., Atwood & Stolorow, 1984; Packer & Addison, 1989; Sarbin, 1986). In these approaches, text is analyzed qualitatively, based on the investigator's personal and empathic understanding of the speakers and knowledge of the circumstances (Stiles, 1990, 1991).

The VRM taxonomy can be a useful adjunct in qualitative analyses; it offers clearly defined categories, which investigators can use descriptively. For example, having explicit criteria for distinguishing an Interpretation from a Reflection in a particular passage of psychotherapy may help an investigator more clearly describe the relationship of the therapist to the client at that moment.

Qualitative applications of coding add the taxonomic criteria to other features of the utterance or passage under study. This type of application has been rare and probably deserves more use. More commonly, coding is used as a step in quantitative measurement of verbal behavior. The quantities derive from counting the frequencies of particular categories in a stretch of discourse.

Coding Versus Rating

Among quantitative approaches, coding should be distinguished from *rating*. Rating involves placing some stretch of text on a continuum (e.g., assigning a number from 1 to 7 to represent how much anger was shown, or the degree to which the speaker revealed personal information, or the skill with which an interview was conducted). Coding involves placing units of text into discrete categories.

Rating scales seem especially appropriate for emotional and evaluative dimensions, perhaps because feelings and values seem to vary on continua rather than discretely. (For example, there are many shades and degrees of anger, friendliness, happiness, improvement, disapproval.) Scales for measuring emotional and evaluative dimensions in interpersonal relationships have been developed to a high level of sophistication (e.g, Benjamin, 1974; Benjamin, Foster, Roberto, & Estroff, 1986). But rating is not confined to emotional and evaluative scales, and there is a seemingly endless list of alternative dimensions on which verbal interaction can be rated. It is even possible to treat response modes as rating dimensions—by rating passages for the degree to which each mode is present (Elliott, 1985; Elliott, Hill, Stiles, Friedlander, Mahrer, & Margison, 1987).

Types of Coding Categories: Speech Act, Content, Paralinguistic

The verbal response modes are categories of speech acts (or more precisely, of *illocutionary* acts; Austin, 1975; Searle, 1969; Stiles, 1981; cf. Russell, 1986). A speech act is what is *done,* as contrasted with what is *said,* when someone says something. For example, in uttering **"What's for supper?"** what the speaker has done is asked a Question. Asking a Question is an example of a speech act. Each of the VRM categories is a different sort of speech act (see Chapters 5 and 6).

Speech act or illocutionary categories, such as VRMs, should be distinguished from categories that code other aspects of meaning. Among the other types of categories, the most common are *content* or *sense* categories and *paralinguistic* or *nonverbal communication* categories (Russell & Stiles, 1979; Stiles & Putnam, 1989). Content categories code the denotative or connotative semantic content of what is said; examples of such categories include "references to mother," "tools," and "human movement." Nonverbal communication categories code communication outside of strictly linguistic channels; examples include "laughter," "hesitation," and various gestures and facial expressions.

In general, an utterance may be coded independently with respect to each of these *metacategories* (i.e., speech act, content, paralinguistic). For example, a particular content may be used in any speech act; each of the following utterances could be coded to the content category "mother," but they have different VRM codes:

Where is your mother? QQ

I am your mother. DE

You wish your mother was here. RR

(Have you seen my mother?) **Yes.** KD

Go tell your mother right away. AA

It may be possible to develop mutually exclusive sets of codes within each of the metacategories. The VRM system does this within the speech act metacategory. But categories from different metacategories are generally not mutually exclusive, as the preceding examples illustrate. Each metacategory provides a different sort of information about the interaction (Russell & Stiles, 1979; Stiles & Putnam, 1989).

I think of the metacategories as representing separate, independent sets of attributes of verbal communication, much as color and size represent separate, independent sets of attributes of physical objects. Red, blue, and green are more or less mutually exclusive categories, as are small, medium, and large. But there is no mutual exclusivity between color and size; red objects can be any size and small objects can be any color.

A ruler can be useful for measuring an object's size, but it is useless for measuring an object's color. In the same way, a speech act coding system such as the VRM taxonomy can be useful for measuring what people *do* in interaction, but it is useless for measuring what they *say*. The distinction between action and content in speech may be less familiar than that between size and color of objects. Consequently, selecting the appropriate measure may take more explicit attention to the nature of the question being investigated. Some of the sorts of questions for which the VRM system is suited are illustrated in Chapter 4.

In the following sections, I focus on systems that, like the VRM taxonomy, are primarily speech act systems. Works by Kiesler (1973); Holsti (1969); Viney (1983); Ekman, Friesen, and Ellsworth (1972); Beattie (1983); Gottschalk and Gleser (1969); Greenberg and Pinsof (1986); Markman, Notarius, Stephen, and Smith (1981); and Russell (1987, 1988; Russell & Stiles, 1979) offer entries into the literature on content and paralinguistic category system.

Conjunctive Categories and Mixed Systems

Most coding systems have respected the boundaries between meta-categories; each system is comprised primarily of speech act categories, or of content categories, or of paralinguistic categories. But some systems contain conjunctive categories, which are defined by some combination of, for example, content and speech act characteristics, and some systems mix categories of different types.

Conjunctive categories may have specific applications, but they are problematic in a general-purpose system. For example, "questions about medications" (Byrne & Long, 1976) conjoins a speech act category (questions) with a content category (medications). This category is useful in medical interviews, where medications are an important topic, but of limited use in most other discourse. Similarly, "forcing client to choose and develop topic" (Snyder, 1945) seems to conjoin an action (forcing client—presumably mainly by Advisements) with a content (choosing and developing topic), and its usefulness is likely limited to psychotherapy and related types of interactions. Separate coding of speech acts (e.g., question, directive) and the contents of interest (e.g., medications, topic development) would accomplish the same purpose and permit greater generality.

Mixed systems contain representatives of more than one metacate-gory; for example, Bales's (1950, 1970) Interaction Process Analysis is composed mainly of speech act categories, such as "asks for opinion," but includes "shows tension," a category based mainly on paralinguistic behaviors (e.g., laughter, nervousness). Such categories are not naturally mutually exclusive (one could ask for opinion and show tension at the same time), so conflicts between codes must be resolved by arbitrary rules of priority (e.g., always code "shows tension" in preference to "asks for opinion" when both are present), which tend to distort the frequencies of the lower-priority categories.

Conceptual clarity is probably best served by coding different metacategories on separate passes through a tape recording or transcript (by different coders, if possible). This allows coders to attend separately to content, speech acts, paralinguistic classifications, or rating dimensions. Categories can then be combined as required at the analysis stage of the research.

Some investigators have constructed *multidimensional* packages of instruments that include speech act, content, and/or paralinguistic coding dimensions, along with rating scales or other measures (e.g., Notarius & Markman, 1981; Pinsof, 1986, Strupp, 1957a). Each dimension can be coded independently. Such an approach to examining diverse features of interaction seems preferable to that of using conjunctive categories or mixed systems. As an alternative to existing packages, investigators can choose already-developed coding systems to measure each metacategory of interest. For example, an investigator might choose a speech act system, a content system, and an affective rating scale system. The VRM system can serve as the speech act component in such a multidimensional package.

Verbal communication is complex and multifaceted, and no coding system or package can characterize it completely. Investigators must select instruments that measure the features most relevant to the topics they are investigating.

Aggregating Across Metacategories

Investigators who code verbal interaction rarely use all of the information that their coding procedures extract. In some cases, categories that distinguish features within one metacategory have been combined during analysis, so that results based on apparently conjunctive categories and mixed systems do not involve conjunctions or mixtures. For example, if Questions about medications and Questions about social or emotional issues are distinguished during coding but aggregated with other Questions during analysis, the results will reflect a simple speech act category rather several speech act/content conjunctions.

Analyses of coding of marital interaction have appeared driven by the core finding that distressed couples tend to exhibit more negative behaviors than do nondistressed couples. The widely used Marital Interaction Coding System (Hops, Wills, Patterson, & Weiss, 1972; Robin & Weiss, 1980) includes about 30 categories, many of which are defined by mixtures of speech act, content, paralinguistic, and evaluative characteristics. Investigators who have used this system have usually collapsed the diverse codes into broad evaluative categories, such as negative verbal behaviors (e.g., put down, disagree), negative nonverbal behaviors (e.g., no response, not tracking), positive verbal behaviors (e.g., agree, paraphrase/reflection), positive nonverbal behaviors (e.g., attention, smile/laugh), and problem-solving behaviors (e.g., accept responsibility, problem solution) (Floyd, O'Farrell, & Goldberg, 1987; Humphrey, Apple, & Kirschenbaum, 1986). The Couples Interaction Scoring System (Gottman, 1979; Notarius & Markman, 1981) uses separate codes for verbal and nonverbal contributions (making this a formally multidimensional system), though its "content" (i.e., verbal) categories are defined by mixtures of speech act, content, and evaluative characteristics: problem information or feelings about problem; mind reading (attributing thoughts, feelings, motives, attitudes, or actions to spouse); proposing a solution; communication talk; agreement; disagreement; summarizing other; and summarizing self. In application, this system has also usually been collapsed into an evaluative dimension (e.g., Gottman, 1979). A similar pattern characterizes research using the Kategoriensystem für Partnerschaftliche Interaktion (Hahlweg, Reisner, Kohli, Vollmer, Schindler, & Revenstorf, 1984; Hooley & Hahlweg, 1989), which includes speech act categories and verbal and nonverbal evaluative codes. The distinctively illocutionary (speech act) information in the codes seems to have been of less interest than the affective and evaluative information in marital interaction research.

Relational Coding Systems

Whereas most coding systems code each individual's verbal productions separately, some investigators have proposed systems for classifying relationships between adjacent utterances by people in conversation (e.g., Fisher & Drecksel, 1983; Hancher, 1979; Millar & Rogers, 1976; Rogers, Courtright, & Millar, 1980; Rogers & Farace, 1975). For example, an utterance may be coded as "one up," "one down," or "one across," depending on whether it takes a superior, inferior, or equal stance with respect to the preceding speaker's utterance.

Categories in relational coding systems depend heavily on speech act characteristics. For example, in one system, giving an order (Advisement) is considered "one up" regardless of what preceded it. At the same time, questions are considered as "one up" if they change the topic but "one down" if they extend the preceding topic (Millar & Rogers, 1976; Rogers & Farace, 1975). Thus, this system incorporates content as well as speech act information.

Speech act systems in general, and the VRM system in particular, encode information about interpersonal relationships. The VRM principles, source of experience, presumption about experience, and frame of reference, trace to the relational or intersubjective nature of speech acts. As reflected in the values of the principles, "speaker" and "other," VRM categories represent classes of "microrelationships" of one party to another (see Chapter 5). Some features of relational coding systems are built into the VRM system. For example, the presumption-about-experience principle is closely related to the "one up" versus "one down" dimension used in relational systems. As reviewed in Chapter 4, relatively greater use of "presumptuous" modes is associated with higher relative status in a wide variety of interactions, and could be considered theoretically as "one up."

Speech Act Categories Are Similar Across Systems

Speech act categories seem limited in number. Although many researchers have developed lists of speech act categories, the lists tend to be manageably short. Typically, lists include about 4 to 20 main categories, and these overlap with each other across lists. Speech act categories seem to be natural categories; utterances fall into relatively few groups that are perceived as coherent and distinct by most people. Consequently, different speech act coding systems tend to be redundant (e.g., Elliott et al., 1987); they are alternative (and hence competing), rather than complementary ways of classifying utterances in discourse.

Categories in other speech act systems tend to resemble the VRM categories or simple combinations or subdivisions of the VRM categories. For example, in Searle's (1976) speech act taxonomy, *directives* encompass VRM Advisements and Questions, while *commissives* and *expressives* are subdivisions of VRM Disclosure (see discussion later in this chapter). Put another way, the VRM principles could be used to distinguish among categories in other speech act systems.

In contrast to the redundancy of speech act systems, content systems seem to have innumerable possible categories, and these do not fall into reliably similar groups across systems. Semantic meaning seems far more variable than speech acts, and it appears unlikely that content can ever be classified as simply as speech acts. As a consequence, content classification systems need not overlap or compete. Each new substantive research area may require construction of a distinct set of content categories. The nearest thing we have to an exhaustive classification of content is an unabridged dictionary.

The paralinguistic metacategory is more heterogeneous than speech acts or content. Grouping facial expressions, pauses, laughter, and speech dysfluencies as "paralinguistic" is a convenience in the context of a book about speech acts, but closer examination reveals great diversity and complex problems of classification and coding. Systematic or even mutually exclusive classification systems may be possible within certain separable types of paralinguistic communication. An example is the classification of emotional facial expressions by Ekman et al. (1972).

OTHER SPEECH ACT CODING SYSTEMS

Principled Versus Empirical Construction

The VRM system is distinguished from most other speech act coding systems by its construction from crosscutting principles of classification, as described in Chapters 1, 2, and 5. The principles are what make the VRM system distinctive (in the sense that other systems have not articulated them explicitly), but at the same time they are what make the VRM system universal (in the sense that they make much the same distinctions as those made descriptively in other systems). Most other systems have been developed empirically—by examining samples of a particular domain of discourse (e.g., negotiation sessions; family interaction; psychotherapy) and by culling categories from work done by others who have previously examined that domain.

An Example of Empirical Construction: The Goodman System

The Goodman response modes system (Goodman & Dooley, 1976) offers an example of empirical construction of a speech act system. This system is of particular interest here because the present VRM was derived from the Goodman system (see Chapter 1).

Goodman developed his list of response modes by observing naturalistic interaction. An important source of observations were brief tape-recorded interactions among college students who had applied to participate in a program providing companionship for troubled preadolescent boys (Goodman, 1972). Students participated in groups, and took turns as "listener," as "discloser," and as "observer" of the interaction. The discloser revealed a personal concern (selected beforehand as a real concern that could be disclosed in this setting) while the listener tried to facilitate and help. The observers rated the listener's performance, and these ratings were used to help select talented companions for the boys. Goodman's attempts to categorize the listeners' interventions led to his response mode framework. This framework was first published by Goodman and Dooley (1976), who reviewed literature on each of their six categories (Question, Advisement, Silence, Interpretation, Reflection, Disclosure; see Chapter 1), showing that each had received attention by earlier theorists and researchers. The framework was a starting point for research by several of Goodman's students (see review by Elliott, Stiles, Shiffman, Barker, Burstein, & Goodman, 1982), who modified the list for their own purposes. It has also been incorporated into a series of audiotape-led group sessions for teaching helping skills (Goodman, 1978) and for developing mutually helpful relationships within groups of people sharing a common concern such as recent bereavement or children with cystic fibrosis (self-help groups; Jacobs & Goodman, 1989), and it has been elaborated as a popular self-help book (Goodman & Esterly, 1988).

Goodman drew on a tradition of process research in client-centered therapy derived from work in the early 1940s by students of Carl Rogers (Porter, 1942a, 1942b; Snyder, 1945). These investigations exploited the opportunity afforded by the advent of a new technology—audio recording of therapy sessions on wire and later magnetic tape. Even at this early stage, however, the speech act categories overlapped substantially with the current VRM categories.

Speech Acts in Philosophy and Linguistics

The philosophical/linguistic study of speech acts seems to have grown from the 1955 William James Lectures by the philosopher J. L. Austin, reprinted in an influential book, *How To Do Things With Words*

(Austin, 1975). Within the general concept of speech acts, Austin (1975) distinguished the *illocutionary* act (the act performed in making an utterance) from the *locutionary* act (simply uttering the words) and the *perlocutionary* act (producing some external effect on the actions or attitudes of others). These acts are performed simultaneously; Austin's analytic distinctions reflect different dimensions along which utterances vary. In uttering, **"The cat is on the mat"** (EE), the speaker simultaneously (a) asserts something, (b) utters a particular series of words, and (c) informs the hearer about the cat's location. In uttering, **"Fetch me some bread"** (AA) the speaker (a) directs someone to do something, (b) utters more words, and (c) elicits fetching behavior (or perhaps refusal) by the other. Asserting and directing are illocutionary acts, called Edification and Advisement in the VRM taxonomy; thus, VRMs are illocutionary categories. The particular words uttered and their actual effect on the other are not crucial to VRM classification or to Austin's concept of illocutionary acts.

Illocutionary acts have been classified in several different ways. Whereas VRM principles are epistemological—based on a distinction between private and public information and who presumes to know it (Chapter 5), philosophical/linguistic illocutionary act categories have been constructed largely on principles of social expectations and conventional use (cf. Russell, 1986). Searle's (1969) explication of "how to promise" is a classic example:

> Given that a speaker S utters a sentence T in the presence of hearer H, then, in the literal utterance of T, S sincerely and non-defectively promises that p to H if and only if the following conditions 1-9 obtain:

1. Normal input and output conditions obtain.
2. S expresses the proposition that p in the utterance of T.
3. In expressing that p, S predicates a future act A of S.
4. H would prefer S's doing A to his not doing A, and S believes H would prefer his doing A to his not doing A.
5. It is not obvious to both S and H that S will do A in the normal course of events.
6. S intends to do A.
7. S intends that the utterance of T will place him under an obligation to do A.
8. S intends (i-1) to produce in H the knowledge (K) that the utterance of T is to count as placing S under an obligation to do A. S intends to

produce K by means of the recognition of i-1, and he intends i-1 to be
recognized in virtue of (by means of) H's knowledge of the meaning of T.

9. The semantical rules of the dialect spoken by S and H are such that T
is correctly and sincerely uttered if and only if conditions 1-8 obtain.
(excerpted from pp. 57-61)

Austin's (1975) concept of the illocutionary act grew from the study
of *explicit performatives*. An explicit performative verb has the curious
property of naming the illocutionary act performed when a speaker
utters it in a first person singular present indicative active sentence. For
example, if I say, "**I promise to buy you a lollipop,**" I have promised
to buy a lollipop. If I say, "**I thank you,**" I have thanked you. If I say,
"**I assert that the world is flat,**" I have asserted that the world is flat.
In the case of explicit performatives, saying makes it so.

Even though Austin showed that illocutionary force is characteristic
of all utterances—not just explicit performative utterances—subse-
quent taxonomists in this tradition (e.g., Green, 1977; Hancher, 1979;
Ohmann, 1972; Searle, 1969, 1976; Vendler, 1972) have been strongly
influenced by the point of origin, and categories based on lists of
performative verbs have been overrepresented (from a VRM perspective) at the expense of other categories. Explicit performatives are
necessarily limited to verbal action by the speaker. Nonverbal mental
or physical actions by the speaker, along with any actions by the other,
by third parties, or by nonhuman agencies, are excluded. Grammatically, all explicit performative utterances are first person singular, and
so would be classified as Disclosure form. In VRM terms, the focus on
explicit performatives has tended to emphasize the "speaker" values of
the principles at the expense of the "other" values (see Table 2.1, p. 16).

Searle's (1976) five major speech act categories illustrate the common ground and the different emphasis. They include *commissives,*
which commit the speaker to some future course of action; *expressives,*
which express the speaker's psychological state; *representatives,* which
commit the speaker (in varying degrees) to the truth of some proposition; *directives,* which are attempts by the speaker to get the other to do
something; and *declarations,* utterances whose "successful performance
guarantees that the propositional content corresponds to the world"
(p. 13). These categories classify the same domain as the psychotherapy
and social interaction speech act coding systems. In VRM terms, commissives and expressives appear to be subcategories of Disclosure;
representatives appear to be Edifications; and directives include both

Advisements and Questions. Searle's declarations appear to be hetero-geneous, including Interpretations (e.g., **"You are guilty,"** "You are out [in baseball]") as well as some Edifications (**"War is hereby declared"**) and Disclosures (**"I resign"**). However, they reflect their origins in the study of explicit performatives by their emphasis on speaker-valued categories. From a VRM perspective, Disclosure ("speaker" on all three principles) has two categories to itself (commissives and expressives), and Edification, Advisement, and Question ("speaker" on two of the principles) are represented in two more (representatives and directives). The remaining four VRM categories (Reflection, Interpre-tation, Acknowledgment, and Confirmation, which are "other" on two or all three of the principles) are ignored except for a few subcategories represented in the heterogeneous "declaration" category.

Systems Emphasize Different Sets of Categories

In general, empirically constructed speech act systems tend to reflect the domain of discourse on which they were developed. Although many categories overlap across systems, empirically constructed systems often emphasize categories that are common or important within a particular domain of discourse, whereas categories of utterances that are rare tend to be collapsed together or omitted.

Counseling and Psychotherapy. In contrast to systems based on explicit performatives, systems developed for analyzing the speech of coun-selors and psychotherapists (e.g., Barkham & Shapiro, 1986; Elliott, 1985; Friedlander, 1982; Goodman & Dooley, 1976; Hill, 1978, 1986; Ivey, 1971; Pinsof, 1986; Snyder, 1945, 1987; Strupp, 1955, 1957a) tend to emphasize other-oriented categories, particularly Interpretation and Reflection. Presumably this emphasis reflects therapists' generic task of understanding clients' experience and helping them reframe it in more satisfying or productive ways. For example, Hill's (1978, 1986) system of 14 categories includes only 3 that concern the speaker's experience (Self-disclosure, Information, and Direct guidance), plus a residual category (Other), whereas the other 10 categories concern the other's experience. From a VRM perspective, these include three sub-divisions of Interpretation (called Interpretation, Confrontation, and Approval-reassurance); three subdivisions of Reflection (Reflection, Restatement, and Nonverbal referent); two subdivisions of Question (Open question and Closed question), and two subdivisions of Acknowl-edgment (Minimal encourager and Silence). Similarly, the Goodman system discussed earlier in this chapter and in Chapter 1 included four categories dealing with the other's experience (Reflection, Interpretation, Question, Silence) and only two dealing with the speaker's experience (Disclosure, Advisement).

Problem Solving in Groups. Bales's (1950, 1970) influential Interaction Process Analysis system was developed particularly for studying problem solving in groups of students, though it was widely modified for application to conversations in diverse settings (Bales & Hare, 1965). The system's origins in problem solving research are recalled in such category names as "gives opinion," "asks for suggestion," and "shows tension."

Like the VRM taxonomy, Bales's system is a general-purpose system that claims to be exhaustive, but its exhaustiveness is empirical rather than guaranteed by analytic principles. It may have adequately classified all or most utterances in student groups, but it had difficulty coping with some other interactions, such as psychotherapy and medical interviews, and investigators who tried to apply it to these areas had to modify the system to accommodate utterances that the VRM system would classify as Interpretation, Reflection, and Acknowledgment (Freemon, Negrete, Davis, & Korsch, 1971; Roter, 1977; Strupp, 1955), which are far more prominent in professional consultations than in discussion groups.

Although the Interaction Process Analysis system was constructed empirically, Bales (1970) identified three "value directions," labeled upward versus downward (roughly, dominance versus submission), positive versus negative (roughly, friendly versus unfriendly), and forward versus backward (roughly, task orientation versus socioemotional orientation). These dimensions are not used as coding principles, but they can be used as summary dimensions. They were based on a factor analysis of ratings, self-descriptions, and test scores, as well as coded utterances, of 60 undergraduate members of self-analytic training groups. Conceptual and empirical comparisons of the VRM and Bales systems have been published elsewhere (Stiles, 1978b, 1980).

Medical Interviews. One important line of extension of Bales's system has applied modifications of Interaction Process Analysis to medical interviews (Brownbridge, Fitter, & Wall, 1986; Carter, Inui, Kukull, & Haigh, 1982; Davis, 1971; Freemon et al., 1971; Roter, 1977; Stewart, 1983, 1984). These and other speech act systems used primarily in medical interview research (e.g., Bain, 1976, 1979; Byrne & Long, 1976; Heszen-Klemens & Lapinska, 1984; Kaplan, Greenfield, & Ware,

1989) tend to emphasize Question-like intents, with subcategories of open questions versus closed questions, for example, or questions distinguished by content features (e.g., questions about symptoms versus medications versus socioemotional issues). Presumably this emphasis reflects the empirical predominance of Question asking by physicians and the importance of information gathering in medical interviews (e.g., Stiles, Orth, Scherwitz, Hennrikus, & Vallbona, 1984; Stiles, Putnam, & Jacob, 1982; Stiles, Putnam, Wolf, & James, 1979b).

Labor-Management Negotiation. Coding systems developed to study negotiation have emphasized Confirmation-like categories—for example, agreement and disagreement (e.g., Donohue, Diez, & Hamilton, 1984; Morley & Stephenson, 1977; Walcott & Hopmann, 1975). Confirmations are not particularly common, even in the speech of negotiators, but they are centrally important. After all, the whole point of negotiation is agreement and disagreement, expressed verbally as Confirmation. For example, in Morley & Stephenson's (1977) Conference Process Analysis system, there are only four categories in the *mode* dimension, which classifies speech acts (other dimensions in this multidimensional system concern the content of the utterance). Two of these may be regarded as subdivisions of the VRM Confirmation category (Accept and Reject), one as corresponding to the VRM Question category (Seek), and one as encompassing most of the remaining VRM categories (Offer). An empirical comparison, based on coding the same negotiation with both VRM and Conference Process Analysis systems, has confirmed these correspondences (Hinkle et al., 1988).

Developmentally Early Language. Systems designed to code the speech of young children (e.g., Dale, 1980; Dore, 1978, 1979; Dore, Gearhart, & Newman, 1978) focus on distinctions that reflect cognitive development. For example, Dale's (1980) list of 14 pragmatic functions includes naming, attributes (descriptive labels), comment, tense (comment on future or past actions), request pertaining to present environment, request for absent object, request for information, nonexistence (e.g., **"all gone"**), rejection, denial of a proposition (**"no"**), affirmation of a proposition (**"yes"**), attention seeking, greeting, and unintelligible. Such categories mirror a widely shared theoretical interest in such issues as the acquisition of object constancy (distinguishing requests for present versus absent objects) and the affirmation and denial of stated propositions. Although they are primarily speech act categories, some of them incorporate content features (e.g., request pertaining to present environment), and one is a purely content category (nonexistence).

Dore's (1978, 1979; Dore et al., 1978) classification of children's conversational acts included six major divisions, which drew on the philosophical/linguistic tradition of Austin (1975) and Searle (1969, 1976): requestives (solicit information or actions), assertives (report facts, state rules, convey attitudes, etc.), performatives (accomplish acts and establish facts by being said), responsives (supply solicited information and acknowledge remarks), regulatives (control personal contact and conversational flow), and expressives (nonpropositionally convey attitudes or repeat others), plus a miscellaneous group that included uncodable utterances, silences, and nonverbal responses. The major divisions were subdivided into 35 subcategories plus 3 residual categories. Many of Dore's subdivisions could also be subdivisions of VRM categories; for example, Dore's seven subdivisions of assertives included five subtypes of Edification (called identifications, descriptions, attributions, rules, and explanations) and two subtypes of Disclosure (called internal reports and evaluations).

Ad Hoc Speech Act Categories. Many studies in many areas have used speech act categories ad hoc, without attempting to develop a comprehensive system. They have used isolated categories or made isolated distinctions. For example, some investigators have simply counted questions or self-disclosures. Some studies have counted particular grammatical features in ways that mimic VRM form categories—for example, first person pronouns (cf. Disclosure form) or interrogatives (cf. Question form). Such categories are designed to address particular hypotheses and research questions without the complexity and expense of comprehensive coding.

A drawback of ad hoc coding definitions is that the results cannot be compared with those of other studies. A term like "disclosure" or "interpretation" may have a wide variety of meanings, so understanding each new study requires that readers understand a new, possibly idiosyncratic meaning for each such term.

It is possible to use VRM categories (or categories from some other general-purpose system) in isolation, provided that coders know enough about the VRM system (or other system) to distinguish the categories of interest from other utterances. For example, an investigator interested in Disclosure might focus on VRM-defined Disclosures alone, consigning all other utterances to an undifferentiated "Other" category. The advantage over an ad hoc category would be that readers could understand the term "Disclosure" in a standard way and directly compare results across studies. Of course, for this approach to be useful, the

VRM system must include the categories and distinctions in which the investigator is interested.

HOW TO ADD CATEGORIES TO THE VRM SYSTEM

Each of the many alternative verbal coding systems has been developed to meet a particular theoretical or research interest. It is possible and often desirable to incorporate categories or distinctions made within some specialized systems, while retaining the advantages (general applicability, exhaustiveness, mutually exclusive major categories, conceptual principles of classification) offered by the VRM taxonomy. Two general strategies to accomplish this are (a) multidimensional measurement—assessing the same material with two or more complementary systems—and (b) subdividing general purpose categories to make particular distinctions that are of theoretical or practical interest.

As noted above, the VRM system can be used as the speech act component in a battery of interpersonal process assessment measures. To avoid duplication, other measures in the battery should be composed of other metacategories—content categories or affect rating scales, for example, rather than speech act categories. To illustrate, the Gottschalk and Gleser (1969) content scales or the Benjamin (1974; Benjamin et al., 1986) SASB affective relationship scales would provide information that is complementary to VRM information; the Bales (1950, 1970) Interaction Process Analysis system is composed primarily of speech act categories and would yield information that is largely redundant with VRM information.

For particular research questions, subdividing categories is often simpler than fully multidimensional measurement. The VRM system can accommodate the addition of most of the coding distinctions made by other systems in the form of subclassifications of the eight basic VRM categories. Such subclassifications can be made on any basis, including content, paralinguistic, or evaluative criteria. For example, agreements may be distinguished from disagreements within Confirmations; questions about medications can be distinguished from other questions within Questions; process (here-and-now) directives can be distinguished from general directives within Advisements; positive Disclosures can be distinguished from negative or neutral Disclosures within Disclosures. Some of the possible subdivisions are illustrated in Chapter 6.

An advantage of constructing formal subdivisions is that it retains the analytic distinctions made by the principles of classification and focuses the final subclassifying on a few relevant criteria. For example, treating confrontation, reassurance, and psychological interpretation as subcategories of Interpretation retains the common psychological features of these utterances—their placing of the other's experience in a frame of reference provided by the speaker—and thus distinguishes them from all non-Interpretation utterances. Distinguishing among the subcategories is then a matter of applying a few relevant criteria: Is the reframing one of "normalizing" (reassuring), pointing out inconsistencies (confrontation), or placing the experience in a theoretical context (e.g., relating it to childhood experience, as in some psychoanalytic interpretations)?

In addition to the advantages for coders, treating further distinctions as subcategories illuminates psychological kinships among categories. It retains the theoretical structure of the three principles of classification (Chapter 5). Adding categories by subclassification retains the possibility of collapsing across the subcategories in order to make direct, quantitative comparisons with VRM profiles from other research.

4

Guide to the VRM Literature and Illustrative Results

To indicate the range of problems that VRM coding can address, I list here the studies I know about that have used this VRM system in research as of this writing (September 1991) and give some examples of VRM research findings. Further information on specific topics is available in the cited literature. I first cite previous VRM coding manuals, published descriptions of the VRM system, and some related theoretical papers, then topics and types of interactions that have been studied using the VRM system. Next, I discuss how VRM profiles characterize roles, relationships, and conversational tasks. Finally, I present illustrations of three alternative approaches to aggregating VRM data: percentage profiles (of psychotherapists' VRM intent), exchange structure factors (in medical interviews), and role dimensions (applied across a wide variety of roles and relationships).

LITERATURE ON THE VRM TAXONOMY

Manuals and System Descriptions

A coding manual for the VRM taxonomy was published in 1978 (Stiles, 1978a); Chapters 5 to 10 of this book constitute a revision and expansion of that manual. Unpublished versions of the manual were circulated beginning in 1975 (Stiles, 1975). The 1978 manual was translated into Dutch (Meeuwesen, 1984). The changes in the present book from the 1978 manual are primarily elaborations and clarifications. There are no major conceptual changes (although the name of one of the principles of classification has been changed from "focus" to "presumption about experience" in order to convey the meaning of the principle better). Research results based on the different versions are directly comparable. Several descriptions of the VRM system have been published (Stiles, 1978b, 1978-1979, 1979, 1981, 1986a, 1987c). Although some of these were addressed to investigators in particular areas, such as psychotherapy (Stiles, 1979, 1986a, 1987c), medical interviews (Stiles, 1978-1979), or linguistic studies (Stiles, 1981), all of them describe the categories and their derivation from the principles of classification.

Several review articles and chapters have sought to place this VRM system in the context of other coding systems used in psychotherapy (Elliott et al., 1982, 1987; Russell & Stiles, 1979) and medical interviews (Stiles & Putnam, 1989, in press[a]). Theoretical articles have examined the concept of intent, as used in the VRM system, particularly distinguishing among on-record and off-record levels of intent (Stiles, 1981, 1986b, 1987b).

There have been a few critiques specifically directed at this VRM system (Denman, 1990; Russell, 1986; Verschueren, 1983). Many of the issues raised by these critiques have been addressed in this book, particularly in Chapter 5.

Topics and Populations Studied With VRM Coding

As described in Chapter 1, the VRM system grew from research on the psychotherapy process. Although it has been applied more widely, it continues to be used in empirical research on psychotherapy and counseling (Burton, Parker, & Wollner, 1991; Cromwell, 1981; Elliott et al., 1987; Knight, 1987; Lane, 1987; McDaniel et al., 1981; Stiles, 1979, 1984a; Stiles, McDaniel, & McGaughey, 1979; Stiles & Shapiro, in press; Stiles, Shapiro, & Firth-Cozens, 1988, 1989; Stiles & Sultan, 1979; Wigutoff, 1988; Winefield, Bassett, Chandler, & Proske, 1987). Theoretical work has examined possible psychotherapeutic effects of Disclosure (Stiles, 1982, 1987a).

Medical interaction has been extensively studied with VRM coding. VRM studies have been conducted on medical encounters in the United States (Caporael & Culbertson, 1986; Carter et al., 1982; Inui, Carter, Kukull, & Haigh, 1982; Orth, Stiles, Scherwitz, Hennrikus, & Vallbona, 1987; Putnam, Stiles, Jacob, & James, 1985, 1988; Stiles, 1985; Stiles et al., 1984; Stiles, Putnam & Jacob, 1982, 1984, 1986; Stiles, Putnam,

James, & Wolf, 1979; Stiles, Putnam, Wolf, & James, 1979a, 1979b), in the United Kingdom (Brownbridge, 1987; Brownbridge et al., 1986; Brownbridge, Lilford, & Tindale-Biscoe, 1988; Burton & Parker, 1988; Burton et al., 1991; Cape, 1988), and in the Netherlands (Meeuwesen, 1988; Meeuwesen, Schaap, & van der Staak, 1991). Some studies have focused on encounters with patients with particular types of problems, including hypertensive patients (Orth et al., 1987; Stiles, Orth et al., 1984), expectant mothers (Brownbridge et al., 1988), breast cancer patients (Burton & Parker, 1988; Burton et al., 1991), patients with a significant psychological component to their physical complaint (Cape, 1988; Meeuwesen, 1988; Meeuwesen et al., 1991), and the institutionalized aged (Caporael & Culbertson, 1986).

Some studies of medical interviews have sought (and some have found) correlations between VRM indexes and measures of outcomes such as patient satisfaction and regimen adherence (e.g., Carter et al., 1982; Inui et al., 1982; Orth et al., 1987; Putnam et al., 1985; Stiles, Putnam, James et al., 1979; Stiles, Putnam, Wolf et al., 1979a). Reconsideration has thrown doubt on this strategy for assessing the importance of medical interview process components (Stiles, 1989), however. Process components such as VRMs are not administered randomly, as the correlational model assumes, but are used responsively to meet participants' requirements as they emerge in the interaction. For example, if a physician needs more information to make a diagnosis, he or she is likely to ask more Questions. Any such responsiveness to participants' changing requirements tends to defeat and may even reverse the process-outcome correlation. For example, negativistic patients may be asked relatively many Questions and still have relatively poor outcomes, leading to a *negative* correlation between Questions and outcome, even though Questions are useful and important components of medical interviewing (see Stiles, 1988, 1989 for further discussion of this issue).

In a variety of studies, people have been brought into psychological laboratories and asked to engage in a conversation or in some verbal task, which was later VRM coded. Although most of these studies have involved conversations between strangers, some have involved intimates, including husbands and wives (Fitzpatrick, Vance, & Witteman, 1984; Premo & Stiles, 1983), parents and children (Stiles & White, 1981), and college roommates (Burchill & Stiles, 1988). The laboratory studies have investigated social-psychological processes and dimensions such as relative status (Cansler & Stiles, 1981; McMullen & Krahn, 1985; McMullen & Murray, 1986), intimacy, solidarity, or familiarity

(McMullen & Krahn, 1985; McMullen & Murray, 1986; Premo & Stiles, 1983), relationship styles (Fitzpatrick et al., 1984), gender differences (McMullen, 1987; Waung, Knight, Lowry, & Stiles, 1987), appropriateness of clothing worn (Solomon, 1981), loneliness (Sloan & Solano, 1984), shyness (Bruch, Gorsky, Collins, & Berger, 1989), state and trait anxiety (Leary, Knight, & Johnson, 1987; Stiles, Shuster, Barth, Joseph, Kappus, Mason, Zimmerman, Lucic, & Harrigan, 1989; Stiles, Shuster, & Harrigan, 1989), awkward silences (McLaughlin & Cody, 1982), and boredom (Leary, Rogers, Canfield, & Coe, 1986). A few laboratory studies have focused on interaction involving individuals with psychological disorders or in psychological distress, including mildly depressed university students (Burchill & Stiles, 1988) and children with school-identified behavior problems (Stiles & White, 1981).

The VRM system has also been applied to public discourse in a variety of real-world situations. These have included U.S. presidential primary speeches (Stiles, Au, Martello, & Perlmutter, 1983), nomination acceptance speeches and inaugural addresses (Miller & Stiles, 1986), courtroom interrogation of rape victims (McGaughey & Stiles, 1983), labor-management negotiation (Hinkle et al., 1988), university classroom lectures and discussions (Stiles et al., 1983; Stiles, Waszak, & Barton, 1979), television commercials (Rak & McMullen, 1987), and psychological radio call-in programs (Henricks & Stiles, 1989).

RESULTS OF VRM RESEARCH

This section illustrates the sorts of results that have been obtained by VRM coding. First, I describe the sharp differences among roles in VRM profiles, then illustrate three approaches to aggregating and presenting the results of coding: (a) percentage profiles of VRM intents, using psychotherapy as an example; (b) the verbal exchange structure (dyadic patterns identified by factor analysis), using medical interviews as an example; and (c) role dimensions (aggregate indexes based on the principles of classification), using presumptuousness in interactions between people differing in status as an example.

Discrimination Among Relationships and Roles

Perhaps the most general finding to emerge from VRM research is that VRM profiles (distributions of modes used in an encounter) discriminate clearly and quantitatively among roles, among relationships, and among verbal tasks. Each role, task, or type of relationship—to the extent that it involves verbal communication—has a distinctive and characteristic profile of mode use. The profiles are distinctive in that they reliably distinguish roles from each other within relationships (e.g., patient versus physician in medical interviews) and they reliably distinguish relationships from each other (e.g., medical interview versus psychotherapy). The profiles are characteristic (a) in the sense that profiles within roles tend to be similar across people and occasions (e.g., one patient's VRM profile in a medical interview resembles other patients' profiles in medical interviews) and more important, (b) in the sense that the profile offers a coherent, intuitively plausible description of the role, including its relationship with other roles.

VRM use in the three segments of initial medical interviews (medical history, physical examination, conclusion) illustrates how the profiles are distinctive and characteristic (Table 4.1). Patients' VRM profiles are very different from physicians' profiles in all three segments, even though they are interacting in the same setting and discussing the same topics (Stiles, Orth, Scherwitz, Hennrikus, & Vallbona, 1984; Stiles, Putnam, & Jacob, 1982; Stiles, Putnam, Wolf, & James, 1979b, 1979c). And the profiles give plausible descriptions of the verbal component of each role in each of these three subtasks; the descriptions are easily recognizable by anyone who has been a participant in a medical interview. To illustrate only the most salient aspects, as Table 4.1 shows in the medical history segment, physicians' speech is dominated by Questions and Acknowledgments, as they gather information, and patients respond with information-giving Disclosures and Edifications, some of which are in the form of yes/no answers (coded KD and KE). In the physical examination, physicians use more Advisements (e.g., "**Take a deep breath**"), and fewer pure Acknowledgments, as they direct patients through examination procedures, and patients continue to give information. In the conclusion, physicians use more Edifications to transmit information about diagnosis and treatment, and patients begin to ask more Questions than previously.

There is variation within roles, of course, and this variation is often of interest to investigators, who may study effects of experimental conditions or individual differences on mode use. But the within-role variation is usually small relative to the huge differences between roles.

The VRM system thus specifies and quantifies the observation that people act differently in different roles. The point is not only that there

TABLE 4.1

Verbal Response Mode Profiles of Physicians and Patients in Medical
History, Physical Examination, and Conclusion Segments of Initial Medical
Interviews

| VRM Category | Percentage of Utterances in Interview Segment | | | | | |
| | History | | Examination | | Conclusion | |
Form/Intent	Dr.	Pt.	Dr.	Pt.	Dr.	Pt.
Question/Question	37	1	22	3	10	6
Reflection/Question	4	0	2	0	1	1
Edification/Question	2	0	2	0	0	0
Acknowledgment/Acknowledgment	16	4	6	3	5	12
Interpretation/Acknowledgment	10	1	12	3	7	12
Reflection/Reflection	6	0	3	0	2	0
Edification/Reflection	4	0	3	0	1	0
Disclosure/Disclosure	3	15	8	9	12	12
Reflection/Disclosure	0	2	0	1	0	1
Edification/Disclosure	0	14	1	15	1	4
Acknowledgment/Disclosure	0	5	0	15	0	3
Edification/Edification	4	15	5	10	23	10
Reflection/Edification	0	2	1	1	2	1
Disclosure/Edification	2	19	1	10	6	10
Acknowledgment/Edification	0	11	0	10	1	5
Advisement/Advisement	2	0	19	1	9	1
Question/Advisement	0	0	2	0	0	0
Disclosure/Advisement	0	0	1	0	2	0
Acknowledgment/Confirmation	0	3	0	5	0	4
Interpretation/Confirmation	0	0	0	1	0	4
Other	10	8	12	13	18	14
Total	100	100	100	100	100	100
Mean number of utterances	105	135	97	47	102	47

SOURCE: Based on 115 initial medical interviews, as reported by Stiles, Putnam, and Jacob (1982).
NOTE: Dr. = physician; Pt. = patient. Form is written first, intent second. "Other" includes modes that
averaged less than 2% by patients and physicians in all segments, uncodable (incomprehensible or
inaudible) utterances, and utterances upon which coders could not agree.

is a difference, but that the difference can be described coherently and
measured precisely.

Because they are quantitative, VRM profiles offer a way to compare
behavior directly across roles. To illustrate, in one study (Henricks &
Stiles, 1989), profiles of psychological radio call-in programs were compared to profiles of a variety of other sorts of interactions (various forms
of psychotherapy; educational interactions; informal conversations),

yielding quantitative indexes of profile similarity. Thus, the roles of caller and program host could be located in relation to other roles, such as client, student, or patient, and therapist, teacher, or physician. Results showed that callers' mean profile most resembled that of clients in cognitive-behavioral therapy, and that the hosts' mean profile most resembled that of rational-emotive therapists and physicians in the conclusion segment of medical interviews. As more types of interaction are coded, the possibility for such comparisons—and their precision—will increase commensurately.

Role Differences in Psychotherapy

One of the first results of applying the VRM system was a demonstration that psychotherapists of different theoretical orientations use dramatically different profiles of mode intents in their verbal interventions (Stiles, 1979). In transcripts of psychotherapy by prominent practitioners representing major schools of therapy, client-centered therapists used mostly Reflection and Acknowledgment intent; gestalt therapists used mostly Advisement, Interpretation, Question, and Disclosure intent; and psychoanalytic therapists used mostly Interpretation, Acknowledgment, Question, and Reflection intent (Table 4.2). Note that in the presentation of these results in Table 4.2, the utterances were aggregated across forms to give percentages for intent codes only.

Importantly, the technical differences among schools were systematic with respect to two of the principles of classification (frame of reference and source of experience). The principles form a bridge between psychotherapy theory and technique; each theory's recommendations, recast in terms of the principles, can be seen as prescribing and proscribing particular modes (cf. Table 2.1, p. 16):

(a) Client-centered theory (Rogers, 1951) holds that change comes from the client's exploring his or her own frame of reference and articulating unsymbolized experiences; the therapist is instructed to respond using the client's internal frame of reference exclusively, to communicate empathy and acceptance. In VRM terms, this allows client-centered therapists to use the four modes that are in the other's frame of reference (Reflection, Acknowledgment, Confirmation, and Edification), though, as shown in Table 4.2, therapists in this sample used mainly only two of them.

(b) Gestalt therapy theory (Perls, 1969; Perls, Hefferline, & Goodman, 1951) holds that change comes from recasting experience into the

TABLE 4.2

Percentage of Therapist VRM Intent Codes in Three Types of Psychotherapy

	Therapeutic Approach		
Mode Intent	Client-Centered	Gestalt	Psychoanalytic
Other's frame of reference			
Other's experience			
Reflection	45.4*	3.7	9.9*
Acknowledgment	46.1*	5.2	17.9*
Speaker's experience			
Confirmation	0.2*	0.0	0.2
Edification	1.9*	0.2	2.1
Speaker's frame of reference			
Other's experience			
Interpretation	0.4	26.2*	48.7*
Question	2.7	.9*	12.2*
Speaker's experience			
Advisement	0.6	36.7*	2.8
Disclosure	1.9	4.8*	1.9
Uncodable and coder disagreement	0.8	3.3	4.4
Number of coded therapist utterances	482	542	616

SOURCE: After Stiles (1979).
NOTE: Data were therapists' interventions in audiotape recorded teaching examples of psychotherapy. These were actual psychotherapy sessions conducted by prominent practitioners of each of the three psychotherapeutic approaches.
* Theoretically prescribed modes.

"now," which may be understood as the therapist's own existential frame of reference. A good gestalt therapist "stays absolutely in the now" and "doesn't listen to the content of the bullshit the patient produces" (Perls, 1969, p. 53). That is, in direct contrast to the client-centered therapist, the gestalt therapist is supposed to hold to his or her own (realistic) viewpoint and not be taken in by the patient's (possibly distorted) viewpoint. This should restrict gestalt therapists to the four modes in the speaker's frame of reference, Disclosure, Question, Advisement, and Interpretation, proscribing the other four, and in this sample, the therapists largely conformed (Table 4.2).

(c) Classical psychoanalytic theory (e.g., Freud, 1912/1958) holds that change comes from making unconscious experience conscious and by modifying the patient's understanding in light of the therapist's interpretations. "The doctor should be opaque to his patients and, like a mirror, should show them nothing but what is shown to him" (Freud, 1912/1958, p. 118). In VRM terms, the therapist should be concerned only with the patient's experience and reveal nothing of his or her own experience. Following this injunction, psychoanalytic therapists in this study used mainly Question, Acknowledgment, Reflection, and Interpretation, avoiding the other four modes (Table 4.2).

The results presented in Table 4.2 were based on actual therapy sessions that were unusually pure examples of the alternative approaches—teaching examples by leading proponents of each school (Stiles, 1979). Typical profiles in psychotherapeutic practice are less extreme. Nevertheless, coding of other samples using this VRM taxonomy and other systems have consistently found large differences among therapists of different schools, and these differences have been consistent with the theoretical principles of the schools (Auerbach, 1963; Brunink & Schroeder, 1979; Cromwell, 1981; Elliott et al., 1987; Hill, Thames, & Rardin, 1979; Snyder, 1945; Stiles, Shapiro et al., 1988, 1989; Strupp, 1955, 1957b, 1957c). This general finding represents one of the strongest and most replicated results in the field of psychotherapy process research. It seems clear that differential VRM use by therapists represents one major way in which alternative therapy theories are implemented.

Whereas these differences among schools are larger for VRM intent than for VRM form (Stiles, 1979), large differences in VRM form use have been found between individual therapists practicing the same approach (Stiles, Shapiro et al., 1989). Psychotherapy theories seem to be cast at the intent level, allowing therapists to use different forms. Forms may be used strategically to shape or soften presumptuous interventions. For example:

You're being too critical of yourself. II

It could be that you're being too critical of yourself. EI

Don't you think you're being too critical of yourself? QI

I wonder if you're not being too critical of yourself. DI

Forms may also reflect personal verbal habits. For example, in many types of therapy, Acknowledgment intents are common, but therapists habitually use different forms to indicate receipt of client communication.

Mm-hm. KK

I see. DK

Right. IK

Okay. IK

Such stylistic differences could have clinically significant consequences, however. For example, pure Acknowledgment (KK, e.g., **"mm-hm,"** **"yeah"**) tends to function facilitatively, to encourage communication, whereas Acknowledgment in the form of an evaluative word (IK, e.g., **"right,"** **"okay"**) tends to truncate communication (Coulthard & Ashby, 1976; Stiles, Putnam, Wolf et al., 1979a). Pure Acknowledgment might be more appropriate in psychodynamic or experiential therapies, to encourage detailed exploration of the client's inner life, whereas IK is more appropriate in cognitive or behavioral therapies, where efficient data gathering is important and long stories may waste time (Stiles, Shapiro et al., 1989).

Client VRM Use. In contrast to therapists' diversity in mode use, clients tend to use similar VRM profiles regardless of their therapist's theoretical orientation (McDaniel et al., 1981; Stiles, 1984a; Stiles et al., 1988; Stiles & Sultan, 1979). Most (60%-80%) client utterances are in the four *exposition* modes, DD, DE, ED, and EE (cf. discussion of verbal exchanges below). Typically, another 10%-15% are in Acknowledgment forms, with the remainder spread across a wide variety of other modes. The common core of exposition modes suggests that if there is a common "active ingredient" among the diverse psychotherapeutic approaches, then it may be more likely to be found in the client's verbal behavior than in the therapist's.

Clients' use of their most prominent mode, Disclosure, is strongly correlated with raters' evaluations of the quality of the psychotherapeutic process, as measured by the *experiencing scale* (Klein, Mathieu-Coughlan, & Kiesler, 1986) and by the subscales for *patient exploration* and *therapist exploration* in the Vanderbilt Psychotherapy Process Scale (Gomes-Schwartz, 1978; Suh, Strupp, & O'Malley, 1986). Clients' percentages of DD were correlated .58 with *experiencing* (Stiles, McDaniel et al., 1979), .66 with *patient exploration,* and .65 with *therapist exploration* (McDaniel et al., 1981). Correlations of these ratings with EE percentages were strongly negative, while correlations with ED percentages were slightly positive and with DE percentages slightly negative. These results suggest that good process, as judged by sophisticated raters, corresponds in part to clients' use of Disclosure intent, as opposed to Edification. In terms of the principles, when clients convey information as seen from their own internal frame of reference, rather than information as seen from an external, objective perspective, they are evaluated as experiencing and exploring more deeply.

A reasonable next question to ask is whether VRM use is important for psychotherapy outcome. Unfortunately, despite a good deal of effort (see review by Orlinsky & Howard, 1986), process-outcome relationships remain poorly understood. This poor understanding probably reflects flaws in the conceptual and statistical approaches that have been used, including the correlation problem noted above in relation to medical interview outcomes (Stiles, 1987a; Stiles, 1988; Stiles & Shapiro, 1989, in press; Stiles, Shapiro, & Elliott, 1986).

Verbal Exchange Structure of Medical Interviews

A robust result of the medical interview work has been the identification of verbal exchanges—clusters of patient and physician VRMs that tend to be used together and appear to serve important medical and socioemotional functions in interviews (Putnam & Stiles, 1991; Stiles, Orth et al., 1984; Stiles & Putnam, in press[b]; Stiles et al., 1982; Stiles, Putnam, Wolf et al., 1979a). Indexes of these exchanges constitute dyad-level measures of verbal interaction, that is, measures that characterize the dyad as an interacting unit rather than each participant as an individual.

According to the exchange structure theory (Putnam & Stiles, 1991; Stiles & Putnam, in press[b]), the dialogue between patients and physicians is composed of verbal exchanges that participants use to accomplish their purposes for the encounter. A verbal exchange is a type of interaction consisting of specific types of speech acts by each participant that tend to occur together in complementary ways. Patients initiate certain verbal behaviors that expect complementary behaviors from physicians and vice versa. Each speech act category has a niche in an exchange; that is, it occurs in association with other speech act categories with which it has functional relationships. For example, physician Questions and patient yes/no answers form one kind of exchange. Physician instructions and patient agreements to comply form another.

Utterances need not be temporally adjacent or in a particular order to be part of an exchange. Although normal speech is composed of turn taking, a response is not rigidly determined by the preceding speech, but may relate to an earlier utterance. For example, when a physician asks, **"Do you have any pain in your chest when you exercise?"** the patient may give several qualifying remarks (**"I know I should exercise more, but I find it very hard to do in the winter"**) before answering the question (**"No, I don't get any chest pain"**). Thus, the "exchange" concept does not require that interactions be analyzed or conducted utterance for utterance, but rather it views exchanges as comprising many utterances within a segment of the interview. Utterances that make up a particular exchange may tend to follow each other immediately or to occur in a particular sequence, but this is not necessary.

Verbal exchanges have been identified by factor analysis of VRM category frequencies within interview segments (i.e., history, examination, conclusion). Factor analysis combines the categories into groups, based on their intercorrelations. Presumably, categories that are used together ("exchanged") will tend to be correlated across interviews and load on the same factor. Thus, each exchange consists of categories whose frequencies tend to go up and down together across interviews. These factors are interpretable as verbal exchanges, and the factors together constitute the medical interview's verbal exchange structure.

The verbal exchange structure of medical interviews has been studied in initial medical interviews—first visits to a hospital walk-in clinic by diagnostically heterogeneous groups of patients—in North Carolina (Putnam et al., 1985, 1988; Stiles, Putnam et al., 1982, 1984, 1986; Stiles, Putnam, Wolf et al., 1979a); in routine visits by hypertensive patients to urban community health centers in Texas (Orth et al., 1987; Stiles, Orth et al., 1984); in general practice patients in and around London, England (Cape, 1988); and in general practice patients in and around Sheffield, England (Brownbridge, 1987; Brownbridge et al., 1986). In view of the heterogeneity of the samples, these studies have yielded a remarkably consistent picture of the patient-physician joint repertoire of verbal exchanges. Almost all of the exchanges shown in Table 4.3 were found in each of the studies.

The seven exchanges summarized in Table 4.3 constitute the bulk of the verbal interaction in the medical interviews studied. Each exchange represents an identifiable clinical function or subtask of the interview. Theoretically, each type of exchange may be considered as an item in a joint repertoire; that is, both participants know the part they must play in a medical interview and expect to play it. Participants adjust the frequency and the content of each type of verbal exchange to meet the requirements of each patient and the situation.

The medical functions represented by the exchanges each involve a constellation of verbal and nonverbal behaviors, not just VRMs, so that factor analyses based on any coding system that measures a sufficient range of behaviors should reveal essentially the same exchange structure. Similarly, other methods of finding associations among physician and patient interview behaviors, such as sequence analysis (Bakeman & Gottman, 1986; Sackett, 1979, 1987) should identify the same set of

TABLE 4.3

Medical Interview Verbal Exchanges and Their Probable Functions

---

EXPOSITION
    Dr: KK   Pt: DD, DE, EE, ED, (QQ)
    Segments: Throughout, but especially in history.
    Description: Patients describe their illnesses and circumstances in their own words; physicians show attentiveness.
    Function: Identify presenting problems, gather background information unconstrained by physician preconceptions, give patients confidence that they have provided full description of illness, catharsis.

CLOSED QUESTION
    Dr: QQ, RQ, EQ   Pt: KE, KD
    Segments: History and conclusion.
    Description: Physicians ask specific questions; patients give brief answers (mostly yes or no).
    Function: Gather data necessary for diagnosis and treatment decisions, fill in gaps in patient's narrative, test hypotheses.

CHECKING
    Dr: RR, ER   Pt: KC
    Segments: Mainly in history.
    Description: Physicians repeat or summarize information provided by patients; patients confirm or disconfirm physician's understanding.
    Function: Check accuracy of communication.

DIRECTION
    Dr: AA, QA, DD, IK   Pt: (nonverbal compliance)
    Segments: Examination.
    Description: Physicians direct patients through examination procedures; patients comply.
    Function: Inform patients how to cooperate in physical examination.

INQUIRY
    Dr: QQ   Pt: ED, KD
    Segments: Examination, somewhat in history.
    Description: Physicians ask about subjective reactions (sensations and perceptions, pain), often in conjunction with examination procedures; patients reveal these.
    Function: Gather subjective data to complement objective examination.

EXPLANATION
    Dr: EE, DE, DD   Pt: KK, QQ
    Segments: Throughout, but especially in conclusion.
    Description: Physicians give objective information about illness and treatment; patients show attentiveness.
    Function: Educate patient about illness, explain and justify treatment procedures, relieve patient worry.

INSTRUCTION/CONTRACTS
    Dr: AA, DA   Pt: IC, IK
    Segments: Conclusion.
    Description: Physicians prescribe tests, treatments, return appointments; patients show attentiveness or (sometimes) agree or comply.
    Function: Instruct patients in treatment regimen.

NOTE: VRM abbreviations: A = Advisement, C = Confirmation, D = Disclosure, E = Edification, I = Interpretation, K = Acknowledgment, Q = Question, R = Reflection. Both the form and intent of each utterance are coded. For example, "**Would you get up on the table?**" is coded QA, Question form with Advisement intent.

exchanges. Very likely there are other actual or potential exchanges that are not represented. Some may be nonverbal or in other ways inaccessible to the VRM coding system. Others may be too infrequently used to have been detected in the analyses.

As an illustration of how exchanges serve clinical purposes, consider the two principal medical history exchanges, Exposition and Closed Question. In order to obtain an understanding of the patient, the illness, and its context, the physician must elicit, organize, and synthesize the relevant data (a task function) and establish a positive, open relationship with the patient (a socioemotional function) in the history segment. Thus, both task-related resources (e.g., information) and socioemotional resources (e.g., support) must be exchanged.

Exposition exchanges, which account for the largest proportion of utterances in the history segment, are composed primarily of patient Edification and Disclosures (in both form and intent) and physician pure Acknowledgments (Table 4.3). Patients describe their illnesses and circumstances (objective and subjective experiences) in their own words (i.e., first or third person sentences), and physicians show attentiveness by saying "**mm-hm**" (KK) or "**yes**" (KK). Physicians use Exposition exchanges to identify problems, gather background information unconstrained by their preconceptions, and allow patients the satisfaction of giving a full description of their illness, including its emotional aspects. Thus, in addition to their data gathering (task) function, Exposition exchanges serve a socioemotional function by giving patients the relief of disclosing their health and personal concerns to an understanding listener. For example:

Pt: **I have the headaches to the point where I throw up with them.** DD

Dr: **Mm-hm.** KK

Pt: **Then I have to go to bed with them.** DD
And then I'll go to sleep for awhile DE
and maybe they'll ease off. ED
But after awhile, they'll come right back again. ED

Dr: **Mm-hm.** KK

Pt: **And my blood pressure last Saturday started dropping.** EE
And that's when they admitted me to the hospital. EE
And I've been in the hospital all week. DE
Well, KK
I've had headaches all week in the hospital. DD

Dr: **Mm-hm.** KK

The Closed Question exchange is defined by physician Questions and patient yes and no answers (coded KD or KE). For example, the physician asks, **"Did you have a pain in your chest?"** (QQ), to which the patient responds **"Yes"** (KD) or **"No"** (KD). In Closed Question exchanges, physicians can pursue hypotheses or conduct a review of systems. Thus Closed Question exchanges give the physician control of the interview, effectively dictating the form of the patient's answer (i.e., yes or no). They are used to gather data necessary for diagnosis and treatment decisions, fill gaps in the patients' narratives, and give physicians a way to test specific hypotheses.

Dr: **Does it hurt to lift the baby?** QQ (pure question)

Pt: **Yes.** KD (subjective information)

Dr: **So you have someone in to help you?** RQ (second person form)

Pt: **Yes.** KE (objective information)

Presumptuousness and Relative Status

Each of the principles of classification can be used as a basis for aggregating utterances (see Chapters 2, 5, and 11). These aggregate indexes are called *role dimensions,* and they reflect broad aspects of interpersonal relationships. For example, the proportion given by the number of a speaker's utterances that presume knowledge of the other (i.e., Reflection, Confirmation, Interpretation, and Advisement) divided by the total number of coded utterances is called *presumptuousness* (Stiles, 1978b). The comparable proportions calculated using the source of experience and frame of reference principles are called *attentiveness* (versus informativeness) and *acquiescence* (versus directiveness), respectively.

One repeated finding based on role dimensions involves the relationship of the VRM role dimension presumptuousness to relative status in face-to-face interaction. The higher-status member of an interacting dyad has been found consistently to be more presumptuous. That is, the higher-status member's proportion of presumptuous utterances is higher than that of the lower-status member (Table 4.4). Physicians were more presumptuous than patients in all three segments of their medical interviews (Stiles, Putnam, James et al., 1979). Psychotherapists were more presumptuous than clients during sessions of various types of psychotherapy (Knight, 1987; Stiles et al., 1988). Parents were more presumptuous than their 10- to 12-year-old children in two laboratory

TABLE 4.4

Presumptuousness by High- and Low-Status Members
of Status Discrepant Dyads

Roles (High/Low status)	Presumptuousness of Role	
	High Status	Low Status
Physicians/patients		
Medical history	.214	.046
Physical examination	.450	.044
Conclusion	.292	.122
Psychotherapists/clients		
Psychodynamic therapy	.313	.109
Cognitive-behavioral therapy	.300	.096
Professors/students		
Classroom discussion	.175	.063
Laboratory interaction	.143	.042
Attorneys/witnesses		
Direct examination	.145	.012
Cross-examination	.229	.042
Parents/children		
Reach agreement task	.351	.177
Tell how you feel task	.270	.094
Management/labor		
Bargaining session	.242	.197
Seniors/freshmen		
Laboratory conversation	.105	.080

SOURCES: Physicians/patients (Stiles, Putnam, James, & Wolf, 1979); psychotherapists/clients (Stiles, Shapiro, & Firth-Cozens, 1988); parents/children (Stiles & White, 1981); attorneys/witnesses (McGaughey & Stiles, 1983); professors/students (Stiles, Waszak, & Barton, 1979); management/labor (Hinkle, Stiles, & Taylor, 1988); seniors/freshmen (Cansler & Stiles, 1981).
NOTE: Presumptuousness was calculated as the proportion of coded utterances that were coded as Advisement, Interpretation, Confirmation, or Reflection, averaged across form and intent codes. Differences between high- and low-status roles were statistically significant in all cases.

problem-solving exercises, (a) reaching agreement on an ongoing source of conflict and (b) telling each other how you feel in the conflictual situation (Stiles & White, 1981). Courtroom attorneys were more presumptuous than witnesses (rape victims) during both direct and cross-examination (McGaughey & Stiles, 1983). Professors were more presumptuous than students both in classroom discussions and in laboratory conversations (Stiles, Waszak et al., 1979). And management representatives were more presumptuous than labor representatives in a negotiation session (Hinkle et al., 1988). In one study, fourth-year university students took part in similar conversations with first-year students and with professors, on different occasions; VRM coding showed the fourth-year students were significantly more presumptuous in the former conversations than in the latter, as well as more presumptuous than the first-year students and less presumptuous than the professors within each type of conversation (Cansler & Stiles, 1981). Thus presumptuousness appears to reflect relative status (i.e., in relation to the other person) rather than some absolute characteristic of the speaker.

As Table 4.4 shows, the size of the differences between interactants was not necessarily large, but it was consistent with respect to relative status. The consistently very low level of presumptuousness by the lower-status member of all dyads suggests that the difference may be maintained by the lower-status member avoiding the use of presumptuous utterances (i.e., Advisements, Interpretations, Confirmations, and Reflections). Perhaps this can be understood as a way of being polite, to avoid giving offense to a superior (Brown & Levinson, 1978; Stiles, 1981). In equal-status dyads, members' presumptuousness has tended to increase with degree of intimacy and to be correlated across dyads (e.g., Premo & Stiles, 1983), suggesting that members adjust their level of presumptuousness reciprocally to reflect their importance to each other (Stiles, 1984b).

5

Conceptualization and Principles of Classification

THEORETICAL BACKGROUND

The taxonomy draws on a conceptualization of verbal communication in which people are seen as centers of experience and speech acts are seen as links between them. Although this conceptualization is not the only possible way to view the VRM coding system, I have found it valuable in considering how and why the taxonomy works as well as it does.

The Stream of Experience

Experience is construed as a stream that is more or less continuous in time and varying in breadth, depth, and intensity. Experience is the contents of awareness. Experience varies as the person encounters new situations and reacts to them. In general, experience has a central topic—some thought, feeling, perception, or intention that is central in awareness. This is surrounded by other thoughts, feelings, perceptions, and intentions that give meaning to the central experience.

Each speech act may be construed as an attempted point of contact between two centers of experience—an attempt to connect one point in the speaker's stream of experience with a point in the other's stream of experience. The nature of these connections varies, and the VRM taxonomy is a classification of the alternative kinds of connections. To illustrate, a Disclosure (**"I'm afraid of the dark."**) attempts to convey the speaker's experience directly to the other, so that the other can have a fragment of the speaker's experience. A Question (**"What was that man's name?"**) attempts to convey an empty space in the speaker's understanding, typically in the hope that the other can recognize it and fill it. An Advisement (**"Please bring me a glass of water."**) attempts to impose an experience—the intention to bring a glass of water—on the other. Insofar as speech acts represent points of connection, or at least intended connection, between human centers of experience, they may be considered as units of interpersonal relationships, or microrelationships.

Although experience is continuous, speech acts are discrete. Each utterance can be considered to concern only a moment of experience. Thus, utterances only sample experience. The point-on-a-stream analogy is meant to suggest that people have experience much faster than they can communicate it. Just as a point on a line has no length, no finite number of utterances can fully convey the continuous flow of a speaker's experience to another person. Even a brief stretch of experience can be unpacked virtually without limit, as illustrated by work with tape-assisted recall, by Labov and Fanshel's (1977) discourse analysis, or by Henry James's novels. People can talk reflectively at length about their experience during the production of any one utterance—particularly if prompted by seeing themselves on a videotape.

This conceptualization of utterances invokes a thought/language dualism by assuming that most of the stream of experience is not communicated by language. Experience proceeds far more rapidly and in greater richness and detail than language can communicate it.

To pursue the analogy one more step, an utterance may be considered as representing a partial cross section of the stream of experience. Though it has no length, it may vary in depth and breadth, analogous to the richness and complexity of the utterance.

Perhaps there are aspects of experience that cannot in principle be communicated in language. Such an assumption goes beyond what is required for the taxonomy. It does seem to me, however, that even the most vivid descriptions of other people's experience fall short of the richness and detail I find in my own experience. I struggle for hours with psychotherapy clients and yet my experience of their experience still seems dim and approximate. Conversely, I seem always able to add things to a description of my own experience, and when I stop adding there are still things left unsaid.

The Speaker-Other Dichotomy

Every speech act may be considered to have a sender and an intended receiver, or as I call them, a *speaker* and an *other*. The speaker may be considered as whoever is the referent for "I" or "we," and the other may be considered as whoever is the referent for "you." The speaker or the other (or both) may be collectivities (as when a speaker addresses a large audience) or may be indistinct (as when an author addresses an unknown readership) or even imaginary or inanimate (as when a speaker addresses a mountain or a tree, or when one fictional character speaks to another).

The VRM taxonomy is based directly on this fundamental dichotomy between speaker and other in the communication of experience. As explained in the next section, it classifies speech acts according to whose experience is the topic of the act, whether or not the speaker presumes to know the other's experience, and whose viewpoint or framework of meaning is used to understand the experience. In this way, the taxonomy classifies the kinds of momentary verbal connections that can occur between two centers of experience. It is a classification of microrelationships—of the momentary relationships that can exist between people in communication.

Theoretically, the modes are coherent and distinct categories (that is, Disclosure, Question, Reflection, and so forth are easily recognizable categories of utterances) because the speaker and the other are coherent and distinct experiencing entities. That is, insofar as there are no plausible intermediate values between speaker and other, VRMs are discrete categories rather than continuously measured attributes.

Thus, the VRM taxonomy is grounded in a theoretical interpretation of the structure of communication, not in external or functional considerations such as what might be therapeutic or what might be done by high-status people. Analogously, the Linnaean biological taxonomy was based on selected morphological features (e.g., the structure of fruits). It was later found to have a basis in genetics and has continued to be refined as genetic mechanisms have become better understood. It was not based on functional characteristics, such as "domestic" versus "wild" or "edible" versus "inedible."

PRINCIPLES OF CLASSIFICATION

The following three principles of classification are the core of this taxonomy of verbal response modes.

Source of Experience

The experience that a speech act concerns may be the speaker's own, as when the speaker reveals his or her own feelings or opinions or information known to him or her ("**I feel great today.**" "**It's 9 o'clock.**"), or it may be the other person's experience, as when the speaker asks a question or describes the other's feelings ("**Where have you been?**" "**You must be famished.**"). Each speech act may be classified by whether it concerns the speaker's experience or the other's experience. Utterances that concern the speaker's experience may be described as *informative,* whereas utterances that concern the other's experience may be described as *attentive.*

Presumption About Experience

In performing a speech act, a speaker may or may not need to presume to know what the other's experience (including the other's intentional behavior) is, was, will be, or should be. Speech acts that do require such presumption are coded as "other." Those in which the speaker need presume to know about only his or her own experience are coded as "speaker." For example, "**You acted foolishly**" presumes knowledge of the other's volitional behavior; "**Make mine medium rare**" presumes to guide the other's behavior (in effect, seeking to impose an experience on the other, the intention to perform some action); "**You probably felt discouraged**" presumes to understand the other's feelings; "**We disagree about the morality of euthanasia**" presumes to know the other's opinion. By contrast, "**I'm sick of spinach,**" "**Fences make good neighbors,**" and "**What does 'laconic' mean?**" require presumptions only about the speaker's own experience. Utterances that require a presumption about the other's experience may be described as *presumptuous,* whereas utterances that require presumptions about the speaker's experience only may be described as *nonpresumptuous* or *unassuming.*

Importantly, this principle concerns only presumptions that are necessary to the meaning of the utterance. As a speaker says, "**I wish I were back in Boston**" or "**Do you want to get a hamburger with me?**" he or she may privately presume to know something about the other's experience, but it is not necessary to presume such knowledge for the utterance to have the meaning it does have. By contrast, the normal meanings of "**You wish you were back in Boston**" and "**Let's go get a hamburger**" (in their normal context) entail specific presumptions about what the other feels or should do, respectively; a speaker cannot mean those things without making those presumptions.

For several years, I called this principle "focus" (e.g., Stiles, 1978b, 1981, 1986a, 1987c). Utterances that presumed knowledge of the speaker's experience only were said to be focused on the speaker, whereas utterances that required presumptions about the other's experience were said to be focused on the other. The name "focus" proved to be uninformative and has been dropped in favor of "presumption about experience." I include this historical note here only to ensure continuity with previous writings about the VRM taxonomy. The crucial concept was presumption all along; only the name has been changed.

Frame of Reference

The meaning that an experience has in a particular speech act derives from the constellation of associated experiences (ideas, memories, connotations, etc.) with which it is linked. In the VRM taxonomy, this constellation is called the frame of reference of the speech act. Each viewpoint, schema, way of looking at, construction, or theory may be considered as a frame of reference. For VRM purposes, frames of reference are considered as either the speaker's or the other's—representing *whose* viewpoint, schema, or theory is used. Speech acts that take the speaker's viewpoint ("**You did a good job.**") are classified as speaker's frame of reference, whereas speech acts that take the other's viewpoint ("**You were proud of your performance.**") are classified as other's frame of reference.

Strictly speaking, in order to understand their own utterances, speakers cannot use a frame of reference that is exclusively the other's. Consequently, the taxonomy distinguishes between use of the speaker's personal frame of reference and use of a frame of reference that is shared with the other. Utterances are classified as speaker's frame of reference if they depend for all or part of their meaning on the speaker's internal (private) frame of reference. The speaker is the presumed judge of such utterances' accuracy or appropriateness (see later discussion of felicity). Utterances that use a neutral, or objective, viewpoint (e.g., statements of fact) are classified as other's frame of reference because the frame of reference is shared with some or all other people. Accuracy or appropriateness is presumed to be judged by the other or by external criteria.

TABLE 5.1

Descriptors Associated With Verbal Response Modes

Mode	Descriptors
Disclosure	Informative, Unassuming, Directive
Edification	Informative, Unassuming, Acquiescent
Advisement	Informative, Presumptuous, Directive
Confirmation	Informative, Presumptuous, Acquiescent
Question	Attentive, Unassuming, Directive
Acknowledgment	Attentive, Unassuming, Acquiescent
Interpretation	Attentive, Presumptuous, Directive
Reflection	Attentive, Presumptuous, Acquiescent

Utterances that use the speaker's frame of reference may be described as *directive,* whereas utterances that use a frame of reference shared with the other may be described as *nondirective* or *acquiescent.*

Table 5.1 lists the eight VRMs with their associated role descriptors (cf. Table 2.1). Aggregate indexes based on these descriptors, called *role dimensions,* are described in Chapter 11.

Selecting Names for Modes and Role Descriptors

The eight verbal response modes are defined by the intersection of the three principles of classification (Table 2.1 and Chapter 6), but they have been given familiar names (Disclosure, Edification, Advisement, Confirmation, Question, Acknowledgment, Interpretation, and Reflection—capitalized in this book, to distinguish them from the colloquial terms). Similarly, the role descriptors shown in Table 5.1 are defined by the principles and the modes (e.g., *attentive* is that which Questions, Acknowledgments, Interpretations, and Reflections have in common—having the other's experience as their topic), but the terms are familiar ones.

In general, in using and developing the VRM system, I have chosen to give formal definitions to familiar English words rather than to invent neutral terms, such as Characteristic Z or Response Type 4. This strategy is intended to make VRM names memorable and accessible. The strategy's weakness is that the terms often have surplus meaning that can mislead some readers (and, initially, some coders). Invented neutral terms are virtually impossible to remember without repeated reference to their definitions, however, and therefore represent a greater impediment to communication, in my opinion.

Formal definitions are a way of moving away from natural language (where categories do not have distinct boundaries) toward axiomatic systems. The advantage is in clarity and in saying the same thing to everybody. The value of the work then depends on how well the system as a whole describes your experience of the phenomenon. Of course, in redefining familiar words I run some risks of confusion—of trying to make claims about disclosures based on findings about Disclosures, for example, or of being misunderstood as making such claims.

One motivation for formal definitions is overcoming variation from person to person in the meanings of such terms as *question, disclosure, interpretation, attentive,* and *presumptuous.* As discussed in Chapter 1, the taxonomic categories overlap the center of the natural language categories surprisingly well, so the VRM meanings for the terms are well within the range of meanings one would encounter naturally. I like to think that the VRM and natural categories overlap because the taxonomy is based on psychological principles that underlie the natural categories.

MEANING AND FELICITY OF UTTERANCES

Illocutionary Force

The aspect of an utterance's meaning that the VRM taxonomy codes is its *illocutionary force* (see Chapter 3). Thus **"Pick up your clothes"** (AA) may be said to have the illocutionary force of an Advisement. More subtly, the illocutionary force of **"Would you pick up your clothes?"** (QA) may be described as a combination of Question and Advisement.

VRM categories do not code all aspects of meaning. For example, the *sense* of an utterance—its denotative and connotative content, which is often considered the central aspect of meaning (see Chapter 3)—is not coded.

Although the taxonomy does group utterances that are similar in force, the force of utterances in each category is not identical; for example, commands (**"Go home!"**), suggestions (**"Perhaps you should go home."**), permission (**"You may go home."**), and prohibition (**"You may not stay out any longer."**) share features defined by the principles and are categorized as Advisements, but clearly their force is not exactly the same. Indeed, no two commands have exactly identical force. In the same way, "**The door is shut**" (EE), "**John shut the door**" (EE), "**I shut the door**" (DE), "**Shut the door**" (AA), "**Is the door shut?**" (QQ), "**You wish the door were shut**" (RR), and (in response to "I wish the door were shut") "**Mm-hm**" (KK) all concern the topic of door shutting, a sense category, but no two of them have exactly the same sense.

Thus, although the VRM system may be described as an exhaustive classification, the VRM categories do not exhaust all possible distinctions among illocutionary forces, much less all meanings. The system is exhaustive in having some category for every comprehensible utterance (with a few qualifications, e.g., see the discussion of expletives in Chapter 10). The same claim could have been made if the taxonomy had only two categories (e.g., speaker's experience versus other's experience).

It is possible to subdivide categories according to further force distinctions or other criteria; for example, commands, suggestions, permission, and prohibition may be subcategories of Advisement (see further examples in Chapter 6). By "subcategory" I mean that all share the defining features of Advisement (speaker's experience, presumptions about other's experience, speaker's frame of reference), but differ from each other in other ways. The relative importance of any category or subcategory depends, of course, on the investigator's theory and purpose. It may be possible to identify a fourth principle that will cut across the other three, yielding 16 categories rather than 8. So far, I have not found another principle that subdivides all modes usefully (for my purposes), though valence (a continuum from positive to negative rather than a dichotomy) would be a popular possibility (see discussion in Chapter 6; Burchill, 1984; Burchill & Stiles, 1988). I have found it useful, however, to construct subcategories of particular modes in particular studies (e.g., Stiles et al., 1988).

Literal Meaning and Pragmatic Meaning

Utterances may have meanings, including illocutionary force, at many levels, and these meanings may be the same or different from each other (Stiles, 1986b, 1987b). The VRM taxonomy codes the illocutionary force of utterances at two levels, the literal level and the pragmatic level, and calls these form and intent, respectively. Literal meaning (form) is what the utterance says based on the dictionary meaning of the words and standard meaning of the grammatical construction. Pragmatic meaning (intent) is what the speaker intends the utterance to mean on the occasion of its use. More precisely, pragmatic meaning is that which is *intended to be recognized as intended to be recognized* (Stiles, 1981, 1986b; after Grice, 1969; and Bach & Harnish, 1979); that is, to mean something by an utterance (in the sense of pragmatic meaning or VRM intent), a speaker must (a) be aware of the content, (b) intend that the other become aware of the content, (c) intend that the communication appear intended, and (d) intend that the communication be attributable to the speaker.

Put more simply, to mean something by an utterance, one must be *on record* as saying it (cf. Brown & Levinson, 1978). On-record meanings are intrinsically public and communicative, at least for the intended audience (i.e., the other). One cannot mean something (in the pragmatic meaning sense) and simultaneously hide or disguise the meaning. Consequently, VRM intent can be validly coded without resort to mind reading, insofar as coders are in roughly the same epistemological position as the other (Stiles, 1987b).

Meanings that do not meet all the conditions for pragmatic meaning are designated *off record*. Off-record levels of meanings may be designated as hint level, manipulation level, secret, or unwitting or subconscious, depending on how many of the conditions they fail to meet (see Stiles, 1986b). Briefly, meanings that are intended to be recognized as intended (but still off record) are hints; meanings that are intended to be recognized, but not meant to be recognized as intended, are manipulations; meanings that are intended in the sense of being central in the speaker's awareness, but not intended to be recognized, are secrets; and meanings that are not even in awareness are unwitting or subconscious.

Note that pragmatic meanings (VRM intents) may be expressed indirectly (i.e., in mixed forms), but they are still on record. For example, **"Could you drive a little more slowly?"** (QA) is Question in form, but the speaker is on record as directing the other to take action, albeit politely. This is distinct from hints or manipulations, which are off record; for example, **"Mary was arrested for speeding here last week"** (EE), may hint that the speaker wants the other to slow down (intended to be recognized as intended) but does not actually direct her or him to do so. Thus, the VRM taxonomy distinguishes between on-record and off-record indirect speech acts (cf. Brown & Levinson, 1978; Searle, 1975).

Off-record meanings are among the many important aspects of communication that are not measured by the VRM taxonomy's form and intent codes. It would be possible, however, to add codes for off-record levels of meanings for many utterances. Such coding would follow principles similar to those for coding on-record intents. For example, in some contexts, the utterance "**I feel a cold draft**" may carry the hint that the other should take remedial action (e.g., shut the window). It could be coded DDA to represent the hint-level Advisement along with the on-record Disclosure. Further, if coders are aware of these additional levels, they may more easily see what is on record and therefore codable. If it is clear that the Advisement meaning in "**I feel a cold draft**" is only a hint—that is, off-record—and not an explicit suggestion, then it is easier to recognize that the on-record intent of the utterance is Disclosure.

Although it is often difficult to code off-record meanings reliably, some off-record meanings can be identified, and their theoretical and practical importance could justify efforts to study them. This book does not address the difficulties of coding off-record meanings. Further conceptual and empirical work on this problem is needed.

Felicity of Utterances

As Austin (1975) noted, utterances in different illocutionary categories must meet different social and epistemological conditions in order to be felicitous, or "happy." Utterances that fail to meet appropriate felicity conditions may be said to be flawed or to misfire. Perhaps the most familiar felicity condition is *truth*—often described as a correspondence between an utterance and a state of the world. (An epistemologically more congenial rephrasing might have this as a correspondence between a shared understanding of an utterance and a shared perception of the world.) A true assertion is felicitous, whereas a false assertion is infelicitous.

Within the VRM system, truth seems to apply most directly to Edification. It applies only with qualification to Disclosure, Interpretation, Reflection, and Confirmation, which seek to represent the speaker's or other's internal states or personal judgments rather than states of the external world. For example, a Disclosure's felicity seems better described as *sincerity* than as truth, for there is no way to demonstrate an objective correspondence between a Disclosure and a state of the world. Truth seems irrelevant to the happiness of Questions or Advisements or Acknowledgments, whose felicity conditions might be better described as answerability, feasibility, and timeliness, respectively.

The taxonomic principles help to specify epistemological conditions that each of the eight mode intents must meet in order to be felicitous.

In each case, felicity depends on the congruence of the central experience with the frame of reference, given the required presumptions. For example, a felicitous (i.e., accurately empathic) Reflection is one in which the other's experience, as expressed by the speaker, is congruent with the other's internal frame of reference, of which the speaker must presume some knowledge. An Acknowledgment need only be timely to be felicitous, insofar as the speaker need not presume knowledge of the other's experience or the frame of reference—that is, the speaker need not have understood the other's meaning. Indeed, most **"mm-hms"** are uttered during the other's speech, before the speaker has enough information to understand the other's meaning. An **"mm-hm"** uttered when the other hasn't said anything would be infelicitous.

In general, an utterance's felicity (truth, sincerity, accuracy, empathy, timeliness, etc.) must be judged from the frame of reference it uses. Thus, the sincerity of **"I'll bring this back tomorrow"** (DD) must be judged from the speaker's frame of reference, whereas the empathic accuracy of **"You wish you could crawl in a hole and die"** (RR) must be judged from the other's frame of reference. Conversely, in coding, asking who is the implied judge of an utterance's felicity is often a valuable litmus test for deciding an utterance's frame of reference. For example, **"You've done more than anyone could expect of you"** is Interpretation (speaker's frame of reference) if the speaker is the implied judge of its accuracy, but Reflection (other's frame of reference) if the other is the implied judge. The felicity conditions of each VRM intent are discussed in Chapter 6. Use of this litmus test (i.e., who is the implied judge of the utterance's truth, sincerity, accuracy, empathy) is discussed in Chapter 8.

Felicity does not affect an utterance's code. An unanswerable Question is still a Question; an untimely Acknowledgment is still an Acknowledgment; an insincere Disclosure is a Disclosure; and a false Edification is an Edification.

6
Verbal Response Mode Intents

This chapter presents definitions and examples of the eight VRM intents. Each intent is defined by the three principles of classification (cf. Table 2.1) as these interact to give each intent its distinctive character.

Most of the examples given in this chapter are pure modes—utterances in which the VRM form matches the VRM intent. Chapter 7 gives VRM form definitions and examples of mixed modes—utterances in which form and intent differ.

WHAT IS INTENT?

VRM intent concerns what is meant, regardless of how it is said (VRM form concerns what is said; see Chapter 7). Thus, coders must judge what the speaker meant in context, using the following three questions, based on the principles of classification: Whose experience is the topic? Does the utterance require the speaker to make some presumption about the other's experience? Whose frame of reference is used to understand the experience?

As explained in Chapter 5 and elsewhere (Stiles, 1986b, 1987a), VRM intents are an aspect of the on-record, pragmatic meaning of the utterance. In simple terms, an utterance is a Disclosure in intent if it is meant as a Disclosure. VRM intent is a *microintent*—an aspect of the meaning of a single utterance. It must be distinguished from the broader concept of intention or purpose.

More technically, VRM intent is what Grice (1969) described as *speaker's occasion meaning,* which in turn is defined as that which is *intended to be recognized as intended to be recognized* (see Chapter 5; Bach & Harnish, 1979; Stiles, 1986b). A consequence of this definition is that VRM intents are public: One cannot mean something (in this sense) and simultaneously disguise or hide it, at least not from its intended audience. Coders are not required to read a speaker's mind in order to code VRM intent; they are required only to understand what he or she meant by the utterance (see Stiles, 1987a, for further discussion). In the VRM system, intent does not refer to deeper motives or purposes, except insofar as these are part of the on-record meaning of utterances.

Off-record meanings of utterances, such as hints, manipulations, secrets, and unintended or subconscious meanings, are not coded as intent (see Chapter 5). It is useful, however, to understand them, because mentally moving them out of the way can help clear one's view of the on-record intent. For example, the utterance **"I feel cold"** (DD) may, in some contexts, carry a hint, such as **"You should close the window and turn up the furnace."** Recognizing that the Advisement is off record helps to make clear that what is left is pure Disclosure. (In the context of some long-established relationships, however, **"I feel cold"** might be an on-record directive for the other to do something about it.)

Although the concept of intent requires that the speaker intend to secure uptake by the other, actual uptake is not necessary. A Question is still a Question even if the other misunderstands it or is distracted and does not hear it.

Meta-Intent

Frequently a whole speech or a whole conversation seems to have some overall intention or *meta-intent*. As an illustration, a person's purpose in having a conversation may be to get the other to do something. This sort of meta-intent should *not* be a basis for VRM coding of utterances within the conversation unless it is on record in a particular utterance. For example, Disclosures and Edifications that are used to convince the other to do something should be coded as having Disclosure or Edification intent, even though there is some element of persuasion in them. The element of persuasion may be considered as an off-record Advisement—a hint or a manipulation— which is not coded directly. In other words, although it is helpful to be aware of meta-intents and other off-record meanings of utterances, VRM coding should proceed one utterance at a time, based on the meaning of that utterance *in its context* (see next section). Intent judgments should be based on the on-record source of experience, presumption about experience, and frame of reference of each separate utterance.

Importance of Context

VRM intent must be judged in context. Ideally, one should consider the entire history of the relationship between speaker and other in coding each utterance. Words or phrases may take on special meanings that are on record for speaker and other, even though they are obscure for coders. In practice, although familiarity with the entire relationship is seldom necessary, accurate VRM coding frequently requires knowledge of previous portions of the conversation in which an utterance occurs, particularly the preceding few utterances. In addition, it is helpful to know the tone of voice, setting, roles of speaker and other, and the purpose of the conversation. For most utterances, it is easy to imagine a different context in which the same words would have a different meaning and merit a different VRM code.

Carl Rogers (1951) offered an illustration of how an utterance's meaning might vary in counseling or psychotherapy:

> A response on the counselor's part might be, "You resent her criticism." This response may be given empathetically, with the tone of voice such as would be used if it were worded: "If I understand you correctly, you feel pretty resentful toward her criticism. Is that right?" If this is the attitude and tone which is used, it would probably be experienced by the client as aiding him in further expression. Yet . . . "You resent her criticism" may be given with the same attitude and tone with which one might announce "You have the measles," or even with the attitude and tone which would accompany the words "You are sitting on my hat." (p. 28)

In addition to knowledge of the immediate context and the relationship, VRM coding requires familiarity with the cultural and linguistic context of the discourse. Insofar as speakers use conventional or idiomatic expressions or assume that their audience shares particular understandings, coders may need to know the conventions and share the understandings in order to code accurately.

VRMs involve only limited aspects of meaning, however, and it is often possible to code an utterance accurately without understanding its full sense. For example, one can code, **"To disable auto-answer, change the value of S0 to its zero default"** (AA) as an Advisement without understanding what "the value of S0" or "zero default" refer to or how one might go about changing the former to the latter.

Subtypes of Intent

The VRM system permits any number of subdivisions within the eight major categories. Such divisions may be made to investigate specific subcategories that have particular theoretical or practical significance in a particular context. For example, in one study, Exploratory Reflections, which seek to show understanding of the client's unexpressed inner thoughts and feelings, were thought to be an important type of intervention in exploratory (interpersonal/psychodynamic) psychotherapy, and so they were distinguished from Simple Reflections, which seek to represent or feed back messages that the client has already expressed (Stiles et al., 1988). In the same study, General Advisements, which seek to guide the client's behavior outside of therapy, were thought to be important in prescriptive (cognitive/behavioral) psychotherapy and were distinguished from Process Advisements, which seek to guide the client's behavior within the therapy session.

In this chapter I suggest several possible intent subtypes within each of the main intent classifications. These examples of subtypes are included to indicate the variety of utterances that fall within each intent classification. For example, closed Questions, short answer Questions, and open Questions all are coded first as Questions. Criteria for coding the listed subtypes are not fully developed in this book; further specification may be needed to obtain reliable coding. Furthermore, many additional subdivisions are possible; subtypes may be developed to meet the requirements of particular research questions or studies by individual investigators.

For investigators who want to make distinctions not present in the VRM system, I recommend that these be made as subdivisions within the main categories, rather than as separate categories (see also discussion of adding categories to the VRM system in Chapter 3). For example, Exploration should be constructed as a subcategory of Reflection, rather than as a separate ninth mode. This strategy preserves (a) the mutual exclusivity of the eight major categories, (b) the possibility of aggregating according to the VRM principles (e.g., into the role dimension indexes; see Chapters 4 and 11), and (c) the possibility of direct comparisons with previous VRM profiles. By aggregating across subcategories, the basic VRM profile of any newly studied type of interaction can be placed, quantitatively, in the context of the wide range of interactions that have been VRM coded (see Chapter 4).

The VRM system does systematically subdivide each of the intent categories according to the grammatical form or literal meaning of the utterance. For example, "**He worries me**" (ED) is distinguished from "**I am worried about him**" (DD); "**Would you shut the door**" (QA) is distinguished from "**Shut the door**" (AA). For details, see the discussion of mixed modes in Chapter 7.

DISCLOSURE INTENT

Disclosure (D) concerns the speaker's experience, requires no specific presumptions about the other's experience (presumes to know the speaker's experience only), and uses the speaker's internal frame of reference. Thus Disclosures reveal the speaker's private thoughts, feelings, wishes, perceptions, and intentions.

Thoughts:

I know the way out. DD
I think the Republicans are to blame. DD
I've solved the problem. DD

Feelings:

I was terrified. DD
I love you. DD
I don't know what I feel. DD

Wishes:

I want a pony. DD
I'd like it if he would be on time just once. DD
I wish I wasn't so shy. DD

Perceptions:

I can't make it out. DD
I saw the boat. DD
I hear what you're saying. DD

Intentions:

> **I'm going to the library.** DD
> **I plan to be rich some day.** DD
> **Now I'll examine your throat.** DD

A defining characteristic of a Disclosure is that one would need access to the speaker's private experience to determine its sincerity. Note that the criterion is the privateness of the information, and not its intimacy, its emotional charge, its psychological depth, or its potential for causing embarrassment, in contrast to self-disclosure categories in some other systems. Thus, revealing intimate facts or describing emotionally significant events is not Disclosure if these facts or events are or were objectively observable in principle. But telling mundane perceptions or intentions is Disclosure, because perceptions and intentions are, in principle, private events. For example, one would have to be able to read the speaker's mind to know for sure whether he or she really saw what he or she seemed to be looking at or to know for sure whether he or she really meant to do what he or she claimed to be intending to do. (See also the following section on Edification intent and the section on distinguishing Disclosure from Edification in Chapter 9.)

EDIFICATION INTENT

Edification (E) concerns the speaker's experience, requires no specific presumptions about the other (presumes to know the speaker's experience only), and uses a neutral frame of reference that is shared with the other. To use a frame of reference that is shared with the other without presuming knowledge of the other's experience is to use a common, objective frame of reference that is shared with *any* other. Thus Edifications are statements of fact—information that is, in principle, public. Edifications need not, however, be true.

> **It hasn't come yet.** EE
> **A White House spokesperson read the President's response.** EE
> **He wandered aimlessly.** EE
> **This morning a flying saucer from Mars landed in New Jersey.** EE
> **The FBI is following me.** EE

The truth of an Edification could, in principle, be assessed by an external observer in the right place at the right time with the right skills and equipment. Or at least such an observer could do as well as the speaker in determining the Edification's truth. In contrast to Disclosures, the speaker claims no epistemological advantage over the other in assessing an Edification's truth.

The name Edification in the VRM taxonomy refers only to the speech act of stating objective information and does not necessarily carry any implication that receiving this will improve the other. In this respect, the term departs from the dictionary meaning of edification.

Third Parties' Private Experience

For purposes of VRM coding, a third party's thoughts, feelings, wishes, perceptions, and intentions are considered to be in a neutral frame of reference. Neither the speaker nor the other has any special access to the third party's private experience—one could not be certain of the truth of a statement like **"She was worried when he was late"** (EE) or **"He wants to come to the party"** (EE) by reading the speaker's mind. Such utterances are, therefore, coded as Edifications.

Intimate, Shocking, or Embarrassing Edifications

Edification need not be emotionally neutral. For example, the following are Edifications:

She loves me. EE

The Japanese are bombing Pearl Harbor. EE

The tumor is malignant. EE

My father raped me when I was 12 years old. EE

There are warts on my genitals. EE

It is important to distinguish between information that is epistemologically private (i.e., subjective, in principle knowable only to the speaker) and information that is socially private (i.e., intimate or embarrassing). Revealing the former is usually coded Disclosure intent; revealing the latter is coded Edification intent if an objective observer in the right place at the right time with the right equipment could, in principle, ascertain whether it was true or false. (See Chapter 9 for further examples.)

Theories and Speculations

Although Edifications state objective information, in the sense of being in principle externally observable, the situation or events need not have actually been observed or even be practically observable. Theoretical generalizations and speculations about external reality are usually Edification intent.

The electrons are arranged in concentric shells. EE

Rats can learn to press a bar to get food. EE

There are no unicorns on the dark side of the moon. EE

ADVISEMENT INTENT

Advisement (A) concerns the speaker's experience (i.e., the content is the speaker's idea), it presumes knowledge of what the other should do or think, and it uses the speaker's frame of reference. Thus, Advisements display the speaker's idea of what the other should do or think. They attempt to guide the other's behavior, to impose experience on the other. Advisements include directives of all kinds: commands, requests, suggestions, advice, permission, prohibition.

Commands and Requests:

Take out the trash. AA

Be seated. AA

Please wash your hands. AA

Help! AA

Suggestions and Advice:

Try doing it slower. AA

Take two of these and call me in the morning. AA, AA

You shouldn't work so hard. AA

See if you can finish it. AA

Permission and Prohibition:

You may leave now. AA

No smoking. AA

Thou shalt not kill. AA

Statements of Obligation:
"Should," "ought," and "must" statements are coded Advisement intent if they seek to impose some way of thinking or acting on the other.

You should stop smoking. AA

You must learn to be more respectful. AA

You really ought to see this movie. AA

Process Advisement Versus General Advisement

Process Advisements attempt to guide the other's immediate, here-and-now behavior, whereas General Advisements attempt to guide the other's later, there-and-then behavior. For example, in a study of psychotherapy (Stiles et al., 1988), Process Advisement intents were defined as therapist utterances that explicitly try to get the client to do something during the psychotherapy session; General Advisement intents were defined as utterances that try to guide the client's behavior outside the session.

Examples of Process Advisements:

Forget about what's going on outside the room. AA

Look at me. AA

I think you ought to listen to what I'm saying. DA

Let's talk about this now instead of next week. AA

You could write it down if that would be easier than telling me. AA

Let's get started. AA

We need to talk about what happened last time. CA

First, I want you to close your eyes. DA

Now, take five deep breaths, slowly. AA

Example of General Advisements:

Try to stay clear of your family while you're feeling this way. AA

Go out and start looking for work tomorrow. AA, AA

Do that. AA

Keep a count of the times you get angry with your brother. AA

You should tell her you're sorry. AA

You ought to think of your mother before you do that. AA

It would probably be a bad idea to continue the relationship. EA

Please consider telling him how you really feel about him. AA

You can always contact me if things get rough. AA

CONFIRMATION INTENT

Confirmation (C) concerns the speaker's experience, presumes specific knowledge of the other's experience, and uses a shared frame of reference. Thus Confirmations compare the speaker's experience with the other's—by expressing shared ideas, memories, or beliefs, or by agreement or disagreement.

We agree that the plan is sound. CC

We believe in a strong America. CC

We've about exhausted that topic. CC

We don't seem to know each other very well. CC

We have a lot in common. CC

We've been through this a hundred times. CC

We'll never understand each other. CC

We both know what it's like to have to diet. CC

You and I make a good team. CC

The term Confirmation as used here does not imply positivity or agreement. **"We disagree"** is just as much a Confirmation as **"We agree."** Both disagreement and agreement entail presuming to know what the other person thinks. The word was chosen to connote existential confirmation—sharing a frame of reference.

The terms agreement and disagreement are used here in a specific sense that may be narrower than their colloquial meanings. They are meant to imply a comparison of the speaker's experience with the other's experience, thus requiring some presumption about the latter.

Thus, they entail more than a positive or negative attitude. In effect, Confirmation intent is the converse of Interpretation intent; in Confirmation, the speaker's experience is viewed from the other's frame of reference, whereas in Interpretation, the other's experience is viewed from the speaker's frame of reference.

Some of the most common sorts of Confirmation intents are usually expressed in other forms. These mixed modes are dealt with in more detail in Chapters 7, 9, and 10. For example, "**I agree with you**" (DC) is Disclosure form. Agreement to do something (e.g., in response to "**Will you please take out the trash?**" [QA]), may be expressed as "**Yes**" (KC) or "**Okay**" (IC).

QUESTION INTENT

Question (Q) concerns the other's experience but does not require presumptions about the other's experience (presumes knowledge of the speaker's experience only), and it uses the speaker's frame of reference. Theoretically, the "seeking" character of Questions (cf. Goody, 1978) reflects the paradox that they take the speaker's viewpoint on the other's experience but need not presume knowledge of that experience. In effect, the speaker attempts to fill a gap in his or her own frame of reference with information or guidance to be supplied by the other.

Are you the owner? QQ

Why did you say that? QQ

Have you ever dreamt you were falling? QQ

Can we please bring in some music? QQ (asking for permission)

What do you want me to do? QQ

You did what to your sister? QQ

You threw it where? QQ

Closed Questions

Closed Questions seek a yes/no answer. The subject-verb order is usually inverted. Characteristically, the words necessary for an adequate answer are entirely contained in the Question. This allows the other to answer completely using a contentless (Acknowledgment form) expression such as yes or no.

Do you feel angry? QQ

Has it stopped raining yet? QQ

Can you see three spots? QQ

May I borrow your umbrella? QQ

Short Answer Questions

Short Answer Questions seek brief answers. The form usually includes interrogative words. These are intermediate between Closed and Open Questions in that they sharply delimit what counts as an adequate answer, yet do not fully contain the words for an answer, so that the other must introduce new words.

How old are you? QQ

What did you have for breakfast? QQ

Where do you live? QQ

When did you first notice this? QQ

How many spots can you see? QQ

Open Questions

Open Questions seek more extended answers. The form usually includes interrogative words.

How have you been feeling? QQ

What is your opinion about the candidate? QQ

Why did he want to leave early? QQ

Test Questions

Question intent may be coded even though the speaker already knows the answer. Examples include test Questions and conversational gambits (aimed at eliciting talk from the other), both of which are common in conversations with young children, from which the following examples were taken:

Is that a baby? QQ

What's this teddy bear doing? QQ

What's over here? QQ

Are you making soup? QQ

Are you going shopping? QQ

Did you get a call on the telephone? QQ

Questions "In Search Of"

Questions can be classified by the mode intent that they seek to elicit from the other. This can be described as the "in search of" relationship. This classification is independent of whether the Question is open or closed.

What do you want? QQ (in search of Disclosure)

Where is he from? QQ (in search of Edification)

May I have a cookie? QQ (in search of Advisement)

Don't you agree? QQ (in search of Confirmation)

In addition, Questions can be classified by the sort of information (content) they seek. For example, in medical interviews, Questions might be classified as biomedical versus socioemotional.

ACKNOWLEDGMENT INTENT

Acknowledgment (K) concerns the other's experience, but makes no presumptions about it (presuming knowledge of the speaker's experience only) and uses the other's frame of reference. To take the other's viewpoint of the other's experience without presuming knowledge of it implies an "empty" utterance. Thus, Acknowledgments express no content—they convey only receipt of or receptiveness to communication from the other. In effect, the content of an Acknowledgment is the preceding (or anticipated) communication from the other.

Receipt of communication:

Mm-hm. KK

Yeah. KK

Well, . . . KK

Receptiveness to communication (salutations):

Hi. KK

Hello. KK

Joe, . . . KK

Floor Holding Versus Floor Relinquishing

Although many Acknowledgments are "back channel" utterances that aim to facilitate the other's communication and do not claim the floor for the speaker, some Acknowledgments do claim and hold the floor. For example, "**Well . . .** " (KK) is often used to signal receipt of a Question and to hold the floor while the speaker thinks of an answer.

Do Not Use Acknowledgment as a Residual Category

Although most Acknowledgments are brief utterances, the converse is not true; that is, many brief utterances are not Acknowledgments. Acknowledgment intent is coded only when the utterance meets the stated taxonomic criteria (e.g., it concerns the other's experience), and it is *not* used merely because the utterance is short or because its intent is ambiguous or difficult to code. See Chapter 10 for a discussion of codes for brief utterances.

INTERPRETATION INTENT

Interpretation (I) concerns the other's experience and presumes knowledge of it but places this in the speaker's frame of reference. Thus Interpretations explain or label the other's thoughts and behaviors. They include psychological interpretations as well as judgments or evaluations of the other, because each of these presumes to view the other's experience (thoughts, feelings, wishes, perceptions, intentions) from the speaker's perspective.

You're a bit modest in how you appraise yourself. II

You are identifying with your mother's hostility. II

You say the nicest things. II

You look like you're in a hypnotic trance. II

You can do anything you set your mind to. II

You're right. II

You're welcome. II

Psychological Interpretations

Interpretations can create meaning for the other by bringing a new perspective or worldview (frame of reference) to bear on the other's experience. The Interpretations used by psychotherapists often use some psychological theory as a frame of reference. That is, they put the client's experience into theoretical terms.

> *Th*: **You are supporting her not eating.** II
> **You are supporting her starving as an attack on your husband.** II

###

You are behaving self-destructively. II

You seem to be reliving your relationship with your father. II

Indirectly, you were rewarded for procrastinating. II

You have a need to unidealize a picture of certain men. II

Judgments and Evaluations of the Other

Evaluations of the other or of the other's thoughts or actions place these in the speaker's personal frame of reference.

You are a nincompoop. II

You've managed to ruin the party. II

You're a good patient. II

Right. II (understood: You're right.)

Judgments and evaluations of third parties or of objects of events (for example, works of art or literature) are *not* VRM Interpretations, even though they might be colloquially described as "her interpretation." These do not presume specific knowledge of the other, nor do they concern the other's experience (see Chapter 9 for discussion and examples).

This is typical of Manet's brushwork. EE

It was a magnificent performance. ED

Naming and Labeling, Praise and Criticism

Naming, labeling, praise, and criticism are variants of judgments and evaluations. Many are Interpretations.

You are a spoilsport. II

You two are really going at it. II

You're manipulating me. II

You're the first person to ask that question. II

You've done a very stupid thing. II

You didn't have to let him walk all over you. II

Predictions of the Other's Experience

Predictions of the other's experience presume to know what the other's experience will be, as predicted by the speaker (see also discussion in Chapter 9).

If you can share your anguish, you will feel less alone. II

You're going to need another year of therapy. II

You'll probably be able to go back to work next week. II

You will soon discover that the main concern of this book is with the theory underlying inferential methods. II

Reassurance and Normalizing

Although utterances in any mode can be reassuring, depending on their content, many utterances that seek to reassure by describing the other's experience or behavior as positive or normal are coded Interpretation intent.

You've got it in you to do it. II

You did the right thing. II

You have a warm and engaging manner. II

You could be in a much worse situation. II

Your worries are perfectly normal. EI

REFLECTION INTENT

Reflection (R) concerns the other's experience, presumes to know what it is, and uses the other's internal frame of reference (insofar as this is understood by the speaker). Thus, Reflections put the other's experience (including intentional behavior) into words. Often they convey empathy. They include repetitions, restatements, clarifications, and exploratory statements about what the other may be experiencing. Thus, a Reflection may go well beyond what the other has literally said, providing that its intent is to portray the other's experience as it is viewed by the other. In effect, in a Reflection, the other is the ultimate judge of the utterance's empathic accuracy.

Other's thoughts and feelings:

You feel confused and alone. RR

You see a lot in her you'd like to have. RR

You wish you had more money. RR

You were very frightened. RR

You think I should stop drinking. RR

Other's intentional behavior:

You jumped on the sand pile. RR

You told her what you thought of her. RR

So you're on two different kinds of drugs. RR

You drove home afterward. RR

You didn't call your mother. RR

Note that Reflection is not restricted to content that the other has expressed verbally. An utterance may be coded as Reflection intent if the speaker intends to put the other's experience into words even if the other has said nothing at all.

You must be exhausted. RR

You must think I'm your worst patient. RR

The following examples are of mothers talking to young children, a rich arena for Reflections that the other has not expressed explicitly. The mother is not necessarily correct in all of her assumptions; in some cases the utterances may represent wishful thinking. They are coded as Reflection because the accuracy of the utterance depends on the child's view of the situation.

> **You know what a ball is.** RR
>
> **You like that little bear today.** RR
>
> **You're going to brush my hair.** RR
>
> **You like strained prunes.** RR

Simple Reflection Versus Exploratory Reflection

Simple Reflections seek to represent or feed back messages that the other has already expressed, whereas Exploratory Reflections seek to show understanding of the other's unexpressed inner thoughts and feelings. In both cases, the speaker seeks to express the other's experience as the other views it, and the other is the judge of the utterance's accuracy. This distinction has been used in research on psychotherapy (Stiles et al., 1988; cf. Barkham & Shapiro, 1986). In what follows, I give a relatively detailed description of these two sorts of Reflections, as an illustration of how VRM subtypes may be distinguished from each other. Applying this distinction would require some notational convention, such as "RRs" for Simple Reflection and "RRe" for Exploratory Reflection, although I have not done this here.

To be a Simple Reflection, an utterance must contain a meaning match between speaker and other. That is, some part of a statement must be matched (or at least the match must be attempted), and no significant new information may be added. The meanings may match at the level of words, content, nonverbal messages, or broad topics. In practice, the match is usually with recent utterances by the other, but it may be with much earlier communication. Do not confuse "meaning match" with "using the same words." The speaker may use different words but add nothing new to the meaning of the other's communication, in which case the intent is Simple Reflection.

> *Cl*: **I just can't get on with the people around me and things.** DD
>
> *Th*: **You mean it's the surroundings.** RR

The therapist added no new information to the client's statement, so the intent is Simple Reflection.

> *Cl*: **And I wonder just what I'm going to have to do to put all the different things I am doing together.** DD
>
> *Th*: **How can I organize it all for myself?** RR

Note that the form of this paraphrasing is Reflection, not Question, because it is a direct quote (there is an understood "You are saying"; see Chapter 7).

Variants within the Simple Reflection subtype include:

Repetition:

> *Cl*: **. . . and it really upsets me.** ED
>
> *Th*: **It really upsets you.** RR

###

> *Cl*: **I'm tired of being alone.** DD
>
> *Th*: **You're tired of being alone.** RR

Paraphrase:

> *Cl*: **I don't know if this is a good thing to talk about.** DD
>
> *Th*: **You're not sure any more that you should talk about what you decided on earlier.** RR

###

> *Cl*: **I'd just like to get away from here, to start afresh in the North.** DD **There's something about the North.** ED
>
> *Th*: **So from the little you know about the North you feel that you would like to live there.** RR

###

> *Cl*: **You know,** RD (filler; see Chapter 8)
> **it just seems impossible to actually get down to it,** ED

you know, RD
if you start something you never get round to sort of finishing because
something else comes up that's got to be done before that is. ED

Th: **Yeah.** KK
**You can't settle your mind on one particular piece of work and get that
done.** RR

Summary:

Th: **You've covered a lot of ground today.** II
First, you talked about how well things were going at your new job, RR
**then you brought me up to date on how things were going with your
wife,** RR
then you led into a discussion about relationships in general. RR

###

Th: **For the past half hour or so you've been telling me about all the things
you're going to miss now that you're graduating.** RR

Nonverbal:

Cl: (sniff) . . . **I** . . . **uh** . . . (sigh) . . . **just** . . . (weeps). (not coded)
Th: **You sound very sad and hurt.** RR

Exploratory Reflection intent must provide an element of news—a
different perspective on, or some new information relating to, the
other's experience. That is, in presuming to understand the other's
experience (however tentatively), the speaker goes beyond what the
other has explicitly stated. It must concern the other's experience,
however, not the speaker's or that of third parties, and it must use a
viewpoint that is shared with the other, not the speaker's own evaluation
of the other's experience. In psychotherapy, Simple Reflections by the
therapist seem to be aimed at "packaging" the client's experience,
whereas Exploratory Reflections are aimed at unfolding or opening up
the client's experience. In this context, Exploratory Reflections are
often marked by tentativeness, which may be expressed via hedges or
by putting the Reflection intent in less presumptuous (e.g., Disclosure
or Edification) forms, for example, "**I guess that . . .**" or "**It's something like**" or by metaphorical language.
Variants of the Exploratory Reflection subtype include:

Reformulations:

> *Cl*: **What I say is very rarely related to what I think I'm going to say.** ED
>
> *Th*: **Mm-hm.** KK
> **It's this sort of irrepressible impulsive view of yourself.** ER

###

> *Cl*: **And it's always been that I had to be the strong one in the family.** ED
> (understood: . . . I felt I had to be . . .)
>
> *Th*: **I guess that means that there was nobody for you when you had problems.** DR

###

> *Cl*: **We don't like to talk about it** DD
> **because it's just going to start everything up again.** ED
> **so we just try to forget it.** DD
>
> *Th*: **Like being put in a cupboard or being swept under the mat.** ER

###

> *Cl*: **I just want to get away from here, to get away from the sort of banal and sometimes sad memories, not only of here but the whole area where I grew up.** DD
>
> *Th*: **You mean something like this is the landscape of your childhood and adolescence,** ER
> **which in some way you feel you've grown up from.** RR (note inverted construction; subject is "you")
> **This is your childhood country or something like that, but also a country associated with pain.** ER

###

> *Cl*: **I think you're touching very closely on the subject there.** DD
>
> *Th*: **Somehow this is important to you, a bit of danger territory.** ER

Inside:

> *Cl*: **I don't know if this is a good thing to talk about.** DD

Th: **You're probably worrying that you're wasting my time.** RR

###

Cl: **I just hurt my child.** DE
Th: **And now I guess you feel like a horrible monster.** DR

###

Cl: **It's just that I don't seem able to do any better at that,** ED
    and this happens with monotonous regularity. ED (or EE?)
Th: **I guess it's this feeling that you fail all the time as a person.** DR

###

Cl: **Other people just go up to people and start talking about what they've
    been doing;** EE
    they don't even wait to be asked. EE
Th: **And you have what feels to you like an insatiable need for attention,** RR
    but you find it hard to ask. RR

###

Cl: **I just find the situation impossible,** DD
    and that's really depressing. ED
Th: **Depressing to feel, "Here it is again, there's nothing I can do about
    it."** ER (understood: It's depressing to feel . . .)

UNCODABLE INTENT

Uncodable (U) is used only for utterances that are incomprehensible
or inaudible. This category is *not* used for utterances that are merely
difficult to code. In cases of difficult utterances, it is usually possible
to narrow the choice to two modes by use of the classification principles. For example, an utterance's source of experience and required
presumptions may be clear even though its frame of reference is not. In
such a case, it is usually best to choose one of the two possibilities (e.g.,

Interpretation or Reflection) rather than failing to code. Note that this preserves much of the VRM information (two of the three dimensions).

VALENCE AND VRM CODING

The VRM system does not incorporate an evaluative, or positive-negative, dimension. Thus, "We agree" (CC) is given the same code as "We disagree" (CC); "You are right" (II) is given the same code as "You are wrong" (II); "I love you" (DD) is given the same code as "I hate you" (DD); and so forth. This feature is not meant to imply that valence, or positivity, is unimportant, but merely that it is an additional dimension that is independent of and distinct from source of experience, presumption about experience, and frame of reference.

Measuring the valence of utterances raises a variety of problems. Unlike the VRM principles, positivity is easily construed as a continuous, rather than a dichotomous, variable. That is, there are degrees of agreement, rightness, love, and so on, conveyed in speech, and many utterances have little or no evaluative force. Like VRM codes and other aspects of meaning, positivity may be assessed at multiple on- and off-record levels (Stiles, 1986b). Statements like "I have great respect for my boss" that are literally positive may be negative at pragmatic or off-record levels (e.g., they may be said sarcastically). Further, even explicitly evaluative utterances can be complex; for example, "You are better than I am" (II) seems to imply a negative evaluation of self.

One approach to measuring the valence of utterances in conjunction with VRM coding distinguished positive, negative, and neutral evaluations by the speaker (Burchill, 1984; Burchill & Stiles, 1988). In general this approach coded the pragmatic (i.e., intent-level) valence applied to the subject of the utterance as evaluated within the frame of reference used for the utterance. For example, "You are better than I am" (II) would be coded as a positive evaluation of the other from the speaker's frame of reference.

FELICITY CONDITIONS OF VRM INTENT CATEGORIES

Each VRM category has associated conditions it requires in order to be felicitous, or happy (see Chapter 5; Austin, 1975; Searle, 1969; Stiles, 1981). These conditions do *not* determine the utterance's VRM code; for example, an insincere Disclosure is still coded as Disclosure, and a false Edification is still coded as Edification.

To be felicitous, a Disclosure must be sincere. That is, the speaker must actually have had an experience with the revealed meaning. The criterion of sincerity is congruence with the speaker's private frame of reference.

To be felicitous, an Edification must be true. The reported information must fit the objective facts.

To be felicitous, an Advisement must be feasible. The speaker must believe it is possible for the other to follow the guidance offered, or to have the experience the speaker seeks to impose. Thus, utterances like **"Please lift that elephant"** (AA) or **"You may not digest that meal"** (AA) are infelicitous, though they are nevertheless Advisements.

To be felicitous, a Confirmation must be both sincere and accurately empathic. That is, the speaker's experience must be accurately rendered, and the speaker must know the meaning of that experience for the other. In other words, the felicity of a Confirmation depends on the accurate representation of the private experience of both speaker and other.

To be felicitous, a Question must be answerable by the other—or at least the speaker must believe it to be answerable. That is, the speaker must believe that the other could have the information that fits into the hole revealed in the speaker's frame of reference.

To be felicitous, an Acknowledgment must be timely with respect to the other's communication (or presence). The speaker must believe that the other has communicated or could communicate something.

To be felicitous, an Interpretation must be acute. It must accurately characterize the other's experience in the frame of reference being used by the speaker.

To be felicitous, a Reflection must be empathic. It must correctly articulate what the other is experiencing from the other's viewpoint.

7

Mode Forms
and Mixed Modes

This chapter presents the grammatical features that define each VRM form, and it describes mixed modes—utterances that have the form of one mode and the intent of another.

GRAMMATICAL FORM AND LITERAL MEANING

Each of the eight mode intents is associated with a more or less distinctive set of grammatical features. For example, inverted subject-verb order and interrogative words are associated with Question; "I" statements are associated with Disclosure. The features, taken together, define the mode's form.

VRM form can be considered as an aspect of an utterance's literal meaning—the conventional meaning of these grammatical features. Literal meaning is distinguished from pragmatic meaning or speaker's occasion meaning (Grice, 1969; Stiles, 1986b)—the meaning intended by the speaker on a particular occasion, an aspect of which is coded as VRM intent (see Chapters 5 and 6).

The principal VRM form criteria were summarized in Table 2.2 and are detailed in this chapter. These definitions represent a consensus of myself, my collaborators, and coders who have applied the system to a wide variety of types of discourse as to which grammatical features literally express each of the eight intents. For the most part, the definitions employ standard grammatical categories, emphasizing person and mood.

The process of determining which grammatical features correspond to each VRM category has involved asking ourselves what the literal meaning of each grammatical expression is when the utterance is taken out of its context. This literal meaning is then given a code following the principles of classification (source of experience, presumption about experience, frame of reference). Ultimately, therefore, the form definitions rest on the linguistic intuitions of those who have collaborated in this process over the past 15 years. It is testimony to the stability of these intuitions that there are only a few, relatively minor changes to the form definitions in this description of the system, as compared with the 1978 manual (Stiles, 1978a). (This book, however, contains a good deal more elaboration and detail.)

The association of each form with the corresponding intent is stronger than an indicator, as some of the illocutionary force is retained even when the form is used to express a different intent. Thus, **"I wish you would stop clearing your throat"** (DA) retains some of the force of a Disclosure even though the utterance evidently has the same intent as **"Stop clearing your throat"** (AA). Utterances in which the form and intent differ are called *mixed modes,* to be distinguished from *pure modes,* in which form and intent match.

GRAMMATICAL FORM SPECIFICATIONS

Disclosure Form

Disclosure form is declarative and first person singular ("I") or first person plural ("we") where the other is not included as a referent.

I wanted to see you. DD

We wanted to see you. DD

When I heard the crack, I knew it was a home run. DD

Theoretically, the pronoun "I" refers to the epistemologically private center of experience of the speaker.

Watch for sentence constructions in which the object or a complement comes before the subject.

You I wanted to see. DD

Sad and disheartened am I. DD

The ball I hit. DE

Compound subjects that include first person pronouns ("I" or "we") are coded Disclosure form so long as they do not also refer to the other (see Confirmation form).

George and I wanted to see you. DD

My mother and I love to talk. DD

Frankie and Tommy and I all saw the ghost. DD

We went to the zoo today. DE (the other stayed home)

An exception to the general rule that first person singular sentences are Disclosure form is when the speaker puts the other's thoughts into words and uses "I" to mean "you" (see Reflection form section below).

Edification Form

Edification form is declarative and third person.

It never stops. EE

He met me at the station. EE

Dinosaurs are extinct. EE

My arm is broken. EE

Broken is my arm. EE

Note that all noun phrases and noun clauses are third person, and hence make an utterance Edification form when used as its subject.

What you said you wanted was a bicycle. EE

That I often wish I were elsewhere is well known. EE

Henry's quitting his job was his first independent step. EE

Relative pronouns are third person.

Henry quit his job, which is why he's home. EE, EE

An utterance with a third person subject is coded Edification form even if it refers to the speaker.

Mother (to child): **Mommy's back now.** EE

Advisement Form

Advisement form is imperative or second person with a verb of permission, prohibition, or obligation (e.g., "may," "must," "should," "have to," "ought to").

Take off your shirt. AA

You must come visit. AA

Let's go for a swim. AA

Imperative forms carry an implied (elliptical) second person subject: **"Take off your shirt"** implies "You take off your shirt." Similarly, **"Let's go for a swim"** implies "You let us go for a swim."

See Chapter 10 for a discussion of discriminating among second person forms.

Confirmation Form

Confirmation form is declarative and first person plural ("we") where the other is a referent (i.e., "we" refers to both speaker and other). Compound subjects that include the speaker and the other (e.g., "you and I") are also Confirmation form.

We're made for each other. CC

We have a quorum. CC

We disagree. CC

You and I disagree. CC

Question Form

Question form is interrogative, with inverted subject-verb order or interrogative words such as "who," "what," "where," "why," "when," or "how."

Have you seen my hat? QQ

Where were you born? QQ

Is that what you meant? QQ

Note that a question mark—which usually denotes a rising inflection in English—is *not* sufficient to code Question form, although it often signals Question intent (see discussion of mixed modes later in this chapter).

Sometimes, in colloquial speech, the initial verb is omitted but understood in context. For example, **"You wanna play blocks?"** (QQ) may be coded Question form if the initial "Do" is omitted but understood (see discussion of elliptical constructions in Chapter 8).

Interrogative words alone are sufficient to code Question form.

What? QQ

You went out with who? QQ

Acknowledgment Form

Acknowledgment forms include nonlexical utterances such as **"mm-hm,"** **"oh,"** or **"ah-hah"**; contentless lexical utterances, such as **"yes,"** **"no,"** or **"well"**; terms of salutation, such as **"Hi"** and **"Hello"**; and terms of address, including names and titles used as forms of address. Coding the intent of Acknowledgment forms depends very heavily on context, since they are essentially empty forms.

(I wish I could visit him.) **Mm-hm.** KK

(I wish I could visit him.) **Yes.** KK

(I don't want to visit him.) **No.** KK

Hi. KK

Well, . . . KK

Hello, Lauren. KK, KK

Dr. Goodman, . . . KK

Nonlexical verbalizations are coded as Acknowledgment form, but only if they have some communicative intent. For example, **"uh,"** **"hmm,"** or **"er"** are coded KK if they are used to convey receipt of communication from the other. They are not coded at all (i.e., they are not utterances; see Chapter 8) if they are noncommunicative noises (e.g., if they signal only that the speaker is trying to formulate something to say).

Interpretation Form

Interpretation form is second person ("you") with a predicate that denotes an attribute or ability of the other.

You are trying too hard. II

You're a liar. II

You can succeed if you really want to. II

Terms of evaluation such as "Right," "Good," "Okay," or "Fine" are also coded as Interpretation form if they are used alone in response to the other. These are pure Interpretations if they are used with their literal evaluative meaning.

Right. II (understood: You're right.)

Good. II (understood: You did good work.)

Nice work. II

Terms of evaluation are often used with other intents, however, and must be evaluated in context. They may also represent other forms—for example, when they are used as tag Questions or as answers to questions. See Chapter 10 for a discussion of these brief utterances.

See Chapter 10 for a discussion of discriminating among second person forms, particularly discriminating Interpretation forms from Reflection forms.

Reflection Form

Reflection form is second person ("you") with a predicate that denotes internal experience (thoughts, feelings, perceptions, intentions) or volitional action.

You're worried about your test results. RR

You had planned a quiet afternoon. RR

You drove to the next town. RR

Literal repetitions (exact repetition of all or part of the other's utterance) and finishing the other's sentences are also coded as Reflection form.

(I feel sandwiched in.) **Sandwiched in.** RR

(When I get nervous, I never seem to be able to . . .) **Finish my sentences.** RR

Speaking for the other—using "I" to mean "you" is also coded as Reflection form. (Such utterances read as if the speaker is quoting the other, although transcriptionists rarely enclose them in quotation marks.)

(I feel ready to punch him.) **I'm not going to take it any more.** RR
(understood: You are saying, "I'm not going to take it any more.")

Note that Reflection and Interpretation forms are sometimes not clearly distinct in English. This is because some verbs (notably *to be* and *to have*) can refer either to externally observable attributes or to private experience. In cases where the intent is clear but the form could be either R or I, I recommend coding a pure mode in preference to a mixed mode.

To illustrate, **"You are angry"** could be either Reflection intent, if the speaker is putting the other's experience into words, or Interpretation intent, if a psychotherapist is explaining a client's inexplicable behavior to the client. In such cases, the utterance should be coded RR or II, depending on which intent is being used, rather than RI or IR.

See Chapter 10 for further discussion of discriminating among second person forms.

Uncodable Form

Form is scored as Uncodable (U) if the utterance cannot be understood or heard clearly. I recommend against using Uncodable for utterances that are merely difficult to code; it is better, in my opinion, to use information that is incomplete or probabilistic—in effect to make an informed guess—than to leave an utterance uncoded. Use Uncodable in preference to wild or uninformed guesses, however.

(inaudible mumble) UU

(inaudible) **his own brother.** UU

Expletives are coded U form because they are formally part of a relationship other than the speaker-other relationship. Often they *formally* invoke God or Fate or other unspecified third parties to do something. For example, **"Damn"** (UD) is formally "May God damn you [or it]." Similarly, some partings are coded U form because they are formally part of another relationship. **"Goodbye"** (UK) is a contraction of "May God be with you [ye]." **"Farewell"** (UK) is a contraction of "May you fare well." This issue is discussed at greater length in Chapter 10.

Do not use the Uncodable designation for elliptical (telegraphic) utterances. See Chapters 8 and 10 for ways of dealing with these.

Pure Mode Rule. As a general rule, when the intent of an utterance is clear but the form is elliptical, code a pure mode. For example, the utterance **"Miserable"** may be coded as DD (not UD) if it is clear that the speaker is describing his or her own internal state (understood as "I feel miserable" or "I was miserable,") even though there are no explicit form cues in the utterance.

MIXED MODES

In the VRM system, each utterance is coded twice, once for its form and once for its intent. As a notational convention, the form code is written first, intent second. Thus, for example, QA means Question form with Advisement intent, which is read, "Question in service of Advisement."

Slow down. AA

Would you slow down? QA

I'd like you to slow down. DA

Because VRM form and intent are coded independently—form based on grammatical features (reflecting literal meaning) and intent based on pragmatic meaning—all combinations of the eight forms and eight intents are possible. Utterances in which form and intent coincide are called pure modes; utterances in which they differ are called mixed modes. With eight forms and eight intents, the taxonomy thus includes 64 possible codes: 8 pure modes and 56 mixed modes, as summarized in Table 7.1.

In practice, the form and intent of an utterance are usually clearly distinct, though in some cases one or the other is unclear and must be guessed at based on whatever information is available. Problems are

TABLE 7.1
Summary of Pure and Mixed Modes

Form	Intent							
	D	*E*	*A*	*C*	*Q*	*K*	*I*	*R*
Disclosure (D)	DD	DE	DA	DC	DQ	DK	DI	DR
Edification (E)	ED	EE	EA	EC	EQ	EK	EI	ER
Advisement (A)	AD	AE	AA	AC	AQ	AK	AI	AR
Confirmation (C)	CD	CE	CA	CC	CQ	CK	CI	CR
Question (Q)	QD	QE	QA	QC	QQ	QK	QI	QR
Acknowledgment (K)	KD	KE	KA	KC	KQ	KK	KI	KR
Interpretation (I)	ID	IE	IA	IC	IQ	IK	II	IR
Reflection (R)	RD	RE	RA	RC	RQ	RK	RI	RR

NOTE: Pure modes are those in which form and intent match (e.g., DD, EE); mixed modes are those in which form and intent differ (e.g., DE, ED). The relation of form to intent is expressed as "in service of." Thus, EI is read as "Edification in service of Interpretation."

most likely to arise in grammatically incorrect or fragmentary utterances. The proposed rules and examples presented in this and succeeding chapters are my attempt to represent what is usually meant by various sorts of fragments or odd constructions.

Mixed Question Forms

The following examples of Question forms and brief answers illustrate a few types of mixed modes. See Chapters 8, 9, and 10 for further examples and discussion.

Advising Questions. Question forms are frequently used to soften the imposition of Advisements. Such constructions are often considered more polite than a bald pure Advisement would be.

Can you move your car? QA

Would you mind turning down the volume? QA

Shall we go now? QA

Mothers talking to young children provided the following examples of QA. In each case, the speaker was seeking an action rather than an answer.

Can you turn the page? QA

Can you make the truck go? QA

How about a kiss? QA

Wanna take him for a stroll? QA

Don't you think he'd like to turn around? QA

Of course, such questions must be interpreted in context.

Do you want to come up here? QA (understood as a suggestion)

Do you want to come up here? QR (child is already trying to climb up)

Rhetorical Questions. The colloquial term "rhetorical question" can refer to a variety of different modes, but many are QD or QE—using a Question form to convey subjective or objective information.

Isn't that weird! QD (understood: That is weird.)

Isn't he cute. QD (understood: He is cute.)

What a day! QD (note interrogative word)

Don't we already have four bottles of oregano. QE (understood: We do . . .)

. . . 'cause why should I work so hard? QD

Don't you think it would be better that way? QD

Is this meeting ever going to end? QD

Do you know what happened next? He fell overboard. QE, EE

So that is my major concern about myself: Can I function as an individual without him? ED, QD

A similar sort of Question mixture is sometimes used to label the other's experience.

Mother (to young child): **Are you tired?** QI

I coded this Interpretation intent on the understanding that the mother was labeling the young child's experience—trying to give a name to something the child was experiencing.

Aren't you a character. QI

Do you think that's funny? QI (understood: that's not funny!)

Reflecting Questions. In the following examples, mothers used Question forms to put their young child's experience into words.

Are you putting them in? QR (to child putting dolls in carriage)

Are you taking him for a stroll? QR

Do you like the teddy bear today? QR (to child hugging bear)

Are you loving your bunny? QR

Do you think that's funny? QR (to child laughing)

Of course, if these utterances were actually seeking information about the child's feelings, they would be coded QQ.

Are we putting our toys away? QR (Mom watching child)

Are we putting our toys away? QC (Mom helping child)

Catalogue of Yeahs

"Yeah" (etc.) is normally Acknowledgment form but may have any intent. For example, indications of receipt of information are KK. Requests for information (e.g., for repetition or elaboration, marked by upward inflection: Yeah?) are KQ. Answers conveying objective information are KE. Answers conveying subjective information are KD. Expressions of sympathy or empathy (other grimaces; speaker says, **"Yeah!"**) are coded KR. Confirmation of accurate Reflections or Interpretations or agreements to perform requested actions are coded KC. Praise (marked by strong inflection) and evaluation (used to mean "correct") are KI. Answers that convey instructions (A: Should I tell Harry? B: **Yeah.**) are coded KA.

"No" and its variants are also Acknowledgment forms. Their intent depends on context, for example, on the Question they answer.

(Is that a telephone?) **No.** KE

(Am I crazy?) **No.** KI

(Do you want to go to the movies?) **No.** KD

(I don't want to do that.) **No.** KR

No, no, Sean (prohibiting). KA, KA, KK.

Are you tired? No. QQ, KR (understood as answering own Question: No, you're not tired.)

Similar considerations apply to other Acknowledgment forms.

(I've got the answer.) **Ah.** KK

Ah! (mock surprise) KD

(My cat died.) **Aw.** (sympathetic) KR

(Are you going home?) **Ahm.** KD (understood: "Yes, I am," expressing intention)

But watch for noncommunicative noises, which are not utterances (see Chapter 8).

I'm going . . . ah . . . to Alaska. DD (the "ah" is not coded)

Asking and Telling

These examples illustrate some of the sorts of distinctions that are made by the mixed modes.

I'm asking you what she said. DQ
I'm telling you that I'll do it. DD
I'm telling you to feed the dog. DA
I wish you would feed the dog. DA

###

May I ask you where you were last night? QQ
May I ask you to help clear the table? QA
May I go to the movies? QQ
May I interrupt you for a moment? QD

###

Can you tell me more about that? QA
Can you pass the salt? QA
Can you tell me why you wanted to do that? QA
Can you tell me what you had for breakfast? QA

###

Let me ask you what you mean by that. AQ

Let me ask you to feed the dog. AA

Let me go to the movies. AA

Let me interrupt you for a moment. AD

Will you let me go to the movies? QA

Will you let me ask you to feed the dog? QA

Will you let me interrupt you for a moment? QD

Formal and Intentional Levels of Relationships

Theoretically, form and intent correspond to two distinct levels of the interpersonal relationship: an explicit, surface, or *formal* level and an implicit, deeper, or *intentional* level. (There are additional, still deeper levels, however, which are not represented by either form or intent codes; see chapter 5 and Stiles, 1986b.) For example, **"I wish you would come to the point"** (DA) formally reveals a wish, whereas intentionally it directs the other to do something. Using the Disclosure form softens the presumptuous intent of the utterance, in contrast to the bald command, **"Come to the point"** (AA). As another illustration, consider the interpersonal microrelationship conveyed by Jill's answer in this exchange:

Jack: **Are you happy?** QQ
Jill: **Yes.** KD

The answer ("Yes") includes attentiveness and acquiescence at the formal level (Acknowledgment), while revealing subjective information at the intentional level (Disclosure). To gain an intuitive idea of the impact of the formal level, imagine a conversation in which all of Jill's utterances were Acknowledgment form (yes or no), as contrasted with a conversation in which all of her utterances were Disclosure form ("I" statements). The information conveyed might be the same, but the relationship would be very different.

Form-intent discrepancies often reflect conflicting interpersonal pressures. For example, the conflicting goals of directing others to do something while avoiding imposing upon or offending them yields a realm of form-intent discrepancies that contribute to *politeness* (Brown & Levinson, 1978;

Stiles, 1981). For example, it is more polite to say **"Could you lower your voice?"** (QA) or **"I'd like some more potatoes"** (DA) than **"Lower your voice"** (AA) or **"Give me some more potatoes"** (AA). In each case, the more polite form puts a presumptuous intent into a nonpresumptuous form.

By using nonpresumptuous forms to carry presumptuous intents, polite utterances attenuate the imposition, in effect diminishing the status of the speaker relative to the other. If the speaker is of higher status or otherwise of acknowledged importance to the other, the speaker can give orders, make judgments, and so forth directly (using pure presumptuous modes). In circumstances where a relatively higher status speaker is constrained to use nonpresumptuous intents (e.g., to give objective information), he or she may use presumptuous forms, in effect reversing the polite strategy, signaling a superior status.

> *Lecturer:* **We see here that the square on the hypotenuse is equal to the sum of the squares on the two sides.** CE

###

> *Lecturer:* **Note well that the square on the hypotenuse is equal to the sum of the squares on the two sides.** AE

###

> *Dr:* **We're gonna back you off this** [medicine]. CD

In the last example, I coded "we" as referring to both doctor and patient—an attempt to use grammar to invoke a sense of shared purpose. (If the "we" referred to the medical establishment—not including the patient—the utterance would be coded Disclosure form.) I coded the intent as Disclosure, expressing the doctor's intention.

Further Examples of Mixed Modes

A few further illustrations of mixed modes follow. Note that, like many of the examples in this book, these are given out of context and hence rely on you, the reader, to use your imagination to fill in the appropriate context. If your imagined context does not match mine, the code shown here may seem wrong. If the code seems wrong to you, try to imagine a context in which the code would be correct.

I went downtown. DE

I did not tell her I was coming to see you. DE

I see. DK

I agree with you. DC

It really bothers me. ED

That's what we did last time. EC

That's something you usually do. ER

We need to hurry. CA

(Are you a sophomore?) **Yes.** KE

(Does it bother you?) **No.** KD

Hmm? KQ

Okay. (no judgment intended) IK

You didn't want to come today? RQ

You know I love ice cream. RD

8
Unitizing

This chapter describes how to divide discourse into units for VRM coding.

UTTERANCE: PSYCHOLOGICAL CONCEPT

Psychologically, a single communicative act concerns one unit of experience. As discussed in Chapter 5, VRM theory views individuals as centers of experience and experience as a continuous stream that takes place within each center. Each communicative act can be construed as a point of contact between two streams of experience. Theoretically, a single communicative act cannot convey more than one point of experience. (Summary utterances like **"I've been feeling depressed all week"** convey the momentary experience of summarizing.) In order to convey two distinct points of experience, two communicative acts are necessary.

The utterance is the grammatical realization of this concept of a communicative act, and is the scoring unit for the VRM taxonomy. Theoretically, each VRM utterance corresponds to one point of contact. The goal of VRM unitizing specifications is to accurately represent one psychological unit of experience communicated between speaker and other.

The prototype of an utterance is the simple sentence, a complete thought with one subject and one predicate. Much discourse is not in simple sentences, however, so a more comprehensive definition is needed. The VRM definition of an utterance has been developed empirically to specify reliably units for which there is one and only one VRM code—and thus to avoid cases in which the sense of one utterance demands two different codes.

UTTERANCE: GRAMMATICAL DEFINITION

In the VRM taxonomy, an utterance is defined as a simple sentence; an independent clause; a nonrestrictive dependent clause; an element of a compound predicate; or a term of acknowledgment, evaluation, or address.

The need for each of these specifications can be illustrated by instances in which failing to make the specification would yield two or more different VRM codes. Independent clauses must be scored separately because of sentences like **"He left me, but I didn't mind"** (EE, DD). Nonrestrictive dependent clauses must be scored separately because of sentences like **"He left me, which didn't bother me"** (EE, ED). ("Which" is the third person subject of the second utterance, a nonrestrictive dependent clause.) Compound predicates must be scored separately because of sentences like **"He left me and made me feel worthless"** (EE, ED). ("He" is the subject of both utterances.) Each term of acknowledgment or address must be scored separately because of sequences like the following:

(Are you voting for Nicholson?) **Well, no.** KK, KD

(Swab the deck.) **Aye-aye, sir.** KC, KK

The following sections consider these specifications in more detail.

Simple Sentences

Most of the examples in the preceding two chapters are simple sentences that demand one and only one VRM code. In coding simple sentences, watch for unusual word orders, such as objects preceding subjects, which do not affect the VRM form code.

I ran home. DE

Home I ran. DE

Independent Clauses

These are normally separated by a comma and a conjunction ("and," "or," "but") or by a semicolon.

You're doing the right thing, and I admire you for it. II, DD

He'd spent all his money, so he had to walk home. EE, EE

You never listen; your head is always in the clouds. II, EI

###

Cl: **I feel I was old enough to bear a baby, and that's surely a lot of pain, but yet they won't leave me make up my mind for myself.** DD, ED, EE

Th: **Here I was old enough to have a child, and yet nobody thinks I can make my decisions or run my own life.** RR, ER

The therapist's first utterance is coded Reflection form because the "I" refers to the client rather than to him- or herself.

There are some important exceptions to the rule that independent clauses are coded separately—"if" clauses and some "because" clauses. In these cases, the thought represented by the sentence concerns the relationship between the two clauses rather than the content of each independent clause, and the VRM code should reflect this. These are discussed in the section on conditional and causal clauses below.

If it doesn't rain tomorrow, I'll play golf. DD

I stopped because I felt tired. DD

Nonrestrictive Dependent Clauses

Nonrestrictive dependent clauses are treated as separate utterances, whereas restrictive clauses are not. Grammatically, a dependent clause is restrictive (and not scored separately) if it restricts the meaning of the term or clause that it modifies. For example, in the sentence, "**I enjoyed the book that he gave me**" (DD), the dependent clause "that he gave me" restricts the meaning of "book" (i.e., it identifies which book is meant), so the sentence is scored only once. "**I enjoyed *Moby Dick,* which he gave me**" (DD, EE) is scored twice, however, because the dependent clause, "which he gave me," is nonrestrictive—that is, it conveys additional information about the book rather than serving to identify it. Nonrestrictive clauses are properly separated by a comma, but usage is inconsistent, so that the psychological concept that each utterance concerns a separate unit of experience (e.g., makes a distinct assertion) is often a better guide than grammatical rules.

Some examples of nonrestrictive dependent clauses:

I go to Miami University, where the dropout rate is low. DE, EE

Your dog dug up my garden, which made me mad. EE, ED

Some examples of restrictive dependent clauses:

When you were cold [toward him] before, why do you think you would have been? QQ ("when" clause is restrictive)

I go to a university where the dropout rate is low. DE ("where" specifies— restricts—the meaning of "university")

When I'm in an elevator, I'm afraid it's going to fall. DD

This is the dog that dug up my garden and made me mad. ED

This last example is coded ED because the accuracy of part of it (i.e., whether the speaker was mad) can be determined only within the speaker's private frame of reference.

The coat that I lent you when you said that you were cold while we were hiking is black and tan, if that is what you wanted to know. EE

The independent clause is "The coat is black and tan" (EE). All of the dependent clauses are restrictive and not coded.

Th: **So those are certainly things we can do, I think, that will be very helpful.** EA, DA

In context, I understood this as a suggestion (Advisement intent) that the client examine the client's reactions of feeling guilty in certain situations. The subject of the main clause is "those"; "we can do" and "that will be very helpful" are restrictive dependent clauses modifying "things." "I think" is a filler, coded DA, which takes its intent from the parent clause (see discussion of fillers and tags later in this chapter).

Unfortunately, in natural speech the distinctions between restrictive and nonrestrictive clauses are not respected consistently.

Th: **So there's already a very clear sort of practical difficulty which we could look at.** EI, CA

I have coded this as if the dependent clause, "which we could look at" is a separate assertion (i.e., nonrestrictive), rather than a restriction on "difficulty" (in effect a definition of "difficulty"). The punctuation makes this ambiguous; properly, a nonrestrictive clause should be separated by a comma. But a restrictive clause should be introduced by "that" rather than "which." Note that the meaning of the sentence is different depending on whether the dependent clause is restrictive (characterizes the difficulty) or nonrestrictive (makes a suggestion).

> **Do you have any questions which perhaps I could answer so that you would feel better?** QQ

I coded this as a single utterance, reasoning that the "which" clause and all that follows were restrictive—specifying (restricting) the meaning of "questions," rather than making a separate assertion. In this interpretation, the invitation is restricted specifically to questions that the speaker might answer to make the other feel better. Note that this use of "which" is technically ungrammatical; if this is a restrictive clause, it should be introduced by "that."

> *Dr:* **So for right now, till we see you, which is gonna be in, oh, let's see, 2 weeks, keep taking two a day.** AA, EE, AE

This is complex. The main clause, with restrictive modifiers, is "So for right now, till we see you, keep taking two a day" (AA). The clause "which is gonna be in 2 weeks" (EE) is nonrestrictive and coded separately. "Let's see" (AE) is a filler that takes its intent from its parent clause. I treated "oh" as a noncommunicative verbalization (uncoded); it could be argued that this is a filler, however, with Acknowledgment form and intent taken from the parent clause, which would be coded KE.

Noun Clauses. Clauses used as subjects or objects of other clauses are not coded separately, though their content may influence the code for utterance intent.

> **I think that it's raining.** DE
>
> **I think it's raining.** DE
>
> **Everything I see reminds me of what I've lost.** ED
>
> **What you see is what you get.** EE
>
> **I can see why you feel like that.** DC
>
> **I don't know whether this makes any sense to you.** DQ or DD

Recall that noun clauses used as the subject of a sentence are third person and so are coded as Edification form.

Whatever I say goes. EA

Whatever you want me to be I will be. DD

In the first sentence, the "whatever" clause is the subject; in the second, the subject is "I," and the "whatever" clause is the complement.

He said that he would be here by 2 o'clock. EE

I suppose I am. DD

You can decide how to live your life. II

I guess we feel the same way. DC

You know that I'm afraid of spiders. RD

I don't want people to do things for me just because I pay them to do it. DD

Adverbial Clauses. Adverbial clauses similarly are not unitized separately, though they may influence the intent of the utterance.

I ran home. DE

I ran home as fast as I could go. DD

Compound Predicates

When there are multiple predicates, each is coded as a separate utterance.

Fran visited me and cheered me up. EE, ED

You don't like him and want to avoid him. RR, RR

I went downtown and bought a camera. DE, DE

I loved her then and still do. DD, DD

You called and spoke to her. RR, RR

People don't just come in and buy things. EE, EE

You were at home and you stood in the door and yelled. RR, RR, RR

Usually all of the individual utterances take the same form code, but it is possible to construct examples of second person sentences in which the same pronoun contributes to more than one form.

You're being too rowdy and have to leave. II, AA

Watch out for complex grammatical constructions that have multiple verb forms but do not involve multiple predicates. Here's an extreme example:

> **I found myself crying for no reason, just standing over my place and crying and crying. And hoping nobody would notice. And finding it very difficult when I'd put in a full day to come in the next morning, just having fallen into bed and not even having cooked or properly eaten, but that I'd made a mistake the night before because I was** *really* **too tired to do it. And just being sort of exhausted mentally, emotionally, physically—all the time.** DD

According to strict grammatical criteria, this can be coded as one utterance; the main verb in the passage is "found." The participles, crying, standing, hoping, finding, and being, are not main verbs. Note that the punctuation does not necessarily alter the coding (this utterance could be punctuated as one sentence). Alternatively, however, the punctuation could be taken to mean that there were distinct breaks between the phrases. If each phase is taken to be a separate thought, preceded by an additional, implicit, repeated "I found myself," then each could be coded separately (as DD). (See the discussion of elliptical constructions later in this chapter.) Listening to a tape recording might help in this case.

Terms of Acknowledgment

Each term of Acknowledgment is coded separately.

Yeah, yeah, mm-hm, okay. KK, KK, KK, IK

Mm-hm, you're feeling sad. KK, RR

(Are you lost?) **Well, yes, I suppose I am.** KK, KD, DD

Multiple Acknowledgments get multiple codes because in some contexts, they could have different intents:

A: **Have you finished with the sports page?** QQ

B: **Oh, yeah.** KK, KD

"Oh" Acknowledges the Question; "yeah" answers it.

Th: **Yes, but being reasonable doesn't take away that feeling.** KK, ER
Cl: **Oh, no.** KK, KC

Here "oh" just Acknowledges the Reflection; "no" Confirms it.

Terms of Address and Salutation

Proper names used to address a person and salutations are coded separately.

Hi there. KK
Hello, Mr. Knudson. KK, KK
Sam, I want you to listen to this. KK, DA
Johnny! KA (understood: Get out of the cookie jar.)

###

Dr: **How are you feeling today?** QQ
Pt: **Oh, pretty good, doctor.** KK, DD, KK

###

Dr: **Have you been doing pretty good?** QQ
Pt: **Yessir.** KD, KK

"Sir" is technically a separate unit even though it is not transcribed as a separate word.

Names and titles are not always used as terms of address, however.

Mr. E: **Mr. Frobisher is it?** QQ
Mr. F: **Um-hmm.** KE

The first utterance is in an unconventional order, but it means "Is it Mr. Frobisher?" (QQ). Thus, the name is not a term of address. The second utterance answers the question. Note that "um-hmm" is one of many alternative spellings of "mm-hm."

Terms of Evaluation

Evaluative words such as right, okay, good, fine, alright, and so forth are often used alone, in response to something said or done by the other. Although they could be considered as elliptical, with an understood "You are" preceding them (see section on Interpretation form in Chapter 7), they occur so frequently that they deserve special mention in a discussion of unitizing. They include no subject or verb, but unlike terms of acknowledgment, they do convey a specific literal content—an evaluation that something the other has done or said is right, okay, good, fine, or alright. Because they literally evaluate the other's experience (in the speaker's frame of reference), they are considered Interpretation form. Despite this literal content, however, these terms are often used to convey other intents.

(Seven times 6 is 42.) **Right.** II

(I've had a hard time adjusting to the new schedule.) **Right.** IK

(Please fill this prescription.) **Right.** IC

Watch out for evaluative words used as tag questions or as answers to questions (see further discussion in Chapter 10). In the latter case, their form is determined by the answer rule (discussed below).

I'm leaving now, okay? DD, QQ (understood: Is that okay?)

(How do you feel now?) **Okay.** DD (understood: I feel okay now.)

SPECIAL PROBLEMS IN UNITIZING

Conditional and Causal Clauses

"If" clauses always, and "because" clauses sometimes, signal a relationship between two parts of the sentence and are *not* coded separately. Instead, the compound utterance is treated as a single unit. The form code is taken from the main clause (i.e., the clause *not* introduced by "if" or "because"), and the intent must take into account the relationship expressed in the utterance as a whole.

If it doesn't rain the crops will die. EE

The crops are dying because it hasn't rained. EE

If I invite her, she'll come. EE

She came because I invited her. EE

If you come any closer, I'll scream. DD (DA?)

To explain the logic for this exception to the usual rule that independent clauses are coded separately, it is helpful to consider conditional and causal clauses separately.

"If" Clauses. "If" clauses describe conditions that may or may not obtain. For example, in the sentence, **"If it rains tomorrow, you'll have to cancel"** (AA), there is no assertion that it will rain tomorrow. (The only possible code for the conditional clause would be EE, yet no statement of fact has been made.) Thus, considering the utterance as separate would misrepresent what was communicated. Note that the "if" clause need not come first, although it usually does.

Let me add something, if I may. AD

I coded this AD because I understood it as expressing an intention ("I want to add something" or "I'm going to add something"). In general, "if" clauses like "If you see what I mean" or "If you like" are not coded separately.

"Because" Clauses. "Because" clauses, used properly, describe relationships between two events or conditions. This expressed relationship may entail a different code than either of the component clauses would have. For example, **"I moved into the other bedroom because my husband snores"** (DD) is coded Disclosure intent because it expresses the speaker's private motivation, even though the two component clauses considered individually depict objective information (separately, each would be coded Edification intent). "Because" is sometimes used not really to assert a causal relationship, however, but merely to connect two independent clauses. In such cases, it seems preferable to code each clause separately. Unfortunately, this distinction is not completely sharp. My suggestion for a litmus test is to ask whether substituting "and" for "because" changes the meaning of the sentence. If it does not, then the clauses may be considered as separate assertions and coded as two separate utterances. If the meaning is changed (i.e., if the point of the sentence is the assertion of a causal relationship), then the two clauses should be coded as a single utterance, with the form taken from the "effect" clause and the intent based on the nature of the causal assertion.

The car stopped because it ran out of gas. EE

I started to worry because it was getting late. DD

I don't talk to my family much, especially since Mom died, because she sat and listened. DD

###

Th: **All I've heard about you really is your form that you filled in, because we keep very distinct from the assessor,** ED
which seems a bit of a drag at first sight, because I know you've spent ages talking to the assessor, ER
but it's better for us really to approach it afresh. ED

###

Th: **Might it be,** QI
could it be that part of that need is so strong because deep down you're not quite sure if it's true? QI

###

Cl (describing how he or she felt as a child): **But of course the feeling at the time is you're a second-class citizen because you get a secondhand bike.** ED

In the following examples, I coded the "because" clauses as separate utterances because they do not really express a causal relationship. I thought I could substitute "and" for "because" without changing the sense of the sentence.

He was at the party, because I saw him there. EE, DD

###

Cl: **I must have wanted it to work badly,** DD
because I resigned my job, DE
and I sent all my gear up there. DE

"I resigned my job" is not a cause for "I wanted it to work badly," so it would not be sensible to consider them as one utterance. Instead the "because" has some more complex (elliptical) meaning involving a psychological inference.

> *Cl*: **I think I've noticed this at school particularly because, uh, it's my second year in this school.** DD, EE

###

> *Cl*: **It's awful** ED
> **because I feel in a way as though I should just move out of the way and let him find somebody who's as uncomplicated and nice as he is.** DD
> (note that the main verb is "feel")

###

> *Cl*: **I still harp on about it** DE
> **because, uh, I'm also still emotional.** DD

###

> *Th*: **Maybe you could talk about the sadness that you feel,** AA (IA?)
> **because that's happening now,** ER
> **isn't it.** QR (tag—see later discussion)

###

> *A*: **Did he ask you to go?** QQ
> *B*: **No, because I would have liked to.** KD, DD

Clauses Introduced by "As," "Since," "So," and "Although"

In general, clauses introduced by "as," "since," "so," "so that," and "although" appear to be separable assertions and should be coded as separate utterances. The distinction between these and the causal clauses described above is not sharp, however, so there may be cases in which these should be conjoined with the main clause as a single utterance. As a litmus test, clauses should be coded separately if "and" or "but" can be substituted without changing the meaning. Sometimes the clauses must be reordered for the substitution to work.

Although I am unaccustomed to public speaking, I would like to say a few words. DD, DD

"As" clauses (or, ungrammatically, "like" clauses) can be treated as independent and coded separately. "As" can also introduce phrases (e.g., "As usual . . . ") that are not coded separately.

Cl: **I'm very cautious about it, thinking about the other, as I told you, about the other people making a stupid mistake.** DD, DE

"As I told you" is a separate utterance, coded DE, and is not a filler. "Thinking about the other people making a stupid mistake" modifies "I" and is not coded separately.

As you know, the meeting is at 2 o'clock. RR, EE

As I've told you many times, I can't see . . . DE, DD

As I say, I can't see . . . DE, DD

The intent of the "as" clause in the last example is difficult because of the present tense of "say." I coded it as meaning "as I have said" or "as I usually say," which are objective reports.

Th (responding to client): **I wonder if it isn't some way of getting over messages to learn,** DI
like, "I can't do everything." RI

In this case, "like" seems to mean "for example" or "that is."

Since you broke it, you must pay for it. AA

I thought that this "since" expressed a causal relationship.

Quoted Statements

Quoted statements or series of statements are not coded separately, regardless of their length. The reason for this is that their content is not part of the speaker-other relationship.

So Henry said, "If you think I'm going to carry that all by myself, you've got another think coming." EE

The whole passage purports to be a report of what Henry said. It is treated as a single utterance.

> **The instructions are, "Turn off the power to the computer. Disconnect any peripherals. Remove the two screws that secure the modem cover. Insert the modem into the modem card guide. . . . "** EE

EE reflects the relationship between the speaker and the other. The Advisements contained in the list of instructions are part of a different relationship—that between the list (or the list's authors) and the reader. That is, the speaker is merely informing the other in this utterance.

> *Dr:* **You tell them that I said I wanted to check, do some tests for anemia, and to ask me about it before they draw blood.** AA

The doctor here gave a single command to the patient, even though the patient was to convey multiple instructions to third parties. The main verb here is "tell."

> **I'm telling you, I walked off.** DE

This is one utterance if it means "I am telling you that I walked off." It could be two utterances if the two clauses express separate thoughts:

> *A:* **Why didn't you tell me you walked off?** QQ
>
> *B:* **I am telling you!** DE
> **I walked off!** DE

Note also that Reflections, which put the other's experience into words, are not considered as quoted statements and are unitized in the normal way.

> *Th* (paraphrasing the client): **This is what I'm saying I'm doing, but actually here I am doing it.** ER, RR

The second utterance is Reflection form because the "I" clearly represents the client's viewpoint. The two clauses are coded separately because they are paraphrases, whereas they would be considered as a single unit if they were a literal quotation:

Th: **You said, " This is what I'm saying I'm doing, but actually here I am doing it." RR**

Embedded Utterances

An utterance is coded only once, even if it has other utterances embedded within it. As a coding convention, I recommend counting interrupted utterances where they begin. Thus, in general, an embedded utterance is scored as *following* the utterance in which it is embedded.

You, sir, should be more attentive. AA, KK

People who use big words, and I probably shouldn't be telling you this, really irritate me. ED, DD

The complete utterance, "People who use big words really irritate me" (ED), is scored only once, before the embedded Disclosure.

Cl: **I can't stand the way he . . . DD**

Th: **You're angry with him. RR**

Cl: **Treats me. He never comes home on time. EE**

The utterance "I can't stand the way he treats me" is coded only once, in the client's first speaking turn.

Appositives

Appositives are words, phrases, or clauses that rename some element in a sentence. Appositives are not coded separately.

I, the emperor, declare this to be so. DD ("the emperor" is an appositive)

It is appropriate that I should be the one to say goodbye. ED

In the second example, the clause "that I should be the one to say goodbye" is an appositive for "it."

Th: **You just feel really surprised at yourself that, by golly, you could tell them some of the things you've been thinking and feeling. RR**

Cl: **Yes, KC**
and I didn't care if I hurt their feelings or not. DD

The therapist's long sentence is a single utterance; the "that" clause is an appositive.

Infinitives

Infinitives are not coded as separate utterances.

Dr: **Why don't you sit on the table and take off your blouse.** QA, QA

###

Dr: **I want you to sit on the table and take off your blouse.** DA

The first example is two utterances because "sit" and "take" are main verbs; the second example is one utterance because "sit" and "take" are infinitives.

FRAGMENTARY UTTERANCES

Natural language is often fragmented—sentences are ungrammatical or incomplete. Thus, the question arises what is the minimum necessary for a verbalization to count as an utterance for VRM coding purposes.

To address this, it is first necessary to distinguish false starts from elliptical or telegraphic speech: In the case of false starts, the speaker did not finish the utterance he or she began, and the utterance is coded or not coded according to the main verb rule. In elliptical or telegraphic speech, the speaker said everything he or she intended to say, but the result was grammatically incomplete. If the speaker said everything he or she intended to say, then the utterance should be coded, even though there may be no verb. Usually elliptical speech can be coded by parallels with other nearby utterances.

False Starts and the Main Verb Rule

False starts are coded if and only if the main verb is present. This rule is somewhat arbitrary, but it can be followed reliably and it usually conforms to linguistic intuition about whether the thought was expressed.

My wife and I have decided to sell our . . . DD

My wife and I have decided . . . DD

My wife and I have . . . (not coded)

My wife and I . . . (not coded)

As this example illustrates, an auxiliary verb ("have" in this case) is not sufficient for a verbalization to count as an utterance.

I'm . . . **I'm afraid to go in the elevator.** DD, DD

I am . . . **I am going to wash the car.** DD

The first example is two utterances because "am" is the main verb; the second is only one utterance because "am" is an auxiliary verb.

Elliptical Speech, Parallelism, and the Answer Rule

Language is elliptical, or telegraphic, when parts of utterances are left unstated but are meant to be filled in by the listener. For deciding whether a fragment counts as an utterance, a litmus test is whether the speaker said everything he or she started to say. If the answer is yes, then the fragment does count as an utterance, regardless of how small the fragment is. (See also the discussion of brief utterances in Chapter 10.)

Elliptical utterances are coded in the VRM system using the following formula: Code what is clearly understood in context.

Dr: **Take a deep breath.** AA
   Again. AA
   Again. AA

In context, the doctor's "Again" is clearly understood to mean "Take a deep breath again" and is unitized and coded to reflect this meaning. As this example illustrates, elliptical utterances often depend upon parallelism for their meaning.

Mother (to child): **Bear?** QQ (understood: Is that a bear?)

Fixed? QQ (understood: Is it fixed yet?)

The Answer Rule. An important example of parallelism is answers to questions. These are coded using the answer rule, which is: Transpose the minimum necessary material from the question and code the result.

(How do you feel?) **Terrible.** DD (understood: I feel terrible.)

(Where are my shoes?) **Right where you left them.** EE (understood: Your shoes are right where you left them.)

Note that the wording of the Question can determine the VRM form code of the answer.

(Where do you live?) **Cincinnati.** DE

(Where is your home?) **Cincinnati.** EE

The first answer is understood as "I live in Cincinnati" (DE); the second is understood as "My home is in Cincinnati" (EE).

(Where shall I take this?) **To the corner of Withrow and College Streets.** AA

(Where do you want me to take this?) **To the corner of Withrow and College Streets.** DA

Here the first answer is understood as "[You shall] Take this to the corner . . . " (AA), whereas the second is understood as "I want you to take this to the corner . . . " (DA).

Note that the answer rule does not need to be invoked to code the form of answers that use Acknowledgment form (e.g., yes and no). From a VRM perspective, these are complete utterances, not elliptical ones. Of course, the content of the Question must be considered in order to code their intent.

(Do you feel terrible?) **Yes.** KD

(Do you live in Cincinnati?) **Yes.** KE

(Shall I take this to College and Withrow?) **Yes.** KA

A: **Is today the 24th?** QQ

B: **Maybe,** EE (understood: Maybe today is the 24th.)
yeah. KE

###

A: **I had Monday off.** DE

B: **Which Monday?** QQ (understood: Which Monday did you have off?)

A: **This Monday.** DE (understood: I had this Monday off.)

###

A: **And you?** QQ (understood: And what did you do?)

B: **Just walked out the door.** DE (understood: I just walked out the door.)

###

Cl: **My dad isn't that way all the time at work.** EE

Th: **And at home?** QQ (coded as a pure mode because the parallelism is ambiguous)

The answer rule can accommodate more than one answer to the same question.

Dr: **When did you run out of pills?** QQ

Pt: **Oh,** KK
not too long ago, DE
last week sometime. DE

I've coded the last two phrases as separate utterances. Alternatively, the second could be considered as an appositive for the first (and therefore not coded).

Th: **But you did get into scrapes?** RQ

Cl: **Occasionally, yeah.** DE, KE

Th: **Mm-hm.** KK

Cl: **When I was very young, yeah.** DE, KE

In the last example, both of the client's DE codes are based on parallel construction: "I did get into scrapes occasionally," and "I did get into scrapes when I was very young." (As an alternative unitizing, these could have been combined into a single sentence, receiving a single code; I separated them because I judged the intervening "yeah" signaled that they were separate thoughts.) The client's "yeah" is coded KE each time, as answering the therapist's Question.

The answer rule can be used even for answers to rhetorical questions.

Student: **What time do I have that class?** QD
   At 9 o'clock. DE

Some responses to questions are not answers, however.

A: **Where do you want me to put it?** QQ

B: **It doesn't matter.** ED

B's response doesn't answer the Question. If B had answered, "In the corner" the code would have been DA (understood as "I want [you] to put it in the corner").

Parallelism in Utterances Other Than Answers. Similar sorts of parallelism can be used to understand elliptical utterances that are not answers to questions.

Th: **Now you're tearing yourself down.** II

Cl: **Of course not, doctor.** DC, KK

Here, "of course not" is understood as "of course I'm not tearing myself down," which disagrees with the therapist's Interpretation.

Th: **So now you've got more confidence.** RR

Cl: **Yeah, however that's going to help.** KC, DD

The client's second utterance is understood as "Now I've got more confidence, however that's going to help" (DD).

Th: **Might it be,** QI
**could it be that part of, you know, that need is so strong that you're
not quite sure that it's true?** QI, RI

The first QI is coded parallel to the second; there are two complete
verbs, as both utterances are obviously saying the same thing. The
whole "that" clause ("that part of . . .) is an appositive for "it," so it is
not coded separately. The "you know" is a filler, coded RI (see section
on fillers and tags). I read this sentence as a (tentative) explanation of
the client's experience, suggested by the therapist (i.e., therapist's
frame of reference, Interpretation intent), rather than as an attempt to
empathize with something already realized by the client. The latter
would have been Reflection intent.

Th: **Normally, I'd see husband and wife together,** DE
but that wouldn't be very good, EE
because I, (false start, not coded)
in a way, in her eyes, (tells us who it wouldn't be good for; this is part of
the preceding EE, not a separate utterance)
and probably difficult for me too. ED

I coded the last phrase as a separate utterance because the grammar is
not strictly parallel, and it can be read as having an additional "would
be" understood (" . . . probably would be difficult for me too"). If the
parallel were sound ("that wouldn't be very good for her or for me"),
there would be only one utterance, which should be coded as ED
because access to the speaker's private experience is implied. The
second utterance is Edification intent because the "good" is judged from
the wife's frame of reference.

Cl: **I don't think the way I used to.** DD
That has bothered me too. ED

Th: **Sort of a feeling that where I used to be pretty clear and sharp, I'm
now confused.** RR

The therapist's response is coded Reflection form because it is understood as "You have sort of a feeling . . . " Note that the speech contains
only one utterance because everything after "that" should have been
enclosed in quotation marks.

Th: **Sounds like you're saying, "I really feel happy."** ER

This utterance is understood as "*It* sounds like you're saying . . . " (ER)—a mixed mode rather than a pure mode—because the verb form ("sounds") calls for a third person subject (i.e., "sounds" is ungrammatical). Context and dialect may have to be taken into account in making this sort of judgment.

Some elliptical utterances can be understood based on social convention or nonverbal context:

Cream and sugar? QQ (understood: Do you want cream and sugar in your coffee?)

Thank you. DD (understood: I thank you.)

Pardon? DQ (understood: "I beg your pardon?" meaning "What did you say?")

Elliptical Questions. As pointed out above and in Chapter 7, Question forms are often elliptical. In colloquial speech, initial phrases may be omitted, as in the following examples.

See the baby? QQ (understood: Do you see the baby?)

See the baby? QA (understood: Look at the baby.)

See the baby? QR (child is already paying attention to the baby)

In each of these cases, the form is Question because the "Do you" is understood in context. See the discussion in Chapter 10 about discriminating among second person forms, however.

You wanna play? QQ

You wanna take this? (handing something to other) QA

The code for each of these assumes that an initial "Do" is understood in context.

You want more? QQ

You want more. RR

If "You want more" is understood as a Reflection, there is no reason to assume that an initial "Do" is understood.

Don't Reconstruct Unless It's Necessary

To repeat, the rule for coding elliptical utterances is to code what is clearly understood in context. *Do not manufacture or reconstruct.* Do not code something that the speaker might have meant. Coding words that a speaker did not actually say raises a danger of imputing communication that was not intended. Although some risks may be necessary in order to code elliptical construction, I recommend doing this as little as possible. In general, if it is not absolutely necessary to infer words that were not said, don't do it.

> *Dr:* **Take one in the morning, one in the evening.** AA

There is only one verb in this example. It is not necessary to construct a repetition of "take."

> **If you mean . . . , no.** KD

The initial fragment is not completed. Unless it were clear from context (e.g., from nonverbal signs) that the speaker had communicated what the other "meant," the "if" clause should not be coded.

Here's a difficult construction:

> *Cl:* **I don't have the time to do that.** DD
> **Give me the time,** AA
> **and I will** DD
> **or try to.** DD

I think "give me the time" is an Advisement, and one should resist the temptation to reconstruct this as "If you give me the time, then . . . " Note, however, the elliptical construction: "And I will [do that] or [will] try to [do that]."

Fillers and Tags

Fillers. Fillers are seemingly empty clauses such as "I mean" and "you know" that are often inserted into other sentences. According to the main verb rule (discussed earlier in this chapter), these count as utterances. The VRM form code is usually obvious; for example, "I mean" is Disclosure form, and "you know" is Reflection form. However, the intent of such utterances is obscure; they seem to be verbal forms with no intent. After much discussion of such utterances with collaborators and coders, I have come around to borrowing the intent of such fillers from the parent clause. Coded in this way, a filler has the force of a repetition—intensifying the effect of the parent clause.

This is, you know, very embarrassing. ED, RD

I really hated him, you know. DD, RD

Although I never realized it, I mean, they never treated me as if they loved me. DD, DE, EE

I mean, it was awful. DD, ED

Guess what, I only had one cavity! AE, DE

Let me tell you, Psych 10 is really boring. AD, ED

See, it's raining outside. AE, EE

It's raining outside, you see. EE, RE

Note that fillers take their intent from the *intent* of the parent clause, not from the form of the parent clause. As a convention, the order of codes for embedded utterances is determined by where the utterance starts. Thus, when the parent clause begins before the filler, the code for the parent clause is written first; when the filler comes before any word of the parent clause, the code for the filler is written first.

So, let's see, you were taking your blood pressure medicine just twice a day before? RQ, AQ

The parent clause begins with "So" and is coded RQ. The "let's see" clause is a filler, which is Advisement form ("You let us see") and takes its intent from the parent clause.

Cl: **I mean,** DE (filler)
   that's what I say, EE
   and that's what some other people say. EE

Fillers must be distinguished from independent clauses that have noun clauses as objects.

You know he was after your money. RE

You know, he was after your money. RE, EE

Guess what I brought back. AA

Guess what, I brought back a puppy. AE, DE

I think he was at Bradford last term. DE

He was at Bradford last term, I think. EE, DE

I mean, he was at Bradford last term. DE, EE

Usually, fillers are properly separated by a comma—reflecting a slight pause or inflection that signifies a separate utterance—whereas noun clauses are not. Transcribers cannot be counted on to make this distinction reliably, however, so coders must use their own linguistic intuition.

I suppose he does what he's capable of doing. DE

However, I suppose he does what he's capable of doing. DE

Although, I suppose, he does what he's capable of doing. EE, DE

In the first two examples, "I suppose" is used to give information about confidence or probability, not to mark subjective information (i.e., the intent is Edification, not Disclosure). In the third example, the filler is coded second because the main clause starts with "although."

The phrases "I think," "I mean," "I suppose," and so forth are not treated as fillers if "that" can be inserted (i.e., if "I think that," "I mean that," "I suppose that," and so forth can be substituted) without changing the sense of the sentence. The substitution should be possible without changing the word order. Thus, "I think" at the end of a sentence is generally a filler; one wouldn't say, "It's raining, I think that," for example. If the substitution can be made, treat the phrase as an introductory clause rather than as a separate utterance; usually this will affect the form of the utterance.

You know [that] I'm not exactly happy with the situation. RD

I'm not exactly, you know, happy with the situation. DD, RD

###

I think [that] Bolivia is south of Peru. DE

Bolivia is south of Peru, I think. EE, DE

###

I mean [that] it would be an honor. DD

I mean, it would be an honor. DD, ED

###

You mean you locked your keys in the car? RQ

You know, it really scares me. RD, ED

###

I wonder, would you shut the door? DA, QA

I wonder if you would shut the door. DA

I am currently coding names and titles used as terms of address as pure Acknowledgments rather than as fillers.

I lay down, doctor, every day, midday, at noontime. DE, KK

I lay down, you know, every day, midday, at noontime. DE, RE

Psychologically, I think, names and titles reach out in a way that fillers such as "you know" do not.

Tags. Tag questions (e.g., "isn't it," "don't you," "haven't I" at the end of sentences) also include a subject and verb (though sometimes only the auxiliary is present and the main verb is elliptical), and they are coded as separate utterances. They may be fillers, in which case they too take the intent of the parent clause, or they may be separate questions. These are fillers:

You're a mean person, aren't you. II, QI

You're pleased with yourself, aren't you. RR, QR

We'll never go back, will we. CC, QC

I've already been to the doctor, haven't I. DE, QE

As these examples illustrate, a question mark is not necessary for an utterance to be coded Question form—the inverted subject-verb order is sufficient. Omitting the question mark helps to signal that the intent is not Question—for example, that the inflection was falling rather than rising. Punctuation tends to be very inconsistent on this point, however, and the presence of a question mark is not sufficient to code Question intent. As always, intent must be judged taking context into account. A litmus test is whether or not the speaker really expects an answer (in which case the intent is Question) or merely agreement (in which case it is not). Tone of voice and inflection may be helpful cues here. If no informative answer is expected, it is not Question intent.

> **You haven't been yet, have you?** RR, QQ (rising inflection)
> **This is the end of the line, isn't it?** EE, QQ

The tag should be coded QQ if the speaker is trying to find out if this is indeed the end of the line; the tag should be coded QE if the speaker assumes that this is the end of the line and is using the tag rhetorically, as a filler. In the latter case, the question mark could have been omitted. Question marks are sometimes used to indicate rising inflections, however, even when no Question is intended.

> *A*: **I'm really sick of my job, right?** DD, QD
> *B*: **Mm-hm, right.** KK, IK

> ###

> *Dr*: **We're working for the same thing, right?** CC, QC

The last example is complex (and I'm not too confident of coding here). Coding "right?" as QC assumes that "is that right?" was clearly understood in context, but that it is used as a filler (not seeking information, but merely intensifying the parent clause).

> *Pt*: **I mean, it could come back, couldn't it?** DE, EE, QQ

"I mean" is a filler that takes its intent from the parent clause. "Couldn't it?" is a tag question that (in my interpretation here) was intended to seek information—checking on whether it could come back. If no such information was sought (i.e., the tag was intended to give emphasis rather than to seek the doctor's view), then this could be punctuated without the question mark, and the sentence could be coded DE, EE, QE, treating the tag as another filler.

Th: **The important thing is to get clear what,** EI
  you know, RI
  what, what you're, (already coded—part of first utterance)
  I mean, DI
  what's reasonable, (already coded—part of first utterance)
  isn't it. QI

The main clause is, "The important thing is to get clear what's reasonable." This could have been EA in some contexts, in which case the three fillers would have been coded RA, DA, and QA.

Ungrammatical Speech

Frequently, natural discourse is ungrammatical, so that VRM form rules based on grammar cannot be applied precisely. Compromises are necessary. Sometimes the best that can be done is to identify the closest possible grammatically correct construction with the same meaning and code that.

Have you, have a letter from them? QQ or QQ, QQ

This is grammatically ambiguous. It could have meant, "Do you have a letter from them?" (QQ) or "Have you . . . Have you a letter from them?" (QQ, QQ). In the latter case, the main verb is repeated, so it should be treated as two utterances.

If that's all you do is lay around, you don't have to eat much. IE

The "if" clause is not strictly grammatical, but it is still not coded separately. The verb phrase "have to" seems to mean "need to"; the sense is one of bodily requirements rather than obligations (so the form is Interpretation rather than Advisement). I coded the intent as Edification on the understanding that the sense of the utterance was "one doesn't have to eat much."

Pt: **Well,** KK
  you won't tell me RR
  and I [inaudible] **that the other doctor told me last time I had to bring it all in,** DD
  he do the same thing you do. EE

I assumed that "inaudible" was an experiential verb like "know" or "remember" and that the last clause, although ungrammatical, was a separate assertion. It is possible that the third utterance could be DE, for example if "inaudible" was a probability marker such as "think"; note that this would change the utterance from a report of subjective experience to a (hedged) report of objective events.

> *Dr*: **There are things, that is, the blood pressure.** EE, EE

The first utterance is "There are things" (EE); the second is a filler, "that is" (EE). "The blood pressure" can be construed as an appositive for "things" or as the complement for "that."

> *Th*: **I find that we can get into a state of mind where we can communicate with that part of you, that private self.** DD

###

> *Th*: **And it seems to me that this idea that you're not very good at seizing opportunities, that is a statement about yourself which may have some validity,** EI
> **but it may be something that's a bit of a self-fulfilling kind of belief, um, that, as you say, serves a function for you.** EI, RR
> **It protects you from taking risks and, uh, branching out.** EI

> *Cl*: **Yes.** KK

> *Th*: **And keeps you perhaps a bit stuck where you are.** EI

> *Cl*: **Okay.** IK
> **Well, actually, . . .** KK

> *Th*: **From my point of view, that's good** ED
> **because that's something we can try these things** [e.g., relaxation procedures] **out on.** EA

Uncodable Utterances

Utterances are unitized if they are complete or have a main verb or if they are elliptical, regardless of whether they can be heard or understood. If a verbalization cannot be heard or understood, but there is reason to believe that it met the unitizing criteria in other respects, it should be given the code U. In some cases, the form of an utterance may be codable even when the intent is uncodable.

> [inaudible]. UU
>
> I [inaudible] **their socks.** DU

###

> *Dr:* **Relax, relax.** AA, AA
>
> *Pt:* **Mummer mummer.** UU (assuming "mummer" means "inaudible mumble")

Uncoded Verbalization

Noncommunicative noises such as "ahh" and "er" are not coded. These must be distinguished from Acknowledgment forms such as "mm-hm" and "oh," however. The distinction is pragmatic; the litmus test is whether or not the speaker intended to acknowledge receipt of or receptiveness to communication from the other. This assessment must be made in context and does not depend rigidly upon how these nonlexical verbalizations happen to be transcribed.

> **I, uh, don't . . . know, uh, what to say.** DD
>
> (Next, Henry will say a few words) **Err. I don't know what to say.** DD
>
> (My mother just died.) **Oh. I don't know what to say.** KK, DD

Laughter, singing, and other nonverbal vocalization is not coded.

> *A:* **Bing de bing ding** (singing). (not coded)

###

> *Dr:* **Say "ah."** AA
>
> *Pt:* **Ah.** (not coded—noncommunicative noise)

Material that is recited or read may or may not be coded, depending on the purposes of the coding. In my research on verbal interaction, I have used VRM codes for measuring the verbal component of the interpersonal relationship between speaker and other. In such relationships, the illocutionary force of utterances that are recited or read usually does not fall on the other. That is, these utterances are not part of the speaker-other relationship. For example, an Advisement read from a book is typically not intended by the reader to impose an experience on the listener. Consequently, in this research, these utterances are not coded.

9

Discriminating Among
Mode Intents

This chapter represents a compilation of reasoning and examples based on the VRM principles and reflecting the types of utterances and discriminations that coders brought for discussion in research projects on which I have worked. Much of this research has been on psychotherapy and medical interviews (see list of studies in Chapter 4). Research in new types of discourse may require new discriminations, but the underlying principles will remain the same.

APPLYING THE VRM PRINCIPLES

VRM intents are defined by the intersection of the three principles of classification, as shown in Table 2.1, and not by verbal descriptions and examples. The verbal descriptions and lists of examples are derived from the principles and should be considered as derivative summaries rather than as definitions. Faced with a difficult utterance, you should first try to understand what the speaker meant and then ask, "Whose experience does this concern?" "Does the speaker presume to know what the other's experience is, was, will be, or should be?" and "Whose frame of reference or viewpoint is used?" The answers to these questions, rather than any superficial similarity to examples in this book, should decide the code.

Th: **If you bullshit in therapy, it's a waste of your time and mine.**

First, unitizing. The "if" clause is not coded separately, so this is a single utterance. Next, form. The subject of this declarative sentence is "it"—third person—so the form is Edification. Finally, intent. This utterance seems to be making some presumptions about the other's experience or intentional behavior, and it is clearly expressing the speaker's viewpoint (speaker's frame of reference). This narrows the choice to Interpretation or Advisement intent, depending on whether this utterance concerned the other's experience or behavior (i.e., something the other had already done) or the speaker's idea of what the other ought to do (i.e., avoid bullshit). This judgment would depend on context. I imagined that this was said by the therapist after the client had wasted some time talking about things that the therapist thought irrelevant, and I understood the utterance as labeling that behavior (i.e., the topic was the other's experience/behavior), so I coded the utterance EI. I did think that there was an underlying directive (i.e., a warning not to bullshit), but I thought this was at the hint level (off record). If I had judged the directive to be on record—so that the utterance was intended not so much to label the client's previous behavior as to direct his or her future behavior (i.e., to impose an experience on the client)—then I would have coded it EA.

Your judgment of the meaning of this utterance may or may not match mine, particularly as the utterance is taken out of context and you and I may imagine different contexts. And, as noted, the VRM code may differ depending on how you and I interpret the meaning. If we can agree on what an utterance means, however, the taxonomic principles should lead us to one and only one VRM code.

This book will not help you understand what people mean when they say things. For this, you must depend on your knowledge of the language, the culture, the setting, and the relationship in which the utterance takes place. As a coder, your job is first to understand what the utterance means and then to apply the taxonomy to that meaning. This chapter and the following one address difficult distinctions and coding situations that have been encountered in several years of using the VRM taxonomy.

DISCLOSURE INTENT VERSUS EDIFICATION INTENT

Disclosure and Edification differ only in frame of reference (Table 2.1). Both concern the speaker's experience and both presume knowledge of the speaker's experience only (no presumptions about the other required).

A litmus test for deciding between Disclosure and Edification intent is to ask if an observer in the right place at the right time with the right skills and equipment could know the accuracy or inaccuracy of the statement as well as the speaker could. If the answer is yes, the utterance is in a neutral or shared frame of reference and is coded Edification in intent. If ascertaining the truth/sincerity of any aspect of the statement would require seeing into the speaker's mind, then the utterance is Disclosure in intent.

Thus, in general, the intent of Disclosure is to reveal oneself, whereas the intent of Edification is to provide data. Disclosure conveys subjective information, whereas Edification conveys objective information. In Disclosure, the speaker reveals his or her own thoughts, feelings, wishes, perceptions, or intentions, whereas in Edification, the speaker provides information that is neutral or objective. In a nutshell:

Disclosure = Subjective = Private

Edification = Objective = Public

I hope I live to be a hundred years old. DD (wish)

I am a hundred years old. DE (observable)

I'm going downtown. DD (intention)

I went downtown. DE (observable)

My worry is that he won't come back. ED (feeling)

He won't come back. EE (speaker has no better access to truth than the other)

I can sew. DD (a claim about ability, not a description of behavior)

I have sewn. DE (observable)

I left early to catch the train. DD (gives speaker's reason)

I left early. DE (observable)

I pull the covers up when I'm cold. DD (requires access to speaker's internal frame of reference)

I pull the covers up at night. DE (observable)

I saw your mother's car at the Irvings. DD (perception)

I waved at your mother when she drove by. DE (observable activity)

A good example of the confusions that can arise is given by reports of reading. Reading may refer to an observable activity (sitting, looking at a book) or to an unobservable activity (gathering information, making sense out of marks on paper). You have to decide which sort of activity is being described.

> **I spent the afternoon reading in the library.** DE
>
> **I've been reading about Soviet agriculture.** DD
>
> **I read a book about it.** DD
>
> **I picked up a book about it.** DE
>
> **I looked at a book about it.** DD or DE (perception versus observable activity)

If any part of an utterance requires access to the speaker's private awareness, then the whole utterance is coded as speaker's frame of reference.

> **I'm a sophomore.** DE (could be checked, e.g., by looking at the class roll)
>
> **I'm a hard worker.** DD (this code presumes that working hard is a subjective matter; the utterance's sincerity does not depend on whether or not others consider him or her a hard worker)
>
> **I'm a sophomore and a hard worker.** DD (one aspect is subjective, so the utterance is coded as speaker's frame of reference)

###

> **I was feverish and sweating.** DE (observable)
>
> **I was feverish and sweating and confused.** DD

Features That Do Not Affect Intent Coding

Some features of utterances that do *not* affect whether the utterances are coded Disclosure or Edification intent (or any other intent) in the VRM system include whether they are true or false, accurate or inaccurate, vague or clear, uncertain or definite, or whether they are emotionally significant, intimate, or embarrassing.

> **There are purple people eaters on Pluto.** EE
>
> **I met a purple people eater at a party.** DE
>
> **I saw a purple people eater last Friday night.** DD (perception)

###

The gorilla was 6 and a half feet tall and weighed 741 pounds. EE

The gorilla was pretty big. EE

###

Fifty-two percent of all marriages end in divorce. EE

My husband left me for another woman. EE

###

I masturbate in the bathtub. DE

I like to masturbate in the bathtub. DD

Perceptions

Whether or not someone sees (or hears or feels or smells or tastes) something is knowable only by that person; for example, one can look at something without seeing it. Because one would have to read the speaker's mind to know for sure if he or she really perceived something, perceptions are considered as speaker's frame of reference. It is thus important in VRM coding to distinguish between assertions of fact and reports of perceptions.

I saw a parade on High Street. DD

There was a parade on High Street. EE

I marched in the parade. DE

I heard the birds singing. DD

The birds were singing. EE

I saw Harry's new bicycle. DD

I met Harry. DE

Harry showed me his new bicycle. EE

Although having "seen" or "heard" something is clearly a perception (private, and hence Disclosure), having "looked" or "watched" or "listened" is more ambiguous. In many cases, these seem to describe observable activities (public, and hence Edification), but in other cases these words describe covert perceptions (private, and hence Disclosure). Coders must decide in each case which meaning was intended.

I watched the parade. DE

I looked at him. DE

I listened to the Ninth Symphony. DE

I felt around under the sofa. DE

Each of the foregoing codes assumed that the utterance's meaning would be the same (describing an activity) even if the speaker had been completely distracted and inattentive during the activity (e.g., "I watched the parade, but didn't see it because I was thinking about what you said last night"; DE, DD).

I was looking straight ahead, but I was watching him out of the corner of my eye. DE, DD

I looked right at her, but I didn't see her. DE, DD

I looked for him in the crowd. DD

I listened to the distant noise of traffic. DD

I felt something soft and furry under the sofa. DD

To complicate matters, perception words are sometimes used in other senses. For example, "I saw Harry" is coded DD if it refers to the speaker's perceiving Harry; it is coded DE if it means only that the speaker met or visited Harry (this could have been determined by an observer). Thus, it is essential to understand what was meant by an utterance before coding it. Usually the meaning is clear in context.

Pain, Discomfort, State of Mind

The speaker's pain and discomfort and state of mind are necessarily private (and hence Disclosure). Observable signs of injury or disease are public (and hence Edification).

My back is killing me. ED

My foot itches. ED

I have a dull ache above my eye. DD

I was confused. DD

I was very busy. DD

This is driving me crazy. ED

My arm is broken. EE

I had a fever. DE

I was sweating. DE

I hit my head, and it raised a lump. DE, EE

My finger got caught in the door, and it hurt like blazes. EE, ED

And I suppose it's a classic Oedipal situation. DD

I coded the last example DD on the understanding that the "classic Oedipal situation" described the speaker's own feelings.

Intentions

Statements of actions intended by the speaker are Disclosure intent rather than Edification intent because one would have to read the speaker's mind (i.e., one would need access to his or her private experience) to know if he or she really meant to do what he or she said. Even though the actions may easily be seen when and if they actually occur, it is always possible that the speaker does not really intend to perform the stated action or that circumstances may prevent the action.

I'm going to ask the nurse to come in now. DD

Lemme explain. AD

I'll tell you how it hurts. DD

I mean, we're going down after Christmas. DD, DD

See you later. DD (understood: I'll see you later.)

She asked me to be her bridesmaid. EE

I'm going to be her bridesmaid. DD (understood as an intention)

Some words can describe either an intention or an observable action. For example, "I tried . . . " is coded Disclosure intent if it refers to effort, but Edification intent if it refers to an observable attempt.

I tried to drink the medicine. DD

I tried to sit up. DD

I tried every door. DE

Predictions

Predictions about events that are external to the speaker-other relationship are generally Edification intent. It is important to distinguish statements about future external events from predictions about the speaker's own experience and future behavior, which amount to intentions (Disclosure intent), from predictions about the other's experience (Interpretation intent), and from predictions about shared experience (Confirmation intent), as well as from directions for the other's future behavior.

Predictions about external events:

All the kids will be there this weekend. EE

The nurse will give you your medication. EE

It may rain tomorrow. EE

High blood pressure is going to kill you. EE (see later discussion of "mind-body distinction")

Predictions about speaker's experience and behavior (intentions):

I'll be there this weekend. DD

I'll be in England next month. DD

That might make me have to change my mind. ED

It would be difficult to maintain this victim stance. ED

I mean, we're going down after Christmas. DD, DD (filler, intention)

Predictions about other's experience and behavior:

You'll undoubtedly be there this weekend too. II

You won't like the taste of this. II

It would be difficult [for you] to maintain that stance. EI

Predictions about shared experience:

We will not get it perfect whatever we do. CC

So we can just see how that's panning out. CC

Directions for future behavior:

Mother (to child): **You won't do that again, IA**
will you. QA

As always, it is necessary to understand the speaker's meaning to make these sorts of discriminations.

I don't think I'll get a vacation this year. DE (prediction)

I don't think I'll take a vacation this year. DD (intention)

I coded the first sentence as referring to circumstances at the speaker's job. In some contexts, it could be used to express the meaning of the second sentence (i.e., the intention), or it could mean "I feel pessimistic today." If either of these is clearly the on-record meaning, the utterance can be coded DD.

Cl: **But it's going to get worse.** ED
It's not solved now; ED
it'll carry on until the weekend, ED
and all the kids'll be there. EE

The client seems to be predicting her or his own feelings.

See also the further discussion of prediction under "Reflection Intent Versus Interpretation Intent" later in this chapter.

Value Judgments and "Should" Statements

Judgments of value (i.e., whether something is good or right or beautiful) are speaker's frame of reference. (People can differ over whether something is good or right or beautiful.) Thus, value judgments are generally coded as Disclosure intent if they concern the speaker's experience, Interpretation intent if they concern the other's experience or behavior.

That was a funny movie. ED

That was a black-and-white movie. EE

That movie was 4 hours long and boring. ED (coded speaker's frame of reference even though only part of it uses the speaker's internal viewpoint)

He's a good person. ED

You're a good person. II

He's really ugly. ED

You're really beautiful. II

By the same reasoning, "should" statements are generally in the speaker's frame of reference.

People should obey the law. ED

Criminals should be made to pay. ED

Nice girls shouldn't do those things. ED

You should pay for what you broke. AA (note that this is also speaker's frame of reference)

You should try to be on time. AA

She (patient) **should keep taking it.** ED or EA

Value-related words can sometimes refer to objective external standards, and these judgments can be coded as Edification intent. For example, "The *Iliad* is a great book" would be EE if the speaker means to state a widely accepted belief that the book is great; it would be ED if the speaker means that he or she enjoyed the book or personally judges it to be a great book. "This meat is good" would be EE if "good" refers to U.S. government standards for grading beef (which include "good" along with "prime" and "choice"); it would be ED if the judgment is based on the speaker's evaluation of the meat.

In medical contexts, "bad" and "good" may denote observable physiological conditions rather than value judgments. Note that these are the exception rather than the rule; code value judgments as speaker's frame of reference (usually Disclosure intent) unless there is a clear reason for doing otherwise.

Your throat doesn't look real red. EE

Your throat doesn't look real bad. EE

It doesn't look like you have strep throat. EE

Your throat doesn't look like a strep throat. EE

There's not a bad infection in there. EE

I don't see anything bad in there. DD

Your throat is in bad condition. EE

Your chances don't seem too bad. EE

Your child has been real bad. ED

Value judgments can also be Interpretation intent if the other's experience or behavior is being evaluated (see Chapter 6).

Your health is, as you know, important. EI, RR

I understood the main clause to be saying that the speaker considered the other's health to be important to the other (other's experience, speaker's frame of reference), coded EI. I think "as you know" represents a separate assertion (i.e., that the other knows that his health is important) rather than a filler. Thus, it is coded RR, rather than taking its intent from the parent clause (see section on fillers, Chapter 8).

Opinion Can Be Any Mode

"Opinion" is generally *not* a useful concept for making VRM discriminations. The term opinion may be used to describe statements that are Edifications, Disclosures, Confirmations, or Interpretations (and perhaps other modes as well). In particular, the concept of opinion does not help to distinguish between Disclosure and Edification, as either may be considered as opinion. The issue is whether the assertion is, in principle, accessible to an outside observer, not whether the speaker would accept the verdict of any particular outside observer.

They gave the game away. EE

They say reverse discrimination is different [from discrimination], **but it's not.** EE, EE

The second utterance is a difficult call. I coded it EE, reasoning that the speaker intends to assert an objective feature of the situation (i.e., that the two situations are alike). This is not explicitly a value judgment, though the speaker's values may influence what aspects of a situation make it like or unlike another.

A: **What has this got to do with the Devil?** QQ

B: **I don't know,** DD
  except maybe that's the way he torments. EE

Did B mean to reveal his or her experience (Disclosure) or to describe the world (Edification)? In this case, I thought the latter.

Metaphors

Metaphors can be difficult, but are treated like other utterances: The form code is based on the literal utterance; the intent code is based on the pragmatic meaning (i.e., the metaphoric meaning, assuming this is on record).

Johnny runs faster than a speeding bullet. EE

"Faster than a speeding bullet" is taken as a description of Johnny's running. The fact that the statement is not literally true is irrelevant. In particular, the use of a metaphor does not in itself place the utterance in the speaker's frame of reference.

Third Parties' Subjective Experience

Statements of what some third party thinks or feels are considered as being in a neutral frame of reference (coded Other). They cannot be determined by reading either the speaker's mind or the other's mind. That is, in asserting something about what a third party thinks or feels, neither the speaker nor the other has privileged access to the truth. Thus, characterizations of third parties' thoughts, feelings, wishes, perceptions, and intentions are generally Edification intent.

My mother didn't love me. EE

He was only having fun, and I was always working. EE, DE

He was absolutely deceitful about the whole thing. EE

They were giving in to their anger. EE

My mom tends to use the children as a way to get to me. EE

Cl: **The sense is that my mother and father haven't really got very much out of life,** EE

and they certainly haven't got very much out of living with each other. EE
They're leading what I would find an intensely boring life. ED
I could accept it if they were both contented, DD
but they're not. EE

If the speaker claims to share an experience with the a third party, however, then the speaker's internal frame of reference is involved.

My brother likes to go to the movies. EE

My brother and I like to go to the movies. DD

My brother likes to go to the movies with me. EE

He felt miserable. EE

He and I felt miserable. ED

They wanted you to come. EE

We wanted you to come. DD

Lots of people are going to Florida. EE

Some of us are going to Florida. ED (includes speaker's intention)

I'm not going to run off with a 20-year-old. DD

He thinks I'm going to run off with a 20-year-old. EE

I'm sure he thinks I'm going to sort of run off with a 20-year-old. DD

"I'm sure" in the last example seems to be more than a probability estimate (cf. next section); what is being asserted is the speaker's belief, not what "he" thinks.

Pt: **My husband had that arthritis in there,** EE
and he might as well live with it. ED

The second utterance is a value judgment by the speaker, so it is in the speaker's frame of reference. It is not Advisement intent because it does not direct the other to do anything (even though it does implicitly direct the husband, a third party, to do something).

Probability Statements, Guessing, Uncertainty, Tentativeness

The distinction between Disclosure and Edification intent does *not* depend on a statement's certainty or uncertainty, precision or vagueness, or tentativeness. Using probability qualifiers like "maybe," "certainly," "probably not," and so forth does not affect the VRM code. In particular, vagueness, tentativeness, or imprecision cannot change an Edification intent into a Disclosure intent.

> **There was whole lots of tigers and lions.** EE
>
> **It looks like there are about 30 in here.** EE
>
> **I don't eat *that* much.** DE
>
> **He is a thoracic surgeon.** EE
>
> **He might be a doctor or something.** EE
>
> **The sky is falling.** EE
>
> **Maybe the sky will fall.** EE
>
> **I was in the store that night.** DE
>
> **I might have been in the store that night.** DE

An imprecise statement of intentions is still Disclosure intent, however:

> **Perhaps I'll take a vacation.** DD

Similarly, tentative or imprecise Advisements are nevertheless still coded as Advisements:

> **You may do whatever you like.** AA
>
> **Could you possibly lend me a dollar?** QA

"I Think" as a Probability Marker

The phrase "I think" (along with other, similar phrases) is often used to indicate probability rather than to reveal thoughts. In this case, it does not affect the VRM intent code.

> **It's raining.** EE
>
> **I think it's raining.** DE
>
> **It might be raining.** EE
>
> **I think it might be raining.** DE
>
> **I know it's raining.** DD
>
> **I think he's planning a party.** DE

I believe she was in line first. DE

I think Belize is in Central America. DE

I think all drugs should be legalized. DD

I know everybody is different. DD

A litmus test is to substitute "probably" or "certainly" or some other probability term for "I think" or "I believe" or "I'm sure that"; if the meaning of the utterance does not change, then the "I think" (or equivalent) does not determine the intent.

She's watching TV right now. EE

I think she's watching TV right now. DE

Probably she's watching TV right now. EE

I'm sure she's watching TV right now. DE

No doubt she's watching TV right now. EE

As always, the issue is whether the speaker is trying to represent the state of the external world (Edification intent) or the state of his or her own thoughts (Disclosure intent). Another litmus test is to imagine what the speaker's predominant attitude would be if the assertion were proved incorrect: If the predominant attitude would be "But that *is* what I thought" (i.e., the utterance was sincere), then the intent was Disclosure; if the attitude would be "I was mistaken," then the intent was Edification.

Of course, probabilistic statements are not necessarily Edifications.

I think I'm in love with her. DD

Maybe I'm in love with her. DD

I think you should be careful. DA

Maybe you should be careful. AA

Dreams and Delusions

Dreams knowingly described by the dreamer are coded Disclosure intent. Thus, **"He was driving a car"** would be coded ED if it described an event that took place in the speaker's dream, even though it would be EE if it described an actual event. One would have to be inside the speaker's head to know if a dream description is true or false. Note that form codes are not affected.

Delusions, by definition, are fantasies that are believed to be fact. Because the VRM system codes the speaker's intention, utterances are coded as having Edification intent if the speaker intends them as Edification. "**The devil spoke to me today**," stated seriously, would be coded EE. ("**The devil spoke to me in my dream**" would be ED, however.)

> *Pt*: **I'm angry because of the force,** DD
> **because they don't realize that they have got that,** EE
> **and they should if they can set up a situation like that so often;** ED
> **they ought to begin to realize what they're doing.** ED

One rule of thumb is, if the speaker thinks it's a fact, the frame of reference is external (i.e., Edification intent).

DISCRIMINATING ADVISEMENT INTENT

Requests Versus Wishes

Context—particularly the nature of the speaker-other relationship—determines whether a speaker's statement of a wish constitutes a directive for the other. "**I want some ice cream**" would probably be a request (DA) if the other has the power to provide ice cream; it would probably be a wish (DD) if the other does not.

> **I want some more of those pills.** DA
>
> **I want some of those sticks you test your urine with.** DA
>
> **I wanted some milk of magnesia.** DD

The first two examples are coded DA assuming that the patient's intent was to request that the physician prescribe (or provide) some more pills or some sticks, respectively. They could be DD if the intent was only to Disclose a wish. The last example seems more likely than the first two to be DD rather than DA; it is more difficult to give orders using the past tense. But in the right context, even this could be DA—if the patient meant "I came to this visit because I wanted you to give me some milk of magnesia, and I still want that."

Th: **I'll see you Monday at 11:30.** DD or DA or even DC

This is DD if it merely states an intention; it is DA if it is meant, "Come to my office at 11:30"; it is DC if it agrees with the client's recently expressed preference to come at 11:30.

Justifications and Reasons: Advisement Meta-Intent

Justifications for taking an action are not coded Advisement even though they are part of an argument to convince the other to do something. They may be described as having a meta-intent of Advisement (see also discussion of meta-intent, Chapter 5).

Write those down in order of priority; AA
it will make it seem clearer. EI

The second utterance is meant to convince, but it is not a suggestion that the other could follow and should not be coded Advisement intent.

Meta-intent refers to the overriding purpose of a conversation, to be distinguished from the VRM intent of an utterance. Quite commonly, people use a variety of modes in seeking to influence others. For this reason, it may be difficult to tell whether an utterance has a directive (Advisement) intent or aims to influence the other's thinking indirectly (possibly with off-record hints or manipulations).

Mother: **Your room is a mess.** EE (understood as a hint: Clean it up!)

This should be coded EE unless it is clear in context that some action is being directed. If the directive is on record, it would be EA.

Your hair is very long. EE
Your hair is too long. ED

Note that "too long" is a value judgment, whereas "very long" is an objective (albeit vague) characteristic. Either utterance could convey a hint ("Get your hair cut"); the utterance should not be coded as EA, however, unless the directive is on record.

Don't you want it [your hair] **to be neat?** QQ or QI or even QA

This utterance has different meanings at different levels; the difficulty is figuring out which meaning is on record. It could be Question intent, with other meanings at the hint or manipulation level. It could mean "Your hair is not neat" (implied evaluation of other's behavior, QI), or it could mean "Get your hair cut" (QA).

> **You need to stand up to him.** IA
>
> **You need a dietician more than anything else in the world.** II

The first example seems to be a suggestion; it would be coded II only if no suggestion were intended. I understood the second example as conveying information about the other's needs (e.g., justifying a referral to a dietician) rather than directing the other to get a dietician.

> Th: **It might be helpful to take the tapes home.** EA

My coding this EA assumed that it was meant as a suggestion to take the tapes home. It would be coded EI if it was meant only as a recommendation that the other construe the experience as helpful.

> *Th*: **Gradually, over the next few weeks, we will get you to start being able to change the thoughts yourself.** CD

I interpreted this as a statement of the therapist's intentions or goals. It is not Confirmation intent because no access to the client's private frame of reference is implied. It is not Advisement because there is no specific instruction given; the client cannot obey this utterance, although he or she has been notified that instructions are likely to be forthcoming.

Instructions to Think or Imagine

Advisements may direct thought as well as action. The difficult discrimination concerns whether the utterance actually imposes a mental action or merely informs.

> **Think of a card.** AA
>
> **Remember, however, that the value of E(M) must be specified when a t ratio is computed.** AA

The second utterance could be coded AE if it conveyed information rather than actually instructing students to remember something.

> *Th*: **Be this incomplete house and repeat the dream.** AA, AA
> **Describe what kind of house you are.** AA
>
> *Cl*: **I am the house and I'm incomplete.** DD, DD
> **But the stairs are there.** ED (the stairs are in the dream)
> **And I don't have the rails to protect me.** DD
> **And yet I do climb, and . . .** DD
>
> *Th*: **No, no,** KA, KA
> **You're the house.** IA
> **You don't climb.** IA

Several of the client utterances would be coded Edification intent if they described real events; they are coded Disclosure intent because they refer to the client's (private) dream. The intent of the utterances in the therapist's last speech are coded Advisement intent because they direct the client's dream work (technically, they seek to impose an experience).

Rhetorical Advisements

> **Now let me see.** AD (this is not really a directive)
>
> **Now take a deep breath.** AA
>
> **Now I'm going to take your blood pressure.** DD (intention)
>
> **Now let me take your blood pressure.** AD or AA

In some contexts, I think, the last utterance could be coded AD, as merely an expression of the physician's intention. The coding issue here is whether permission is being actually requested; if the patient is being asked to let the physician do something, then the utterance should be coded AA.

DISCRIMINATING CONFIRMATION INTENT

Agreements and Disagreements

Probably the most common types of Confirmation intents are agreements. These may be cast in a variety of forms.

I agree with you. DC

You and I agree. CC

(We have to work together.) **Amen!** KC

You can say that again. AC

If you've ever had the flu, you know how you ache. RC (understood: you know how I ache.)

###

A: **I don't have anything to say about basketball.** DD

B: **Well, we'd have a pretty brief conversation about basketball.** KK, CC

###

A: **It's nice to meet you.** ED

B: **Yes, it's nice to meet you.** KC, EC

Not everything that concerns agreement or disagreement is coded as Confirmation intent. Watch out for agreements and disagreement with third parties.

My brother and I disagree about everything. DD

My brother and sister disagree about everything. EE

Brief Agreements: KC and IC

Agreement or disagreement with a Reflection or Interpretation is coded as Confirmation intent because such agreements must concern the speaker's experience (that's what the other was talking about in the Reflection or Interpretation) and must presume knowledge of the other's experience (which, paradoxically, concerned the speaker's experience).

Jack: **You wish this semester was over.** RR

Jill: **Yeah.** KC

"Yeah" is coded KC because it conveys Jill's feelings and presumes understanding of what Jack is thinking. In this case, Jack's thoughts concerned Jill's wishes, so Jill's presumption was not difficult. By contrast, "Yeah" is coded KK if it communicates only receipt of the other's communication.

Jack: **He visited me last Saturday.** EE

Jill: **Yeah.** KK

Here "Yeah" is coded KK because it requires no presumption of knowledge beyond what was said. (Jill need not even know who "he" is.)

Jack: **Dr. Black is a dull lecturer.** ED

Jill: **Yeah.** KC or KK

This "Yeah" is coded KC if it means that Jill thinks so too; it is coded KK if it means only that Jill heard what Jack said. Evidence favoring KC would include an emphatic tone of voice, knowledge that Jill had attended lectures by Dr. Black, and other indications that she felt negatively about her experience with Dr. Black. Evidence favoring KK would include an even tone of voice, knowledge that Jill had had no experience with Dr. Black, or indications that she enjoyed Dr. Black's lectures.

Cl: **I'm depressed.** DD

Th: **You're really feeling down.** RR

Cl: **Yeah.** KC

###

A: **You've had a hard day.** RR

B: **Yes, that's right.** KC, EC

###

A: **You must be mistaken.** II

B: **No, I'm not.** KC, DC

Acknowledgment and Confirmation differ in source of experience and in presumption. To distinguish them, ask "Whose experience is the topic of this utterance?" or "Does the utterance presume knowledge of the other's experience?" If the utterance concerns the speaker's experience, it cannot be Acknowledgment (cf. Table 2.1).

(I wish I could run away.) **Yeah.** KK

(You wish you could run away.) **Yeah.** KC

Similarly:

(I love peanuts.) **Right.** IK (could be coded IC if the speaker means that he or she loves peanuts too)

(You love peanuts.) **Right.** IC

Confirmation intent is coded for agreeing to do something, as well as for agreeing with something. In both cases, the speaker places his or her own experience in the other's frame of reference.

(Get me some peanuts.) **Right.** IC

(Take two of these.) **Okay.** IC

(Shine your shoes, sailor.) **Aye-aye, sir.** KC, KK

These responses presume understanding of the other's experience—the command. They are agreements to do something.

A: **Well, I hope.** KK, DD
   Of course, we always live on hope. CC
B: **Yes.** KC

###

A: **Astronomy was awful at 8:00.** ED
B: **It would be bad to teach a class early in the morning.** EC

###

B: **No, no. I don't think so. That's not what I think, no.** KC, KC, DC, EC, KC

All of the utterances in the last speech are disagreements with whatever the other had just said.

A: **We can talk about exams and grades.** CA

B: **Oh, alright.** KK, IC

"Oh" acknowledges the suggestion; "alright" agrees to it.

A: **All you got to do is love them** [children]. EE (Subject is "All"; "you got to do" is a restrictive clause)

B: **That's right.** EC

A: **They** [children] **only repeat what they hear.** EE

B: **That's right.** EC

I've coded "That's right" as Confirmation intent here on the assumption that B was citing her or his own experience with children (i.e., agreeing). If, instead, B was evaluating A's knowledge, then "That's right" should have been coded EI.

Confirmation Intent Versus Disclosure Intent

Confirmation and Disclosure differ in their presumptions and frame of reference, but both concern the speaker's experience. In Confirmation intent, the speaker presumes knowledge of the other's experience and uses it to express or give meaning to his or her own experience. To distinguish Confirmation intent from Disclosure or Edification intent, ask whether access to the other's private experience would help determine the truth or accuracy of the utterance (i.e., Does the meaning require presumptions about the other's experience?).

If the speaker assumes that the reader already shares knowledge or beliefs, so that the utterance is understood to mean, "We agree (or disagree) about this" or "We're looking at this the same way," then the intent is Confirmation. If the speaker is expressing his or her own viewpoint or suggesting what the other *should* think, then the intent is Disclosure.

Being yelled at makes me feel that way too. EC

I feel the same way. DC

Me too. DC

I am here too, and we can do our business. DE, CC

We do not have the luxury of a paradigm, as enjoyed by some other professions. CC

We can and should do more for the poor. CD (note only one main verb)

Neither we nor anyone else should be complacent. CD

You've got to balance the budget. AD

I find that we can get into a state of mind where we can communicate with that part of you, the private self. DD

I judged that the last example asserted the speaker's personal view, independently of what the other thought. Of course, in some contexts, the meaning might be different.

Suggestions for Joint Activities

Suggestions that involve both the speaker and the other are coded Advisement intent, not Confirmation Intent.

We could also make a chart on this. CA

We ought to make a rule that we do it after supper. CA

We are just going to have to waste some blocks here. CA

We might as well [do it]. CA

We could put the yellow one on top of the TV set. CA

Maybe we should start with it the long way. CA

We could tackle that in a fairly direct way. CA

Confirmation Intent Versus Reflection or Interpretation Intent

Confirmation concerns the speaker's experience. Thus, an utterance that concerns the other's experience cannot be coded Confirmation intent. Conversely, an utterance that concerns the speaker's experience cannot be Reflection or Interpretation.

It sounds like you support this. ER

###

Student: **This is a very difficult test.** ED
Teacher: **That's right.** EI (other's experience is difficult)

###

Th: **You've had a very difficult day.** RR
Cl: **That's right.** EC (speaker's experience is difficult)

###

Cl: **I actually find that quite difficult.** DD
Th: **Mm-hm, very difficult.** KK, RR (other's experience is difficult)

###

Cl: **I actually find that quite difficult.** DD
Th: **Mm-hm, very difficult.** KK, RC (speaker's experience is difficult)

The choice of Reflection or Confirmation intent here depends on whether the therapist is conveying his or her own experience. If context or paralinguistic cues indicate that the utterance means that the therapist independently knows "that" to be very difficult, code Confirmation intent. Otherwise code Reflection intent.

> **Try to remember to do this every day so we don't eat more calories than what our body burns up.** AA, CI

My CI code assumes that the "we" and "our" are really meant as "you" and "your."

DISCRIMINATING QUESTION INTENT

"Tell Me" and "I Wonder"

"Tell me" Advisement forms and "I wonder" Disclosure forms often function to elicit information from the other, but they may or may not express on-record Question intents. "Tell me" forms seem most often to express Advisement intents.

Tell me about your mother. AA

Tell me everything you've heard. AA

I think it is justifiable to code Question intent when the object of the verb "tell" is an interrogative (I'm not too confident about this, however):

Tell me how you feel. AQ

Would you tell me how you feel? QA

Can you tell me how you feel? QA

You feel how? QQ (here the form is determined by the interrogative word)

"I wonder" Disclosure forms may or may not seek information.

I wonder how you feel. DQ

I wonder why you decided to go there. DQ

I wonder what your feelings are about meeting. DQ

The interrogative words seem to justify the Question intent. These could be DD, however, if they mean to convey only the speaker's curiosity without seeking an answer.

I know you won't tell me, but I do wonder how you feel. DD, DD

In psychotherapy, "I wonder" is often used to soften the presumptuousness of Interpretation intents.

I wonder if there's a link between some of the feelings about what you didn't have with your father. DI

I wonder if there's a sense of something missing from your life. DI

Some other information-gathering constructions:

Please try to describe your impressions. AA

How about the Fish Camp? QA

Let's see how it works for you. AA

Answering Questions With Questions and Answers to Questions About Questions

Th: **So how's it fantastic?** QQ

Cl: **What, the relaxation?** QQ

Th: **Hmm.** KD

The therapist's answer is coded KD because it concerned what she meant by her Question (e.g., "Yes, I meant, 'how's the relaxation fantastic'").

Th: **So it** [client feeling] **has happened once?** EQ

Cl: **Yeah, er mm, do you want to know all about it?** KD, QQ

Th: **Yes.** KD

Questions in response to questions may be coded RQ if they are exact repetitions, if they finish the other's utterance, or if "You are asking" is understood.

Pt: **I didn't like the feel of it, to tell the truth.** DD

Dr: **Why didn't you?** QQ

Pt: **Like the feel?** RQ

Dr: **Mm-hm.** KD

The second patient speech formally finishes doctor's question, while intentionally it asks what the doctor meant.

Dr: **Why didn't you call us last month?** QQ (possibly QA = "You should have called.")

Pt: **Why I call last month?** RQ

Dr: **Uh-huh.** KD

I coded the form of the patient's (ungrammatical) response as Reflection because I understood it as "You are asking, . . . "

DISCRIMINATING INTERPRETATION INTENT

Interpretation Intent Versus Edification or Disclosure Intent

In distinguishing Interpretation from Edification or Disclosure, ask whose experience is being discussed and whose frame of reference is being used to judge it. For example, if the topic of the utterance is the other's experience, the intent cannot be Edification or Disclosure.

> *Th*: **That's very good.** EI
> **It's always better to talk to someone.** EI

The client's experience is being evaluated by the therapist.

> **If you are in love then it's hard to be objective.** ED

I understood this utterance as meaning "I'm in love and it's hard for me to be objective." It would be EI if the *other* were the one in love. It would be EE if this were a discussion between researchers who were studying the psychology of love.

> **That's right.** EI
> **That's interesting.** ED

###

> **You nagged.** II (concerns other's behavior)
> **You hurt my feelings.** ID (concerns speaker's experience)

###

> **She's bitchy.** ED (value judgment)
> **She's sloppy.** EE (observable characteristic)
> **You're bitchy.** II (evaluation of other)
> **You're sloppy.** II (evaluation of other's volitional behavior)

###

> *Cl*: **I don't wanna say goodbye to you.** DD

Th: **What do you want?** QQ

Cl: **I really don't know. Okay. Bye.** DD, IK, UK

Th: **When you said goodbye you crossed your legs.** RI

Presumably, the client knew that she or he said goodbye and crossed her or his legs, but the juxtaposition of the two implies some connection between these actions. I judged that this interpretive connection was on record.

The VRM Mind-Body Distinction in Medical Contexts

Even though Interpretation and Edification differ in all three principles of classification, confusion between them often arises when the speaker is giving the other information that pertains to the other's body. This happens frequently in medical interactions, when the physician gives the patient medical information.

Solution to the mind-body problem (philosophers have tried for years to solve it; here's VRM's answer):

Body, Physical = Edification

Mind, Experience, Intended Actions = Interpretation

When the physician is giving the patient information about the patient's physical condition (his or her body), the intent is Edification.

You have diabetes. IE

Now you just got a bad miserable cold. IE

You will probably throw up from this medicine. IE

These are coded IE because it is the patient's body that has diabetes, vomits, and so forth.

When the physician is telling the patient about the patient's experience (his or her mind, who he or she is as a person), the intent is Interpretation.

This will make you feel better. EI

You will get nauseous from this medicine. II

The second example is coded II because it is the patient as a person who experiences the nausea (source of experience is the other).

A litmus test for Interpretation versus Edification intent in medical contexts is to ask if the physician's statement would hold true while the patient is asleep (i.e., when the patient as body and person are, in effect, unconnected). If the answer is yes, the intent is Edification, for example, **"You have a fever"** (IE). Fever can be measured regardless of whether the patient is awake or asleep. If the answer is no, the intent is Interpretation, for example, **"You feel hot because you're angry"** (II).

> **With that bump on your head, you are a good candidate for a headache.** II

Although the bump on the head is physical (body), the ache is experienced by the person (mind).

> **If you feel worse, you will need some medicine.** II

Here I assumed that "worse" is subjective and "need" refers to the patient's psychological experience of wanting relief. If the medicine would be needed just as much if the patient were asleep, the utterance would be coded IE.

> **If the boil rises, you will need some medicine.** IE

Here I assumed the need was biological. Note that "you need" is Interpretation form if it expresses the speaker's judgment. It could be Reflection form if it was repeating a need already expressed by the patient.

> **Your mood change might be chemical.** EI
>
> **It's to stop** [taking lithium] **that would more likely be a problem.** EI

I coded these Interpretation intent, rather than Edification intent, because they seek to explain or predict the client's internal experience.

> **I'll be with you in a minute.** DD (an intention, not a prediction)
>
> **I suspect it** [the drug] **will work fine.** DI

In the second example, "fine" seems to refer to the patient's experience.

REFLECTION INTENT VERSUS INTERPRETATION INTENT

Reflection and Interpretation both concern the other's experience and presume knowledge of it; they differ only in frame of reference—whose viewpoint is used in expressing the other's experience. Thus a litmus test for distinguishing between them is: Who gets to say whether the utterance is correct? Reflection intent implies that the other makes this judgment, whereas Interpretation intent implies that this judgment is made, however vaguely or tentatively, by the speaker.

In this taxonomy, Reflection and Interpretation are distinct modes; there is *not* a continuum from one to the other. In particular, the distinction does not rest on the psychological depth of the utterance or whether the speaker uses the different words or the same words as the other. An utterance can be a Reflection even if it goes far beyond what was expressed by the other; a deep Reflection may put into words experiences that the other had not fully articulated to him- or herself (see section on Exploratory Reflection in Chapter 6).

Statements about the other's volitional behavior are Reflection; judgments about the other's behavior are Interpretation.

You ran down the street. RR

You ran very well. II

Particularly in "psychological" contexts, such as psychotherapy, the same words can be either Interpretation or Reflection, depending on the attitude of the speaker, as conveyed in tone of voice, posture, and particularly in adjacent utterances. For example, **"You feel angry"** could be Reflection if the speaker is communicating empathy but Interpretation if the speaker is explaining or judging the other's experience.

The following mental experiment can be a litmus test for deciding between Reflection and Interpretation intent: Imagine that following an utterance characterizing the other's experience, the other replies that the statement is wrong. What would the speaker's attitude be? If the speaker would consider him- or herself mistaken, then the intent was more likely Reflection; if the speaker would consider that the characterization may have been correct even though the other disagrees or doesn't understand, the intent was more likely Interpretation.

Only you know what you enjoy eating. RR

I hear the tremor in your voice. DR

So you're worried about that again! RR

It must have felt good to yell at me. ER

You feel that anyone who gets close to you risks dying. RR

I'm very sure that when people who are meaningful to us die, it's very hard to go through. DR

You didn't have to smother me. II

I don't think you need to worry about that. DI

That's what I hear you saying. EI

It seems to me that what you can change is you. EI

The Rorschach shows you have an ability to see things as a whole. EI

It's very human to cry. EI

It's okay to be angry [in general]. EI (could be EA if it gives specific permission)

I'm sure people don't die just because they're close to you. DI

Your personal relationship with her did not have anything to do with the fact that she died. EI

As long as you live, there will be people you care about who die for one reason or another. EI

Utterances are coded Reflection intent if they repeat (paraphrase, summarize, etc.) information that the other has already conveyed. Reflections can be incorrect and they are still Reflections. Reflections need not be positive, but can be accusatory. Nevertheless, the truth of the assertion can be known only by the other (whether or not the other admits it).

A: **I don't know.** DD

B: **You feel confused.** RR (speaker is mistaken)

A: **No, I'm not confused.** KC, DC

You never listen. RR (accusatory)

Utterances that are factually about a third party may be coded Reflection intent if they articulate the other's experience.

Th: **Sounds like she knows how to get to you.** ER

Th: **He needs to rely on you,** ER
 at least, he feels that now that he's threatened with losing you. ER

I coded these ER because they were a recapitulation of what the client had said before. That is, they concerned the client's experience and viewpoint rather than information known independently by the therapist.

A: **I now get your point.** DD
 He's just there. ER
 You've done all this for him and everything. RR
 My cousin's done the same thing. EC

Th (repeating information): **So, John is going to think about that.** ER
Cl: **Yes.** KC

But there's no one with whom you feel you can get upset. ER

But there's no one with whom you feel you can get upset? EQ

Predictions About Other's Experience

Future tense statements in the second person are scored Interpretation if they make a prediction. Such predictions represent the other's future experience as viewed within the speaker's frame of reference (see also discussion of prediction in "Disclosure Intent Versus Edification Intent" earlier in this chapter).

When you take this, you will be drinking more water. II

You will meet a tall, dark man. II

You'll probably have difficulty with the second problem. II

You're gonna be sorry. II

If you write down a long list and don't manage to cross any off, then you will feel that you haven't achieved anything. II

Second person statements about the future can be Reflections if they restate intentions of the other.

So you're going to be leaving us. RR

You'll be afraid to confront him. RR

###

Th: **Gradually, over the next few weeks, we will get you to start being able to change the** [dysfunctional] **thoughts yourself.** CI

The subject is "we," which I took as a slightly patronizing reference to both therapist and client. I coded the intent as Interpretation because this is a prediction of the client's experience rather than merely a statement of the speaker's intentions (which would be Disclosure intent) or a specific suggestion (which would have been Advisement intent).

Th: **Write those down in order of priority;** AA
    it will make it seem clearer. EI (prediction about other's experience)

For further information on discriminating Reflection and Interpretation, see the section on discriminating second person forms in Chapter 10.

10

Brief Utterances and Other Difficult Forms

Many of the most difficult coding problems involve very brief utterances that have conventional meanings or whose meaning is minimal or obscure. This chapter addresses some common instances of short or telegraphic utterances, along with other difficult forms, including the problem of discriminating among second person forms.

CODING BRIEF UTTERANCES

Don't Overuse Acknowledgment

Although most Acknowledgments are one- or two-word utterances, the reverse is not true: Many brief utterances are *not* Acknowledgment. *Do not code Acknowledgement form or intent just because the utterance is short.* Furthermore, Acknowledgment is not a residual or junk category. Acknowledgment forms include nonlexical utterances (mm-hm, ah, oh) and contentless lexical utterances (yes, no, well, hello) and terms of address (names and titles). Acknowledgment intent is coded only for utterances that concern the other's experience and use the other's frame of reference without making presumptions about the other's experience (coded speaker on the presumption principle). Do not code Acknowledgment just because you don't know what else to code.

Yes and No Answers

Yes and no and all their variations (yeah, yep, yah, uh-huh, nope, naw, nyet, etc.) are Acknowledgment forms. When they are used to answer a question, their intent depends on the information that they convey, which in turn depends on the Question (or other mode) to which they respond.

(Do you want to go to the movies?) **Uh-huh.** KD

(Have you seen my puppy?) **No.** KD

(Is 6 the square root of 36?) **Yes.** KE

(Were you the first one in line?) **Nope.** KE

(Shall I get you some coffee?) **Yah.** KA

(Do you agree with me?) **Yep.** KC

(Hello.) **Yes.** KK

(I'm a [inaudible]) **Huh?** KQ

(Am I being unreasonable?) **Yes.** KI

Oh, Mm, Ah, Um, Etc.

These nonlexical sounds are coded Acknowledgment form if they are communicative utterances. Coding the intent, as always, depends on their meaning in context. They are coded KK if used to express receipt of communication from the other, KD if used to convey subjective information, and so forth. They are not coded if they are noncommunicative noises (e.g., if they are used only to fill silence while the speaker searches for the right words).

(I've been away for a week.) **Oh.** KK

(Are you feeling better now?) **Mm.** KD

(I've got the evidence.) **Ah.** KK

I've had . . . ah . . . just about enough from you. DD ("ah" is not coded)

Well

"Well" is an Acknowledgment form that is often used to hold the floor rather than to relinquish it to the other.

A: **Where are you going?** QQ

B: **Well, I'm going home.** KK, DD

"Well" acknowledges the Question, "I'm going home" answers it.

A: **You're feeling resentful.** RR

B: **Well, no.** KK, KC

"Well" acknowledges the Reflection, "no" disagrees with it.

I am, well, going home. DD, KK

"Well" formally acknowledges the other.

Please

"Please" is generally understood as "if you please." Like other conditional clauses, it is not coded separately. Often it signals Advisement intent.

Please pass the butter. AA

Pass the butter, please. AA

Could you pass the butter, please. QA

Okay, Right, Etc.

"Okay," "right," and other terms of evaluation are coded as Interpretation form if they formally respond to the other's communication (see sections on Interpretation form in Chapter 7).

(And that's what happened.) **Okay.** IK

(And that's what happened.) **Right.** IK

(Turn down that radio.) **Okay.** IC

(Turn down that radio.) **Right.** IC

These words can be used in other ways, however; for example, as a Question or as a Disclosure. Pay attention to context. For example, "okay" or "right" used as a tag signals Question form:

Your appointment is on Tuesday, okay? EE, QQ (understood: Is that okay?)

I'll be there in a minute, okay? DD, QQ

When "okay" (or any other word that is not an Acknowledgment form) is used in answer to a Question, the form depends on the construction of the Question (see section on the answer rule in Chapter 8).

(How are you?) **Okay.** DD (understood: I am okay.)

(How is he?) **Okay.** EE (understood: He is okay.)

###

(May I borrow your rake?) **Okay.** IA

(Are you coming?) **Okay.** ID

In the last two examples, "okay" doesn't answer the Question grammatically. The Question is closed (seeking a yes or no answer) rather than open, so the form of the answer cannot be based on parallel construction. (The parallel form doesn't work, for example, "You okay borrow my rake.") Instead, the form is treated formally as an evaluative response to the other's communication.

> *Dr:* **You want us to give you a sinus pill, right?** RR, QQ
>
> *Pt:* **Right.** IC

The doctor's "right" is really seeking an answer, so it is coded pure Question (understood as "Is that right?"). The patient's "right" formally evaluates the other's statement (Interpretation form), but it concerns the patient's own experience, so it could not have Interpretation intent. Note that grammatically the patient's "right" is a response to the doctor's Reflection, not the Question (to which the grammatically appropriate response would have been "Yes").

> *Dr:* **Have you felt this way more than a week?** QQ
>
> *Pt:* **That's right.** EC

The patient evidently presumed that the doctor already thought she or he had felt this way for a week or more. Grammatically, the response does not answer the Question but confirms an understood Reflection.

> *Cl:* **He can't contribute much to the conversation.** EE
>
> *Th:* **That's right.** EI or EC

The question is whether the therapist's judgment is an evaluation of the information provided by the client or an agreement with it. The therapist's judgment can be coded EC (agreement) only if she or he means to describe personal experience with the person in question. If the client's experience is at issue, the code is EI.

See also the section on brief agreements in Chapter 9.

Brief Evaluations

In general, evaluations are coded as speaker's frame of reference (cf. section on value judgments in Chapter 9). If the speaker is evaluating the other, the intent is Interpretation. If the speaker is evaluating something else, the intent is generally disclosure. Elliptical (one- or two-word evaluations) are coded as pure modes if there is no subject or verb. If there is a subject, of course, the form code will depend on that.

That's good. EI

That's nice. EI

That's beautiful. EI

Good. II (understood: You've done something good.)

Very good. II

Good throw. II

Good girl. II

But don't forget that evaluative words frequently express other intents, including receipt of information and agreement to comply. That is, "good," "okay," "right," and the like can be coded as IK or IC (see preceding section and Chapter 7).

Here and There

"Here" and "there" used alone (i.e., elliptically) can have any of a variety of meanings, depending on context.

Here, I'll show you. AA, DD

I think "here" means "look here" or some similar command that the other pay attention; "I'll show you" discloses the speaker's intentions.

Here [are a few more examples] (EE):

[Look] **Here.** AA

[Come] **Here.** AA
[Put it] **Here.** AA
Here [take this]. AA
Here [let me help you]. AA
Here [it is]. EE
Here [it's ready for you]. EE
Here you are (showing the other something). RE
Here you are [take this]. RA

Note that in the two last examples, the utterance is not elliptical. The subject is "you," so the form cannot be Edification. It could be argued, however, that these are Interpretation rather than Reflection form.

There, there [you're okay]. II
There you go [you got it right]. II
There you go (child placed in car seat). RR
There you go [whee!]. RR

###

Here we go (starting off on family trip). CC
Here we go (child placed in car seat). CR
Here we go (urging child to pick up toys). CA

In the last set of examples, the intent distinction rests on whether the speaker is describing a shared experience or only the other's experience. In the last two sentences, although "we" grammatically refers to both speaker and other, the meaning of the utterance would not change if "you" were substituted.

Other Adverbs Used Alone: "Really," "Sure," "Seriously," "Exactly"

Adverbs like "really" used alone generally stand for some understood sentence or clause. Use parallelism to identify both form and intent. Coding depends heavily on context.

A: **It really is hot out.** EE

B: **Really.** EC (understood: It really is.)

Note that in this case, "really" concerns the speaker's experience.

Cl: **So that's what annoyed me.** ED

Th: **Sure.** ER

"Sure" is an adverb, and the utterance it represents is understood by parallelism: Roughly, "**That's sure what annoyed you**" (ER).

A: **I have a terrible pain.**

B: **Really.** RR (understood: You really have a pain.)

###

A: **Are you going to the dance?**

B: **Sure.** DD (understood: I sure am going to the dance.)

###

Dr: **So you've had headaches all week.** RR

Pt: **Exactly.** DC (this is an adverb, not a term of evaluation)

###

Really? QQ or QK

Use QQ if the speaker is seeking information, QK if the speaker is just expressing receipt.

When adverbs are used as modifiers within a sentence, they are not coded separately.

I don't know, really. DD

Incidentally, consider the phrasing. AA

Anyway, I was going to tell you something else. DD

"Really," "incidentally," and "anyway" in these cases are adverbs used as modifiers within the sentences and are not separate utterances.

Telegraphic Questions

In English, the intent to gather information (a hole in the speaker's frame of reference) is often signaled by a rising inflection, and this is transcribed by a question mark. Often, speakers omit the complete subject and verb of Questions (elliptical or telegraphic speech), but these utterances are clearly understood in context. Using the pure mode rule, code QQ if the intent is clearly Question, but there is no information by which to judge form.

> **More soup?** QQ (understood: Do you want some more soup?)
>
> **Age?** QQ (understood: What is your age?)
>
> **Little welts?** QQ
>
> **Wheezing?** QQ
>
> **Live in Ashboro?** QQ
>
> **And then Number 3?** QQ

If the context offers evidence of other forms, code the appropriate mixed mode.

> *Pt*: **I was covered by little welts.** DE
>
> *Dr*: **Little welts?** RQ

###

> *A*: **I live in Shbrow.** DE
>
> *B*: **Live in Ashboro?** RQ

###

> *A*: **I just feel so grouchy.** DD
>
> *B*: **Grouchy?** RQ

These forms are Reflection because (a) they literally repeat the other's words and/or (b) they have understood subjects, for example, "You live in Ashboro?" As these examples illustrate, RQ has a "checking" quality: Formally, the speaker repeats something known or suspected while pragmatically seeking information.

> *Dr:* **That rash is on both legs?** EQ
>
> *Pt:* **Sir?** KQ
>
> *Dr:* **On both legs?** EQ (by parallel with own utterance)

The last utterance could alternatively be coded QQ on the argument that it is merely a telegraphic version of "Is that rash on both legs?"

Question Marks: Caution

A question mark is not sufficient to code Question form. Question form requires inverted subject-verb order or interrogative words (see Chapter 7).

> **You're afraid of spiders?** RQ
>
> **You aren't coming this morning?** RQ
>
> **It was a white car?** EQ
>
> **It's raining outside?** EQ

Note the "checking" quality of these examples, which derive from the Reflection form (checking on other's intentions) and Edification form (checking on objective information), respectively.

The question mark not an infallible index of Question intent either, so you must judge for yourself whether you can trust the transcriber in each situation.

> **Could you carry this for me?** QA
>
> **Blow the candle out?** AA

If the context indicates that the second utterance was a command, it should be coded as AA despite the question mark. But some utterances are Question form even without a question mark. (Remember that Question form may be signaled either by an inverted subject-verb order or by an interrogative word.)

> **So what!** QD (interrogative word)

How about that! QD

Clarification Requests

Forms used frequently to ask the other to repeat something tend in conversation to be abbreviated. Retain the form code if the form is unambiguous. If the utterance is so abbreviated that the form is no longer clearly implied, then code the utterance as a pure mode.

I beg your pardon? DQ
Beg pardon? DQ
Pardon? DQ
I'm sorry? DQ
Pardon me? AQ
Sorry? DQ (understood: I'm sorry?)
Please? QQ
Huh? KQ
Hmm? KQ

Telegraphic Advisements

Hey! KA (understood: Stop that!)

Obviously, a code for "hey" depends on how it is used in context.

Lauren, get off the table. KK, AA
Lauren, I'm warning you. KK, DD
Lauren! KA

In the first two examples, "Lauren" is an Acknowledgment whose function is establishing that communication exists.

Speaking for the Other

As noted in Chapter 7, finishing the other's sentence or quoting the other is Reflection form.

Th: **You feel that you can't be wanted just for yourself.** RR

    Cl: **Unless I could give something or just please people.** RC

The client's response is coded Reflection form because it is finishing the therapist's sentence. It is coded Confirmation intent because it concerns the speaker's experience and presumes knowledge of the other's experience (i.e., the other's empathic understanding); in effect, it agrees with the therapist's Reflection (see also Chapter 9).

    A: **And so I got a C in the course.** DE
      I just really felt . . . DD

    B: **. . . screwed over. Yeah.** RR, KK

B's response here could be enclosed in quotation marks—formally, B was quoting A—but transcribers are unlikely to do this.

    A: **So I told her what she could do if she was gonna take that attitude.** DE

    B: **Yeah. "Take a walk, sister."** KK, RR

Forms of Idiomatic Expressions

Some brief forms are idiomatic and so do not fit grammatical rules. The codings here are my best guesses at this point. Maybe you can come up with a different code or a better rationale. As always, intent may vary depending on context.

    Not that I know of. DD
    Me too. DD
    Good for you. II
    Good on you. II
    Pretty girl. II (addressed to young child)
    You stinker. II

In the following pair of sentences, the first is technically in Question form because "what" is an interrogative word. In the second, "what" is a relative pronoun.

    She's what now, about 47. QE
    She's what she says she is, about 47. EE

Forms Imported From Other Relationships:
Expletives and Partings

Expletives present a difficult problem for VRM coding. Although some appear at first glance to be Advisements (e.g., "damn," "fuck you"), closer consideration suggests that the other is not actually being directed to do something. Instead, some third party (God, fate, or some unspecified person or thing) is being directed to do something. For example, "damn" seems to be short for "May God damn it [or you]" or something of this ilk. Formally, then, such utterances are not part of the speaker-other relationship—they are part of a relationship between the speaker and the third party—even though pragmatically they seem to express the speaker's experience in the speaker's frame of reference.

Viewed in this way, such expletives present a dilemma. They could be considered as part of a relationship between the speaker and the third party, and hence omitted from the speaker-other protocol. But this would overlook the important expressive function they serve pragmatically in the speaker-other relationship. Until someone finds a better solution, I recommend including such utterances, coding the intent according to the principles as usual, but treating the form as Uncodable.

Bless your heart. UD (formally, this is a directive to someone besides the other)

May he [patient] **be well.** UD

May Nixon find peace. UD

More power to him. UD

Damn. UD

Fuck you. UD

Goodness gracious. UD

May God bless you, doctor. UD, KK

Oh, my ears and whiskers. KD, UD(?)

Hot damn! UD (could be UI if it concern's other's thoughts or behavior)

Oh, God, how do I describe this? UD, UD, QD

In the last example, I understood the initial "Oh, God" as expletives—addressed formally to God and hence not formally part of the speaker-other relationship, though in intent they convey the speaker's feeling of frustration to the other. The Question form is rhetorical—the speaker was conveying her difficulty in description rather than seeking help.

Parting phrases such as "goodbye" and "farewell" are constructed similarly to expletives. "Goodbye" is a contraction for "May God be with you [ye]"; "farewell" is a contraction for "May you fare well." In each case, the formal Advisement is not directed to the other, but to third parties (God and fate, respectively), and hence the utterance is formally part of a different relationship. Again, I recommend retaining such utterances, recognizing their pragmatic contribution (in most cases, I think this is either Acknowledgment or Disclosure), and treating the form an Uncodable.

Goodbye. UK

Farewell. UK

Sometimes, speakers formally address an imaginary third party as a way of making a joke or saying something that is difficult or embarrassing to say to the other directly.

Th (to animated patient): **Give that lady a shot of Thorazine.** UI (a joke, addressed to an imaginary third party)

In context, this meant something like "You're being very expressive," so that the therapist could make a joke that the client was acting psychotic enough to warrant a dose of a major tranquilizer. The form is U because the utterance is formally addressed to someone other than the client. The utterance is coded, however, because it is pragmatically addressed to the client. If this were uttered seriously, for example, to an attendant on a psychiatric ward, it would be an Advisement to the attendant, but would not be coded as part of the therapist-patient relationship.

Not all emotional ejaculations are formally part of another relationship, however:

Oops. KD

Uh-oh. KD

Oh dear. KD

Unlike expletives, these do not invoke third parties (cf. "Damn"). They are contentless communications that reveal a current feeling to the other. The alternative would be to consider these as speaker's communication to him- or herself, and hence not coded as part of the speaker-other relationship.

> *Cl*: **What will I do if anything happens?** QD
> **Oh dear,** KD
> **It's one thing after another.** ED

The first sentence is rhetorical; the client is not really asking what she or he will do. I understood the utterance as meaning, "I don't know what I'll do."

> *A*: **Bah!** KD
>
> *B*: **Bah, yourself.** RD? (I'm not sure how to code this one)

Mixed Pronouns

When speakers refer to themselves in second or third person, the form code follows the literal meaning, and the intent code follows the pragmatic meaning.

> **In this [my] situation, you [I] could do anything.** ID
>
> **In this situation, one [I] could do anything.** ED
>
> **At this university, you [one] have to study hard.** AE
>
> **You [one] have to go to grad school to become a licensed psychologist.** AE

###

> *Mother*: **Your mother [I] wants you to clean your room.** EA

###

> *Mother* (to Mark): **Other people's children pick up their clothes, but not Mark.** EE, EI

###

> **There's nothing you [one] can do.** EE
> **There's nothing you [you] can do.** EI

###

A: **Maybe** [you should do that], **like you said, due to your religious beliefs.** AA **But, uh, I would sort of work that out with him.** DA

DISCRIMINATING SECOND PERSON FORMS

Because they are all second person ("You"), Advisement, Interpretation, and Reflection forms are sometimes difficult to distinguish. The differences among these three forms are not well marked in English. The definitions given in Chapter 6 use classes of verbs to distinguish among modes. These definitions cannot be applied rigidly, however, because the same words may be used in different senses. As a rule of thumb, prefer a pure mode to a mixed mode when the form is ambiguous. That is, do not use the codes RI, IR, AI, IA, AR, or RA unless there is a strong argument that the utterance is not a pure mode.

The Rhetorical "You"

Discriminating second person forms is particularly difficult when the intent is Edification or Disclosure and "you" really means "one" or "I." In such cases, the distinction must rest on the meaning of the verb or verb phrase in the utterance. Verbs (or verb phrases) that describe internal experience or volitional behavior (i.e., behavior that is intended or of which the other is aware) signal Reflection form. Verbs that describe attributes or abilities of the other signal Interpretation form. Verbs that describe permission, prohibition, or obligation signal Advisement form. Unfortunately, these rules still leave some utterance forms ambiguous.

When the intent of a second person utterance is some mode other than Reflection, Interpretation, or Advisement (i.e., where "you" really means "one" or "I"), the following mental experiment may be helpful: Imagine the utterance out of its context, with "you" to be understood as referring to the other person (rather than to the speaker or to people in general), and consider what its form would be. That is, code the form as if the utterance had its literal meaning.

If you want to take the shortcut, you turn left at the first light. AE

The Advisement form stands out more clearly by considering, "You turn left at the first light." This tells the other to do something. Suppressing the "if" clause helps one to perceive the form.

If you want to stay alive in the Yukon, you learn to keep yourself warm.
AE

The main clause, "You learn to keep yourself warm," reads like a command if it is taken out of context.

A: **When you're a doctor, you spend a lot of hours seeing patients,** RE
   and you're on call all the time, RE
   and you have a lot of responsibility for the health of a lot of people. RE
   You're an awfully important person. ID
   You have to deal with a lot of people who are pretty bad off. AE
   And you have to listen to a lot of hypochondriacs too. AE
   And you gotta deal with a lot of red tape in Medicare and Medicaid and Blue Cross and that stuff. AE
   You have to go to medical school for 4 years, AE
   and then you must do an internship, AE
   and you usually do a residency after that. RE

Because the activities of doctors, such as spending a lot of hours, are in principle observable, the intent of utterances describing them is Edification.

According to the principles of classification, Reflections put the experience of the other into a frame of reference shared with the other, whereas Interpretations tell the other what significance the other's experience has in the speaker's personal frame of reference (see Chapter 6). Therefore, Reflection forms, taken out of context, often have the sense of voicing something of which the other is aware or could be aware, whereas Interpretation forms often have the sense of the speaker telling the other something that the other did not already know.

Sometimes you can get your exams changed. IE

Once it starts rolling, you can't stop it. IE

You have a fever. IE

You left your raincoat. RE

You wonder why you need experiments in memory. RD

You might say that this is typical of a Republican administration. RE

###

You're gonna be at the beach this weekend, I hear. RR, DR

You're gonna be sorry if you don't make a reservation. IA

The last two examples illustrate that (a) very similar verbal constructions can have different codes in different contexts, and (b) intended actions like going to the beach signal Reflection form, whereas predictions of future feelings signal Interpretation form. The Advisement intent of the second example is based on the understanding that the speaker was overtly trying to influence the other's behavior—not merely predicting the consequences of his or her failure to act.

> *Cl*: **You go around saying, you know, "Hey folks, you talk about supervision and how important it is to you as higher managers"** RE, RE (filler; note that quoted material is not part of speaker-other relationship) **and really you're doing little more than saying the emperor got a new suit on.** RE

###

A: **The fruit buds all froze off,** EE
so you have a lot of trouble getting work these days. RD

The RD code assumes that the speaker is describing his or her own difficulties finding employment (intended as "I have a lot of trouble . . . "). The form is clearer, however, if we pretend that "you" actually refers to the other, describing the other's experience of trouble.

You're a sitting duck when you're up there. IE

You feel like a sitting duck when you're up there. RD

These codes presumed that the speaker is describing his or her own experience when he or she was "up there."

Patients who monitor their physical condition may be aware of such indexes as their weight and blood pressure, and physicians may or may not assume such knowledge. The physician's assumptions are crucial in assessing the intent of such utterances as the following:

You've lost weight. RR

You are keeping your weight down. RR

You now weigh 174 pounds. RE

You are keeping your blood pressure down. RE

You are keeping your blood sugar down. RE

I assumed the other was aware that he or she had lost weight or was keeping weight down, but did not know his or her exact weight, blood pressure, or blood sugar. Out of context, however, it is hard to be sure. For example, the last two utterances could be coded RR if they were acknowledging the other's efforts at self-care.

Ability Versus Permission and Obligation

"You can" signals Interpretation form if "can" means "able." A person's capacities exist whether or not that person is aware of them. "You can" can be Advisement form if it means "you may," as in giving permission.

You can probably lift 100 pounds easy. II

You can try to lift those weights if you like. AA

Note that one sense of "must" in conjunction with "be" does not denote obligation, but is merely an intensive form of "are."

You must be a psychology major. RR

You must be mad. II

You must be here by 9 o'clock sharp. AA

###

Dr: **You're left-handed, aren't you.** RR (or IR?) QR

Pt: **Right.** IC

"You're left-handed" could conceivably be coded IR; it is grammatically parallel to a diagnosis, which would be coded Interpretation form, for example, **"You have a heart murmur"** (IE). As noted earlier, I have preferred to avoid IR and RI codes. An exception, however, is using RI for "you see" or "you know" used as a filler:

Th: **You see,** RI
if you're forever looking at the time, it prevents you from being relaxed. EI

###

Th (summarizing client's communication): **Well,** KK
you've, often when you get up a bit higher, got to organize your own thing, AR
I guess. DR (filler)

"You've got to" is technically an Advisement construction. In another context, "You've, often when you get up a bit higher, got to organize your own thing" might be AE—giving information about what it's like "a bit higher."

Second Person Questions

Watch for elliptical utterances, particularly questions, that begin with "you," because some initial material may be understood only in context.

You've been checking your urine every day? RQ

You been checking your urine every day? QQ

Grammatically, the second sentence requires an initial "Have" ("Have you been checking . . . "), which makes the form Question (inverted subject-verb order). Allowance for dialect must be made sometimes, however, and the second utterance could be RQ if its psychological sense is clearly one of checking something the speaker already believes rather than asking for information.

You have any chills or fever? QQ

This makes grammatical sense only with an initial "do."

You are taking your medications every day? RQ

Note that grammatically, this could not take another initial verb, so the form is unambiguously Reflection.

You have some orange tablets you were taking? RQ or QQ

This sentence is ungrammatical and ambiguous; the phrasing makes it seem more like checking (RQ) than inquiring to me. Coding would depend on context.

You off the salt, Mr. Brown? QQ, KK

I understood this as "Are you off the salt?" In some contexts or tones of voice, it could have been meant as "You are off the salt?" (RQ)—checking on something already guessed to be the case. In general, if the intent of an utterance is clear but the form cues are missing or ambiguous, I recommend preferring pure modes (i.e., QQ in this case).

You know what it is? QQ or RQ ?

The decision whether to code QQ or RQ depends on context. Grammatically, this utterance could be elliptical, with an initial "do" understood. If the speaker is asking, it is QQ; if the speaker is checking it is RQ; if the speaker is telling (in which case the question mark should not have been used), it is RR.

CONTEXT AND AMBIGUITY

Often the briefest, most telegraphic exchanges are the most difficult and complex for coding. This is because speakers each presume that the other understands the unstated meanings (whereas coders may be left in the dark).

Dr: **Travelin'?** QQ
Pt: **No.** KD
Dr: **Just for the day, huh?** RR, KR
Pt: **Just for the day.** RC

There are a variety of ways of understanding this brief exchange, and in isolation, we cannot be sure we have got it right. I coded "No" as expressing the continuing intention of the patient (Disclosure intent). I understood the doctor's second speech as presuming knowledge of what the patient's intention was (following the Disclosure that the patient was not traveling). I considered the "huh?" (KR) as a filler rather than as a question, despite the question mark. I considered the patient's last utterance as a repetition of the doctor's words in service of agreeing with the doctor's presumption.

In this section, I have collected a few illustrations of how brief utterances often depend heavily on context for their interpretation. Keep in mind the limited context it is possible to include in this book; examples in real relationships may be more complex.

Dr: **You are living with your husband.** RR

Pt: **No.** KC

Dr: **No.** RR

Pt: **Uh-uh.** KC

I coded the Dr's "No" as RR rather than KR because it seems to be a repetition of the Pt's "No" rather than a new utterance.

Dr: **I see you came in last week also.** DR

The intent is Reflection because the utterance concerns the other's experience (coming in last week) and presumes knowledge of it. It would be Disclosure intent only if it primarily revealed the speaker's perception (cf. **"I saw you come in last week"** DD).

Dr: **Other thing,** ED (?)
      no salt, AA
      and I want you to lose weight. DA

I think that "Other thing," understood in context, means, "There's one other thing I want to tell you"—conveying an intention. I'm not very confident of this, however. Alternatively, DD would be appropriate if the form of the utterance is not clearly understood in context, but the intent is clear. "No salt" is clearly intended as an Advisement, even though there is no verb; in the absence of any form cues, it is coded as a pure mode.

> *A* (spelling word for B to copy): **S-t-r-a-b-i-s-m-u-s.** AA
>
> *B* (repeating as she or he writes): **S-t-r-a-b-i-s-m-u-s.** RC

I understood A's utterance as a directive and B's utterance as agreement to comply—coded Reflection form because it is an exact repetition.

> **He is one of those kind.** EE or ED

The intent of this utterance depends on whether "those kind" refers to an observable characteristic or some private feeling or evaluation by the speaker. For example, if "those kind" means "people who wear brightly colored ties" then the code is EE; if "those kind" means "people who make me mad" then the code is ED.

> **Your turn.** EE (or AA?)

I think that in context this would be understood as "It's your turn" (EE). I think the implicit Advisement (i.e., to perform some action) is off record, though I may be wrong here; an alternative reading would be that this is understood as "Take your turn" (AA).

> *A*: **You want to put it on top?** QQ or QA or RQ or RA
>
> *B*: **On top of what?** QQ

A's utterance could be intended as seeking information (Question) or as a suggestion to put "it" on top (Advisement). In form, it could be understood as a Question (with an initial "Do" understood) or as Reflection phrased as a check. The context provided (i.e., B's response) seems to rule out another possibility, RR, which would have appeared possible if B had responded "Yes" (KC).

> *Th*: **Well,** KK
> **you see,** RD (filler)
> **what I'm trying to get you to do is to sort of come off all that in some way.** ED

On record, the therapist is here disclosing her or his intentions. The subject of the last utterance is the noun clause, "What I'm trying to get you to do." There may be an off-record Advisement that the client should "Come off all that."

Parent: **What are you supposed to do when you break something?** QQ

Child: **Tell you or mom.** DC

Parent: **Yes.** KI

A: **What color block should I use?** QQ

B: **Yellow.** AA

A: **Okay.** IC

B: **No! Blue.** KA, AA

Complex Causal Constructions

Here are a few complex speeches involving "because." See the section on conditional and causal constructions in Chapter 8 for a discussion of coding causal clauses.

Cl: **So that's why I was re-deployed,** EE
　　because I was lucky to get a contract again. DE
　　And that's why I'm just a teacher, ED
　　I suppose, DD (filler)
　　because, uh, as soon as they give me any responsibility, I seem to resign.
　　(not separate; an appositive for "that")

Grammatically, both of these "because" clauses could be read as appositives for "that," in which case they should not be coded separately. However, for the first "because," the appositive reading does not make sense, so I considered it as a separate utterance (substituting "and" actually helps the sense). The second "because" is more clearly an appositive.

Cl: **When I relax into this relationship, it's super,** ED
　　y' know, RD (filler)

    because I feel quite . . . uh, DD
    I can be myself. DD
    I don't have to pretend, DD
    y' know. RD (filler)

  Th: **If you want to cry, there's some tissues there.** EE or EA

  Cl: **I always do.** DE

In my reading, substituting "and" for "because" would not change the meaning. Note also the therapist's intervention could be considered as on-record permission (EA) rather than merely giving information (EE) with the permission at the hint level (see Stiles, 1986b).

11

Preparation and Analysis of VRM Data

This chapter describes techniques I have found useful for preparing and analyzing VRM data. They include (a) some suggestions for transcribing and numbering utterances to facilitate coding and analysis, (b) ideas for training and supervising coders, (c) ways to assess the reliability of VRM coding, and (d) approaches to aggregating and summarizing VRM data.

PREPARING TRANSCRIPTS FOR VRM CODING

Rules for Transcribing

The following suggestions deal with the need that arises in transcribing naturalistic interaction for arbitrary decisions. They are intended to make VRM coding of the resulting transcripts easier and more accurate. For more detailed rules, see Auld and White (1956).

1. Above all, be accurate. In particular, be careful to include brief acknowledgments, such as "mm-hm" and "yeah."
2. Prefer short sentences to long ones.
3. Use commas to separate independent clauses and nonrestrictive dependent clauses, but not restrictive dependent clauses. (This is consistent with proper usage.)
4. Indicate inflections and special emphases by question marks, exclamation points, underlining, and so forth. The goal is to convey to coders what was actually said and how it was said.

5. Indicate nonverbal and paralinguistic features of the interaction, such as pauses, laughter, coughing, facial expressions, and so forth, in parentheses.

6. Indicate inaudible utterances or parts of utterances in parentheses, for example, "He (inaudible) to me later." This conveys to coders that the speaker said something, even though the recording of it was defective.

7. Indicate unfinished sentences with ellipses (three dots) and a period (a fourth dot). Pauses within speeches may be indicated by ellipses, dashes, or parenthetical notations, for example, "(45 sec. pause)."

8. Remember that because natural language is often irregular and ungrammatical, grammatical rules will not cover every case. The goal of an accurate rendering takes precedence over other rules. It is helpful, though not essential, for transcribers to be familiar with the taxonomy, particularly with the principles of unitizing described in Chapter 8.

Numbering Utterances

Analysis of VRM data often requires that utterances be numbered to permit later comparison of the codes with the text, to compare the work of different coders, or to keep track of the order of the codes. The optimum numbering system may be different in different circumstances.

Utterance Numbering on Transcripts. One system that I have used works as follows: (a) Number each line on the transcript. (b) The utterance number is the line number plus one decimal place that signifies its order of occurrence in that line. Thus, the first utterance to begin on line 29 is numbered 29.1. If a second or third utterance begins on line 29, they are numbered 29.2 and 29.3, respectively. (c) Each utterance is numbered according to where it begins, regardless of how long it is. For example, if the third utterance to begin on line 29 continues for four more lines, it is still numbered 29.3. Here's an example of a fragment of a transcript in which a dating couple is deciding whose college formal to attend:

51 *M*: (sigh) **We'll decide** (pause), **umm, we'll decide**

52   **yours, that is, if you want to do that.**

53 *F*: **Well, if we would have went to one of the two**

54   **other things, I would say I'd want to go to yours**

55 *M*: **Umhmm.**

56 *F*: **For sure. And the only reason why I'd choose yours**

57   **over mine is because you're going to Chicago, and**

58   maybe that's not a good enough reason. You know
59   what I mean?
60 *M*: Yeah. Chicago's always going to be there. We can, I
61   mean, I don't know. I think it's more important that
62   you attend yours. . . .

This could be numbered and coded as follows. Note that I have included a code for who the speaker was, along with a recapitulation of the text and alternative codes for a few of the utterances (in parentheses).

51.1 M CC **We'll decide,** (parenthetical material not coded)

   No code **umm,** (noncommunicative noise)

51.2 M CC **We'll decide yours, if you want to do that.**

52.1 M EC **that is,** (filler—takes intent from parent clause)

53.1 F KK **Well,**

53.2 F DD **if we would have went to one of the two other things, I would say I'd want to go to yours for sure.**

55.1 M KK **Umhmm.**

56.1 F ED **And the only reason why I'd choose yours over mine is because you're going to Chicago,**

57.1 F ED **and maybe that's not a good enough reason.**

58.1 F QQ **You know what I mean?** (RQ?)

60.1 M KC **Yeah.** (coded as agreeing; answering the question would be KD)

60.2 M EC **Chicago's always going to be there.** (coded as agreeing with "that's not a good enough reason"; alternative could be EE)

   No code **We can,** (no main verb)

60.3 M DU **I mean,** (filler; parent clause intent is unclear)

61.1 M DD **I don't know.**

61.2 M DD **I think it's more important that you attend yours.**

Utterance Numbering on Audiotapes or Videotapes. When VRMs are coded directly from audiotape or videotape, it may not be feasible to assign numbers in advance. Sequence information can be preserved, however, by coding procedures that simply list the codes (with speaker identification) in order. For example, coded from tape, codes for the preceding fragment of conversation could be recorded as:

MCC MCC MEC FKK FDD MKK FED FED FQQ MKC
MEC MDU MDD MDD.

Sequence information can be recovered by assigning numbers to utterances during analysis (e.g., as they are read by a statistical program).

Keeping Track of Multiple Speakers

In general, it is essential to keep track of who is being addressed, as VRMs measure the relationship between a speaker and an other. Keeping track is easy in a dyadic interaction or in other cases where all of a speaker's utterances are addressed to the same person (or collectivity). It becomes much more complex in a group, where utterances may be addressed to any combination of the others. The different relationships a speaker has with each group member are reflected directly in the different profiles of VRMs that characterize each dyadic combination (see Stiles, 1986a, for an example).

SELECTING, TRAINING, AND SUPERVISING CODERS

Selecting Coders

VRM coding demands good verbal comprehension, sensitivity to nuances, an ability to attend to details, and persistence. Knowledge of grammar is very helpful. Professional training in psychology, communication, or linguistics is not necessary. Most of the coders I have worked with have been university undergraduates or recent graduates. VRM coding demands careful and precise attention to what people mean by what they say, and a capacity for empathy is essential. The VRM system, despite its detail, takes a commonsense approach to understanding conversation. Individuals whose approach to understanding what people mean is either very global and impressionistic or very intricate and layered may have difficulty with VRM coding.

It is desirable for coders to come from the same language community as the speakers being coded.

Coding is not for everyone. Although a surprising number of people find VRM coding interesting and challenging, others find it extremely tedious. Of the people who initially assure me they are interested in working as coders, only about half stay interested throughout training and work. I have not found any quick way to distinguish who will stay interested, so I structure coder recruitment and training as a gradual process, with several points at which individuals can withdraw with minimal loss of face or damage to the integrity of the research work.

Coder Training

A copy of this book and the computer-assisted training program on the accompanying disk are all that is required to begin coder training. The training program runs on MS-DOS (IBM-compatible) computers. To use the disk, insert it in the default drive, type "START," and press Enter. The training exercises on the disk can be completed without direct reference to the book, but I recommend using both together. The book offers conceptual background that will make the coding principles seem more sensible. Coders report that reading Chapter 1 gives them a helpful perspective on the training program's distinctions. Also, the book (particularly Chapters 5 to 10) addresses many details that are not in the training program but are likely to be encountered in coding new material.

The computer-assisted training program is organized to introduce coders first to the principles of classification (source of experience, presumption about experience, frame of reference), then to form classification, and finally to full form/intent classification. The program is self-paced, allowing extended practice applying coding principles to sample transcripts, and individuals vary a good deal in how long it takes them to master it, as well as in the way they use the materials (e.g., the order of tackling the principles and of using the disk and the book). In my experience, a majority of coders can complete the program in about 30 hours, but some excellent coders take longer.

In my university, I have found it convenient to train students in VRM coding in a one-credit 5-week "sprint" course. Students read this book, work on the computer-assisted training program for 6-8 hours per week (this requires that they have access to an IBM-compatible microcomputer), and attend regular class meetings at which coding problems are discussed. Students complete and turn in activity log sheets on which they record the principle they applied, the transcript, and the percent correct (provided by the program). Consultation (with me or experienced coders) is available by telephone.

The disk training program aims to give coders a grounding in the logic of the principles of classification before they attempt to use the mode names, even though the mode names may seem simpler and intuitively more appealing. As discussed in Chapter 5, the mode names (Disclosure, Interpretation, etc.) have colloquial meanings that do not coincide precisely with their technical meanings in the VRM taxonomy. If coders first learn to apply the principles, they will be less prone to being misled by the mode names or by other idiosyncratic misunderstandings of the VRM categories. I encourage coders to continue to remind themselves about the principles even after they have mastered the whole system and can code most utterances virtually automatically.

The practice transcripts in the training program are already divided into units, and training in unitizing is not included in program. In the later weeks of my "sprint" course in VRM coding, I distribute ununitized transcripts for practice and discussion. Although most unitizing decisions are simple, the difficult minority require time and careful attention. Learning both coding and unitizing seems much facilitated by having pairs of coders work together on transcripts, as this encourages them to articulate their reasoning and justify their decisions.

By the time coders have spent 30 or more hours learning the principles of classification and the mode forms and intents, they will have nearly memorized the sample transcripts in the training program and will be ready for new material. Because the amount of practice material in the program is limited, coders using it will not encounter many of the kinds of utterances they will encounter in other discourse. To become competent in coding for a particular project, therefore, coders should also read this book (particularly Chapters 5 to 10), practice on samples of the type of discourse to be coded, and engage in discussion of problematic utterances they encounter.

VRM coding is a skill that is acquired gradually, not a concept that is grasped all at once. Like all skills, VRM coding requires coaching and regular practice. Coders tend to continue to improve for a period of months with daily practice. Put another way, the learning curve is a long one.

Separate Unitizing and Coding?

Coding and unitizing are different skills. Individuals with good grammatical skills can divide text into utterances (following principles described in Chapter 8) without understanding VRM coding. Although coders can perform both tasks simultaneously (as they have in most of the VRM research I have done), accuracy can be improved by separating the tasks. In a university community, students in English departments often have a background in grammar that makes it relatively easy for them to learn to apply unitizing rules (Sloan, 1989). They can unitize transcripts, for example, by marking a slash ("/") between utterances and lines to connect parts of an utterance separated by embedded material. Transcripts prepared in this way can be coded more easily, quickly, and reliably than can un-unitized transcripts by coders who understand VRM principles but have a weaker knowledge of grammar.

Coding Directly From Tapes

Coding directly from audio- or videotapes requires additional practice. Coders must be competent at coding and unitizing before they begin to learn this additional skill. Expect some initial frustration. Skill at coding from tapes does improve sharply with practice, however. Experienced coders say they find it much easier to unitize and code from tapes than from transcripts because of the additional cues provided by phrasing and inflection.

The success of coding directly from tape depends heavily on the audio quality of the recording. Using suitable equipment—particularly tape players with foot pedal control, automatic rewind, and variable speed control—can make large differences in the speed of coding.

Before microcomputers were easily available, coders used paper-and-pencil tallies to record their codes (e.g., Putnam et al., 1988). This approach preserves aggregate data for each marked tape segment, but it loses information on the sequence of codes within segments. More recently, I have had coders enter codes in microcomputers using simple entry programs that check for illegal codes and record entries on disk. Typically coders enter three keystrokes for each utterance—a speaker code, the VRM form code, and the VRM intent code. These trigrams are saved in sequence for later analysis.

In direct audio coding, separate unitizing is not possible, and there is no simple way to match the work of one coder with that of another utterance by utterance. Intercoder reliability must be assessed using aggregated data (e.g., by correlating across tapes or marked segments of tapes; see below).

Supervising Coding

Every type of conversation or discourse has peculiarities. Typically, a new type of discourse (that is, new to VRM coding) will include a few unusual types of verbal constructions whose VRM code must be identified by reasoning from the principles of classification. This reasoning can be done as a group discussion involving all coders on a project. Once the logic of an unusual construction has been understood, coding repeated instances is a simple matter.

For additional training, identifying new or difficult constructions, and preventing "coder drift" (development of idiosyncratic ways of coding particular constructions), regular feedback and discussion of coding is essential. Feedback can consist of comparison with other coders' work on the same tape or transcript. A simple expedient is having groups of two or three coders review the codes on a stretch of discourse they have each coded; any disagreement is cause for discussion. I have often used computer-generated utterance-by-utterance comparisons of samples of coders' work.

Coder meetings also can maintain social contact and morale of coders whose main task (i.e., coding) involves little interaction with people. Support from other coders can prevent their feeling isolated. Furthermore, depending on the material that is coded, VRM coding can be emotionally involving. Coding requires empathy with the speaker, and if speakers are expressing psychological conflict and pain (e.g., in psychotherapy), then coders may empathically experience the conflict and pain. Such issues need to be acknowledged and discussed in meetings or informally.

How Long Does Coding Take?

Time requirements vary. Some of the factors that influence how long it takes to code a stretch of discourse include the skill and experience of the coders, whether material is tape recorded or transcribed, the quality of the recording or transcription, the mechanical system for recording codes, and how fast and how grammatically the speakers speak. In my experience, coding times have varied from less than twice the speaking time to more than ten times the speaking time. That is, coding a 10-minute stretch of discourse might take 15 minutes or less if coded by a highly experienced coder working from clearly recorded audiotape, using a foot-pedal control dictating machine for tape playing and entering three-stroke codes (speaker-form-intent) into a computer, coding material that is clearly understandable, paced evenly and lei-surely, and expressed grammatically. Another 10-minute stretch might take 2 hours or more if coded by an inexperienced coder working from poor-quality recordings or dense transcripts, using awkward playback equipment, hand writing utterance numbers or times along with VRM codes, coding material that is fragmented, rapid, and ungrammatical.

Although this list of factors may not seem surprising, I have been surprised at how much difference some of the factors make. Formal speeches and lectures tend to be even, clear, and grammatical, and large parts can often be coded live; conversations of parents and children negotiating about rules tend to be fast, fragmented, and ungrammatical, and they take far longer to code. Clear recordings are surprisingly easier to code than indistinct ones; for researchers, investments in recording quality, such as lapel microphones where they are feasible, are well worthwhile. Finally, VRM coders improve a surprising amount in both speed and accuracy with extended practice. For example, over the course of 6 months of coding 10-20 hours per week, coders in a psychotherapy study (Stiles et al., 1988) improved from averaging more than 5 hours to code a 1-hour session just after training to averaging less than 2 hours per 1-hour session. Accuracy (as indexed by intercoder reliability) also improved substantially over this period.

RELIABILITY OF VRM CODING

Like coding speed, VRM coding reliability is greatly affected by the coders' talent and experience, and by the difficulty and variability of the material being coded. More formal speech (complete sentences, conventional grammar) can be coded more reliably than speech that is fragmented, ungrammatical, frequently interrupted, or indistinct. In the case of coding from audio recordings, the quality of the recording (whether the speech is clear or muffled and whether speakers are distinctly identifiable) has a large impact on intercoder reliability.

Some categories are more easily identified in certain material, whereas other categories are easier in other material. In general, more common categories tend to be identified more reliably, whereas modes that are rare in a particular corpus may be overlooked and hence coded unreliably.

For illustration, the mean percentage of utterances on which a pair of coders agree has ranged from 95% for form and 85% for intent on a study of courtroom interrogations of rape victims (McGaughey & Stiles,

1983), to only 81% for form and 66% for intent in a study of parent-child interaction (Stiles & White, 1981). The courtroom interrogations were highly structured, with a narrow range of modes, and with most responses clearly and fully articulated. The parent-child interactions were fragmented and hard to understand, and they used a very wide range of modes.

In many transcript-based VRM studies, three coders have independently coded each transcript, and their work has been combined on a two-out-of-three basis. Utterances on which all three coders disagree are classified as "Disagreement." These make up fewer than 5% of the utterances in most studies. Even the unusually unreliable coding for the parent-child study (Stiles & White, 1981) yielded two-out-of-three agreement for 97% of the form codes and 92% of the intent codes. In a study of 115 transcripts of medical interviews, two-out-of-three agreement was 99% for form and 97% for intent (Stiles et al., 1982). The two-out-of-three agreement is so much higher than the pairwise agreement because most VRM disagreements are between two of the eight modes. Coders may disagree about whether an utterance is Reflection or Interpretation, but they agree it is not Question or Disclosure (in terms of the principles, they agree that it concerns and presumes knowledge of the other's experience).

For estimating the reliability of particular modes, the most appropriate measures are Cohen's kappa (Cohen, 1960; Fleiss, 1971; Tinsley & Weiss, 1975) and the intraclass correlation coefficient (Shrout & Fleiss, 1979). Kappa is a chance-corrected measure of agreement on nominal scales, which can be used where utterance-by-utterance comparisons are possible. The kappa value for agreement between two coders is given by:

$$\text{Kappa} = \frac{P_0 - P_c}{1 - P_c}$$

where P_0 = the proportion of codes in which the two coders agree, and P_c = the proportion of codes for which agreement is expected by chance. See Cohen (1960) for computational formulas and Fleiss (1971) for a generalization to the case of multiple coders.

The intraclass correlation coefficient gives an estimate of the reliability of the mean of κ coders' results (e.g., of the two-coder mean percentage of Disclosures in each encounter) or of a single coder. It can be used when only summary data (i.e., frequencies for each category) for each encounter (or segment) are available. For example, it can be used when VRM coding is done from audio- or videotape and particular utterances cannot be matched across coders. Note that although VRM categories themselves are nominal measures, the frequencies or percentages of each category in an encounter are ratio measures.

The intraclass correlation coefficients I recommend are those designated by Shrout & Fleiss (1979) as ICC(1, 1) and ICC(1, k). (The first number in parentheses indicates the statistical model used; the second indicates the number of coders whose results are to be averaged.) ICC(1, 1) gives the estimated average reliability of a single coder's VRM percentages in a session. The formula, based on a one-way ANOVA with sessions as the independent variable, is:

$$ICC(1, 1) = \frac{MS_{sessions} - MS_{error}}{MS_{sessions} + (k-1)\, MS_{error}}$$

where MS = mean square and k is the number of times each target (session, tape, transcript) was coded. It is not necessary for the same k coders to code each target. The formula for ICC(1, k), which gives the reliability of the k-coder average percentage for each mode, is:

$$ICC(1, k) = \frac{MS_{sessions} - MS_{error}}{MS_{sessions} + MS_{error}}$$

Based on a model in which coder is considered as a random effect, ICC(1, 1) and ICC(1, k) are conservative indexes, which treat constant coder biases (e.g., tendency to code too many or too few utterances as Disclosure) as error.

As discussed by Shrout and Fleiss (1979), there are alternative models for calculating intraclass correlation coefficients, in which the coder is considered as a fixed effect—ICC(2, k) and ICC(3, k). Computationally, these alternatives require that every coder code every target (to estimate the coder effect). Fixed effects models give the reliability of discriminating among transcripts, and this is usually higher than the reliability estimates given by the random effects model, but they treat VRM variables (e.g., the percentage of utterances coded as Disclosure) as if they were unanchored ratings.

TABLE 11.1

Illustrative Category-by-Category VRM Intercoder Reliabilities

Mode	Cohen's Kappa		ICC(1,1)		ICC(1,2)	
	Form	Intent	Form	Intent	Form	Intent
Disclosure	.95	.74	.97	.69	.98	.87
Edification	.91	.79	.92	.87	.98	.87
Advisement	.71	.58	.83	.96	.94	.76
Confirmation	.66	.33	.88	.42	.93	.86
Question	.93	.93	.98	.90	.98	.91
Acknowledgment	.98	.88	.93	.94	.91	.91
Interpretation	.62	.45	.96	.84	.52	.35
Reflection	.60	.63	.68	.73	.94	.81

NOTE: Cohen's kappa (Cohen, 1960) reliabilities were taken from a study of laboratory interactions of university students and professors (Cansler & Stiles, 1981). ICC = intraclass correlation coefficient (Shrout & Fleiss, 1979). ICC(1,1) reliabilities were taken from a study of psychotherapists' responses (Stiles, Shapiro, & Firth-Cozens, 1988). ICC(1,2) reliabilities were taken from a study of political campaign speeches (Stiles, Au, Martello, & Perlmutter, 1983).

I believe that the random effects model, $ICC(1, k)$ is more appropriate because VRM coding assumes that there is a correct code for each utterance. If two coders differ on a VRM code, at least one must wrong, even if they differ by a constant across transcripts (and hence discriminate transcripts equally well). For example, if a coder consistently codes too many utterances as Disclosure, then that coder should be considered as mistaken, even though his or her aggregated codes may distinguish among transcripts just as well as a coder who has no such bias.

Table 11.1 gives some illustrative reliabilities. The kappa values are from a study of interactions of college students and professors (Cansler & Stiles, 1981); the intraclass correlation coefficients are from a study of psychotherapists' responses in 84 psychotherapy sessions (Stiles et al., 1988) and from a study of political campaign oratory (Stiles et al., 1983). As Table 11.1 illustrates, form codes were generally more reliable than intent codes, and reliability varied across modes. These figures reflect the particular coders and transcripts involved, and should not be taken as characterizing VRM coding by other coders in other applications.

AGGREGATING VRM CODES

The VRM system offers a wide array of aggregate measures for characterizing an encounter. These include:

TABLE 11.2
VRM Role Dimensions

Role Dimension	Constituent VRMs
Informativeness	Disclosure, Edification, Advisement, Confirmation
Attentiveness	Question, Acknowledgment, Interpretation, Reflection
Unassumingness	Disclosure, Edification, Question, Acknowledgment
Presumptuousness	Advisement, Confirmation, Interpretation, Reflection
Directiveness	Disclosure, Advisement, Question, Interpretation
Acquiescence	Edification, Confirmation, Acknowledgment, Reflection

NOTE: Each role dimension index is calculated as the proportion of coded utterances (i.e., omitting uncodable utterances) that is in one of the designated modes.

1. The frequency or percentage of each pure or mixed mode, for example, the frequency of KK or the percentage of DE. See Table 4.1 for an example of this sort of profile.

2. The frequency or percentage of each form or intent, for example, the frequency of Acknowledgment form aggregated across intents or the percentage of Edification intent aggregated across forms. See Table 4.2 for an example.

3. Role dimensions. The principles of classification are another, theoretical basis for aggregating VRM data. Three role dimensions, (a) Informativeness versus Attentiveness, (b) Unassumingness versus Presumptuousness, and (c) Directiveness versus Acquiescence, correspond to the proportion of speaker versus other values on source of experience, presumption about experience, and frame of reference, respectively. This is summarized in Table 11.2. See also Table 4.4.

In Table 11.2, Informativeness, for example, is calculated as the proportion of utterances in the modes Disclosure, Edification, Advisement, and Confirmation (all speaker's experience; cf. Table 2.1). Attentiveness is calculated as the proportion of utterances in the other four modes, Question, Acknowledgment, Interpretation, and Reflection (all other's experience), or equivalently, as one minus Informativeness. The role dimension indexes may be calculated for form and intent separately or averaged across form and intent. The construct validity of these indexes has been supported by research in a variety of settings (e.g., Cansler & Stiles, 1981; McGaughey & Stiles, 1983; McMullen & Krahn, 1985; McMullen & Murray, 1986; Premo & Stiles, 1983; Stiles, 1979; Stiles, Putnam, James et al., 1979; Stiles, Waszak et al., 1979; Stiles & White, 1981; see Chapter 4).

The role dimensions were generated from theoretical constructs rather than from intuitive impressions. For example, Attentiveness refers to the proportion of utterances that concern the other's experience, not to a rater's impression of how attentive a speaker was. The role dimension names were chosen to approximate the interpersonal impact of using the designated modes, but the names do not *denote* that impact. It is an empirical question whether a speaker with high VRM Attentiveness indexes would be described as attentive by observers. Construct validity of the attentiveness-informativeness dimension is supported by a variety of findings. For example, interviewers such as psychotherapists and physicians taking medical histories are highly attentive, whereas interviewees such as psychotherapy clients and medical patients are highly informative (Stiles et al., 1988; Stiles, Putnam, James et al., 1979). See Chapter 4, especially Table 4.4, for further findings of construct validity for the role dimensions.

Computational Formulas for Role Dimensions

For convenience, I include a list of computational formulas for calculating the VRM form and intent aggregates and the role dimension values for each speaker within a summarizing unit (e.g. a transcript). With minor modification, these are suitable for inclusion in a statistical package program. The list uses the following abbreviations:

DD, DE, DA, etc. = frequency of DD, DE, DA, etc., in the summarizing unit.
DFM = Disclosure form; EFM = Edification form; etc.
DIN = Disclosure intent; EIN = Edification intent; etc.
TT = Total number of utterances in the summarizing unit.
INFFM = Informativeness form proportion.
ATTFM = Attentiveness form proportion.
UNAFM = Unassumingness form proportion.
PREFM = Presumptuousness form proportion.
DIRFM = Directiveness form proportion.
ACQFM = Acquiescence form proportion.
INFIN = Informativeness intent; etc.
INFAV = Informativeness average; etc.

Mode forms:

DFM = DD + DE + DA + DC + DQ + DK + DI + DR + DU;

EFM = ED + EE + EA + EC + EQ + EK + EI + ER + EU;
AFM = AD + AE + AA + AC + AQ + AK + AI + AR + AU;
CFM = CD + CE + CA + CC + CQ + CK + CI + CR + CU;
QFM = QD + QE + QA + QC + QQ + QK + QI + QR + QU;
KFM = KD + KE + KA + KC + KQ + KK + KI + KR + KU;
IFM = ID + IE + IA + IC + IQ + IK + II + IR + IU;
RFM = RD + RE + RA + RC + RQ + RK + RI + RR + RU;
UFM = UD + UE + UA + UC + UQ + UK + UI + UR + UU.

Mode intents:

DIN = DD + ED + AD + CD + QD + KD + ID + RD + UD;
EIN = DE + EE + AE + CE + QE + KE + IE + RE + UE;
AIN = DA + EA + AA + CA + QA + KA + IA + RA + UA;
CIN = CD + EC + AC + CC + QC + KC + IC + RC + UC;
QIN = DQ + EQ + AQ + CQ + QQ + KQ + IQ + RQ + UQ;
KIN = DK + EK + AK + CK + QK + KK + IK + RK + UK;
IIN = DI + EI + AI + CI + QI + KI + II + RI + UI;
RIN = DR + ER + AR + CR + QR + KR + IR + RR + UR;
UIN = DU + EU + AU + CU + QU + KU + IU + RU + UU.

Total utterances:

TT = DFM + EFM + AFM + CFM + QFM + KFM + IFM + RFM + UFM.

Role dimension forms:

INFFM = (DFM + EFM + AFM + CFM)/(TT − UFM);
ATTFM = 1 − INFFM;
UNAFM = (DFM + EFM + QFM + KFM)/(TT − UFM);
PREFM = 1 − INFFM;
DIRFM = (DFM + AFM + QFM + IFM)/(TT − UFM);
ACQFM = 1 − DIRFM.

Role dimension intents:

$$INFIN = (DIN + EIN + AIN + CIN)/(TT - UIN);$$
$$ATTIN = 1 - INFIN;$$
$$UNAIN = (DIN + EIN + QIN + KIN)/(TT - UIN);$$
$$PREIN = 1 - INFIN;$$
$$DIRIN = (DIN + AIN + QIN + IIN)/(TT - UIN);$$
$$ACQIN = 1 - DIRIN.$$

Role dimensions averaged across form and intent:

$$INFAV = (INFFM + INFIN)/2;$$
$$ATTAV = (ATTFM + ATTIN)/2;$$
$$UNAAV = (UNAFM + UNAIN)/2;$$
$$PREAV = (PREFM + PREIN)/2;$$
$$DIRAV = (DIRFM + DIRIN)/2;$$
$$ACQAV = (ACQFM + ACQIN)/2.$$

Note that these indexes must be calculated separately for each speaker.

Verbal Exchanges

VRM categories can also be aggregated on an empirical basis. As described in Chapter 4, in studies of the verbal exchange structure of medical interviews (Putnam & Stiles, 1991; Stiles, Orth et al., 1984; Stiles & Putnam, 1991; Stiles et al., 1982; Stiles, Putnam, Wolf et al., 1979a), we used factor analysis to identify verbal exchanges—clusters of patient and physician modes that are used responsively to accomplish a particular subtask of the medical interview. For example, the *closed question* exchange included several forms of physician Question intents, coded QQ, RQ, EQ, physician truncating Acknowledgments, coded IK, and patient yes/no answers, coded KE and KD (see Table 4.3). An index of the closed question exchange (based on the frequency or percentage of all constituent modes), thus represents the extent to which a *dyad* engaged in a particular type of interaction (see Chapter 4).

COMPARISONS OF VRM PROFILES

Because the VRM system can be applied to any discourse, it permits direct, quantitative comparisons across different roles and relationships. As an example, one study (Henricks & Stiles, 1989) assessed the similarity of VRM profiles of hosts and callers on psychological radio call-in programs with profiles of participants in a variety of other help-intended interactions, including psychotherapists and clients, physicians and patients, and university professors and students. This comparison used as a statistic the geometric mean difference between profiles, calculated as the square root of the sum of the squared differences of the eight VRM intent percentages. This geometric mean difference is a generalization of the Pythagorean theorem and may be interpreted as a conceptual distance between speakers. Just as the Pythagorean theorem yields a hypotenuse based on coordinates in two-dimensional space, the geometric mean difference yields an analogous straight-line distance between two sets of "coordinates" in eight-dimensional "VRM space." Thus, this procedure gives a quantitative estimate of how similar or different each role is from each other role.

Chapter 4 lists roles and relationships that have been coded with this VRM system and cites references that contain VRM profiles for comparison.

References

Atwood, G. E., & Stolorow, R. D. (1984). *Structures of subjectivity: Explorations in psychoanalytic phenomenology.* London: Analytic Press.

Auerbach, A. H. (1963). An application of Strupp's method of content analysis to psychotherapy. *Psychiatry, 26,* 137-148.

Auld, F., Jr., & White, A. M. (1956). Rules for dividing interviews into sentences. *Journal of Psychology, 42,* 273-281.

Austin, J. L. (1975). *How to do things with words* (2nd ed.). Oxford, UK: Clarendon.

Bach, K., & Harnish, R. M. (1979). *Linguistic communication and speech acts.* Cambridge, MA: MIT Press.

Bain, D.J.G. (1976). Doctor-patient communication in general practice consultations. *Medical Education, 10,* 125-131.

Bain, D.J.G. (1979). The content of physician/patient communication in family practice. *Journal of Family Practice, 8,* 745-753.

Bakeman, R., & Gottman, J. M. (1986). *Observing interaction: An introduction to sequential analysis.* New York: Cambridge University Press.

Bales, R. F. (1950). *Interaction process analysis: A method for the study of small groups.* Reading, MA: Addison-Wesley.

Bales, R. F. (1970). *Personality and interpersonal behavior.* New York: Holt, Rinehart & Winston.

Bales, R. F., & Hare, A. P. (1965). Diagnostic use of the interaction profile. *Journal of Social Psychology, 67,* 239-258.

Barkham, M., & Shapiro, D. A. (1986). Counselor verbal response modes and experienced empathy. *Journal of Counseling Psychology, 33,* 3-20.

Beattie, B. (1983). *Talk: An analysis of speech and non-verbal behaviour in conversation.* Milton Keynes, UK: Open University Press.

Benjamin, L. S. (1974). Structural analysis of social behavior. *Psychological Review, 81,* 392-425.

Benjamin, L. S., Foster, S. W., Roberto, L. G., & Estroff, S. E. (1986). Breaking the family code: Analysis of videotapes of family interaction by structural analysis of social behavior (SASB). In L. S. Greenberg & W. M. Pinsof (Eds.), *The psychotherapeutic process: A research handbook* (pp. 391-438). New York: Guilford.

Brown, P., & Levinson, S. (1978). Universals in language usage: Politeness phenomena. In E. N. Goody, (Ed.), *Questions and politeness: Strategies in social interaction* (pp. 56-324). Cambridge, UK: Cambridge University Press.

Brownbridge, G. (1987). *Doctor-patient communication and the consulting room use of computers in general practice.* Ph.D. thesis, University of Sheffield, Sheffield, UK.

Brownbridge, G., Fitter, M., & Wall, T. (1986). Doctor-patient communications and the consulting room use of computers in general practice. (DHSS Supported Research Project Final Report). Sheffield, UK: MRC/ESRC Social and Applied Psychology Unit, University of Sheffield.

Brownbridge, G., Lilford, R. J., & Tindale-Biscoe, S. (1988). Use of a computer to take booking histories in a hospital antenatal clinic. *Medical Care, 26,* 474-487.

Bruch, M. A., Gorsky, J. M., Collins, T. M., & Berger, P. A. (1989). Shyness and sociability reexamined: A multicomponent analysis. *Journal of Personality and Social Psychology, 57,* 904-915.

Brunink, S. A., & Schroeder, H. E. (1979). Verbal therapeutic behavior of expert psychoanalytically oriented, gestalt, and behavior therapists. *Journal of Consulting and Clinical Psychology, 47,* 567-574.

Burchill, S.A.L. (1984). *Valence coding manual for verbal response mode taxonomy.* Unpublished manuscript, Miami University, Oxford, OH.

Burchill, S.A.L., & Stiles, W. B. (1988). Interactions of depressed college students with their roommates: Not necessarily negative. *Journal of Personality and Social Psychology, 55,* 410-419.

Burton, M. V., & Parker, R. W. (1988). A randomized controlled trial of preoperative psychological preparation for mastectomy: Preliminary report. In M. Watson, S. Greer, & C. Thomas (Eds.), *Psychosocial oncology* (pp. 133-158). Oxford, UK: Pergamon.

Burton, M. V., Parker, R. W., & Wollner, J. M. (1991). The psychotherapeutic value of a "chat": A verbal response modes study of a placebo attention control with breast cancer patients. *Psychotherapy Research, 1,* 39-61.

Byrne, P. S., & Long, B.E.L. (1976). *Doctors talking to patients.* London: Royal College of General Practitioners.

Cansler, D. C., & Stiles, W. B. (1981). Relative status and interpersonal presumptuousness. *Journal of Experimental Social Psychology, 17,* 459-471.

Cape, J. D. (1988). *General practice consultations with patients with psychological problems.* Ph.D. thesis, University of London.

Caporael, L. R., & Culbertson, G. H. (1986). Verbal response modes of baby talk and other speech at institutions for the aged. *Language & Communication, 6,* 99-112.

Carter, W. B., & Inui, T. S., with Kukull, W. A., & Haigh, V. H. (1982). Outcome-based doctor-patient interaction analysis: II. Identifying effective provider and patient behavior. *Medical Care, 20,* 550-566.

Cohen, J. (1960). A coefficient of agreement for nominal scales. *Educational and Psychological Measurement, 20,* 37-46.

Coulthard, M., & Ashby, M. (1976). A linguistic description of doctor-patient interviews. In M. Wadsworth & D. Robinson (Eds.), *Studies in everyday medical life* (pp. 69-88). London: Martin Robinson.

Cromwell, D. (1981). *Therapists' responses to confrontation: An analogue study comparing theoretical orientation, level of self-actualization, and experience level.* Ph.D.

thesis, Boston University, 1981. *Dissertation Abstracts International, 42,* 2522B. (University Microfilms No. 8125621)

Dale, P. S. (1980). Is early pragmatic development measurable? *Journal of Child Language, 7,* 1-12.

Davis, M. S. (1971). Variation in patient's compliance with doctor's orders, medical practice, and doctor-patient interaction. *Psychiatry in Medicine 2,* 31-54.

Denman, C. (1990). *The verbal response mode system: A case study in taxonomising language.* Unpublished manuscript, Department of Psychiatry, Guys Hospital, London.

Donohue, W. A., Diez, M. E., & Hamilton, M. (1984). Coding naturalistic negotiation interaction. *Human Communication Research, 10,* 403-425.

Dore, J. (1978). Variation in preschool children's conversational performances. In K. E. Nelson (Ed.), *Children's language* (Vol. 1, pp. 397-444). New York: Gardener.

Dore, J. (1979). Conversational acts and the acquisition of language. In E. Ochs & B. B. Schieffelin (Eds.), *Developmental pragmatics* (pp. 339-361). New York: Academic Press.

Dore, J., Gearhart, M., & Newman, D. (1978). The structure of nursery school conversation. In K. E. Nelson (Ed.), *Children's language* (Vol. 1, 337-398). New York: Gardener.

Ekman, P., Friesen, W. V., & Ellsworth, P. (1972). *Emotions in the human face: Guidelines for research and a review of findings.* New York: Pergamon.

Elliott, R. (1985). Helpful and nonhelpful events in brief counseling interviews: An empirical taxonomy. *Journal of Counseling Psychology, 32,* 307-322.

Elliott, R., Hill, C. E., Stiles, W. B., Friedlander, M. L., Mahrer, A. R., & Margison, F. R. (1987). Primary therapist response modes: Comparison of six rating systems. *Journal of Consulting and Clinical Psychology, 55,* 218-223.

Elliott, R., & Shapiro, D. A. (1988). Brief structured recall: A more efficient method for identifying and describing significant therapy events. *British Journal of Medical Psychology, 61,* 141-153.

Elliott, R., Stiles, W. B., Shiffman, S., Barker, C. B., Burstein, B., & Goodman, G. (1982). The empirical analysis of help-intended communications: Conceptual framework and recent research. In T. A. Wills (Ed.), *Basic processes in helping relationships* (pp. 333-356). New York: Academic Press.

Fisher, B. A., & Drecksel, G. L. (1983). A cyclical model of developing relationships: A study of relational control interaction. *Communication Monographs, 50,* 66-78.

Fitzpatrick, M. A., Vance, L., & Witteman, H. (1984). Interpersonal communication in the casual interaction of married partners. *Journal of Language and Social Psychology, 3,* 81-95.

Fleiss, J. L. (1971). Measuring nominal scale agreement among many raters. *Psychological Bulletin, 76,* 378-383.

Floyd, F. J., O'Farrell, T. J., & Goldberg, M. (1987). Comparison of marital observational measures: The marital interaction coding system and the communication skills test. *Journal of Consulting and Clinical Psychology, 55,* 423-429.

Frankel, R. M. (1984). From sentence to sequence: Understanding the medical encounter through microinteractional analysis. *Discourse Processes, 7,* 135-170.

Freemon, B., Negrete, V. F., Davis, M., & Korsch, B. M. (1971). Gaps in doctor-patient communication: Doctor-patient interaction analysis. *Pediatric Research, 5,* 298-311.

Friedlander, M. L. (1982). Counseling discourse as a speech event: Revision and extension of the Hill Counselor Verbal Response Category System. *Journal of Counseling Psychology, 29,* 425-429.

Freud, S. (1958). Recommendations to physicians practicing psycho-analysis. In J. Strachey (Ed. and trans.), *The standard edition of the complete psychological works of Sigmund Freud* (Vol. 12). London: Hogarth. (Originally published 1912)

Gomes-Schwartz, B. (1978). Effective ingredients in psychotherapy: Prediction of outcome from process variables. *Journal of Consulting and Clinical Psychology, 46,* 1023-1035.

Goodman, G. (1972). *Companionship therapy: Studies in structured intimacy.* San Francisco: Jossey-Bass.

Goodman, G. (1978). *SASHATapes: Self-led automated series on helping alternatives.* Los Angeles: UCLA Extension.

Goodman, G., & Dooley, D. (1976). A framework for help-intended interpersonal communication. *Psychotherapy: Theory, Research and Practice, 13,* 106-117.

Goodman, G, & Esterly, G. (1988). *The talk book: The intimate science of communicating in close relationships.* New York: Rodale. (Reprinted as a Ballentine paperback)

Goody, E. N. (1978). Towards a theory of questions. In E. N. Goody (Ed.), *Questions and politeness: Strategies in social interaction* (pp. 17-43). Cambridge, UK: Cambridge University Press.

Gottman, J. M. (1979). *Marital interaction: Experimental investigations.* New York: Academic Press.

Gottschalk, L. A., & Gleser, G. C. (1969). *The measurement of psychological states through content analysis of verbal behavior.* Berkeley: University of California Press.

Green, O. H. (1977). Semantic rules and speech acts. *Southwestern Journal of Philosophy, 8,* 141-150.

Greenberg, L. S., & Pinsof, W. M. (Eds.). (1986). *The psychotherapeutic process: A research handbook.* New York: Guilford.

Grice, H. P. (1957). Meaning. *Philosophical Review, 66,* 377-388.

Grice, H. P. (1969). Utterer's meaning and intentions. *Philosophical Review, 78,* 147-177.

Hahlweg, K., Reisner, L., Kohli, G., Vollmer, M., Schindler, L., & Revenstorf, D. (1984). Development and validity of a new system to analyze interpersonal communication (KPI). In K. Hahlweg & N. S. Jacobson (Eds.), *Marital interaction: Analysis and modification* (pp. 182-198). New York: Guilford.

Hancher, M. (1979). The classification of cooperative illocutionary acts. *Language in Society, 8,* 1-14.

Henricks, W. H., & Stiles, W. B. (1989). Verbal processes on psychological radio call-in programs: Comparison with other help-intended interactions. *Professional Psychology: Research and Practice, 20,* 315-321.

Heszen-Klemens, I., & Lapinska, E. (1984). Doctor-patient interaction, patients' health behavior and effects of treatment. *Social Science & Medicine, 19,* 9-18.

Hill, C. E. (1978). Development of a counselor verbal response category system. *Journal of Counseling Psychology, 25,* 461-468.

Hill, C. E. (1986). An overview of the Hill counselor and client verbal response modes category systems. In L. S. Greenberg & W. M. Pinsof (Eds.), *The psychotherapeutic process: A research handbook* (pp. 131-160). New York: Guilford.

Hill, C. E., Thames, T. B., & Rardin, D. K. (1979). Comparison of Rogers, Perls, and Ellis on the Hill Counselor Verbal Response Category System. *Journal of Counseling Psychology, 26,* 198-203.

Hinkle, S., Stiles, W. B., & Taylor, L. A. (1988). Verbal processes in a labour/management negotiation. *Journal of Language and Social Psychology, 7,* 123-136.

Holsti, O. (1969). *Content analysis for the social sciences.* Reading, MA: Addison-Wesley.

Hooley, J. J., & Hahlweg, K. (1989). Marital satisfaction and marital communication in German and English couples. *Behavioral Assessment, 11,* 119-133.

Hops, H., Wills, T. A., Patterson, G. R., & Weiss, R. L. (1972). *Marital interaction coding system.* Unpublished manuscript, University of Oregon, Oregon Research Institute.

Humphrey, L. L., Apple, R. F., & Kirschenbaum, D. S. (1986). Differentiating bulimic-anorexic from normal families using interpersonal and behavioral observational systems. *Journal of Consulting and Clinical Psychology, 54,* 190-195.

Inui, T. S., & Carter, W. B., with Kukull, W. A., & Haigh, V. H. (1982). Outcome-based doctor-patient interaction analysis: I. Comparison of techniques. *Medical Care, 20,* 535-549.

Ivey, A. E. (1971). *Microcounseling: Innovations in interviewing training.* Springfield, IL: Charles C. Thomas.

Jacobs, M. K., & Goodman, G. (1989). Psychology and self-help groups: Perspectives on a partnership. *American Psychologist, 44,* 536-545.

Kaplan, S. H., Greenfield, S., and Ware, J. E., Jr. (1989). Assessing the effects of physician-patient interactions on the outcomes of chronic disease. *Medical Care, 27,* 110-127.

Kiesler, D. J. (1973). *The process of psychotherapy: Empirical foundations and systems of analysis.* Chicago: Aldine.

Klein, M. H., Mathieu-Coughlan, P., & Kiesler, D. J. (1986). The experiencing scales. In L. S. Greenberg & W. M. Pinsof (Eds.), *The psychotherapeutic process: A research handbook* (pp. 21-71). New York: Guilford.

Knight, D. P. (1987). *Verbal response mode correlates of status and gender in psychotherapy.* Master's thesis, Department of Psychology, Miami University, Oxford, OH.

Labov, W., & Fanshel, D. (1977). *Therapeutic discourse: Psychotherapy as conversation.* New York: Academic Press.

Lane, T. W. (1987). *On predicting level of patient verbal involvement in a psychotherapy interview.* Manuscript submitted for publication.

Leary, M. R., Knight, P. D., & Johnson, K. A. (1987). Social anxiety and dyadic conversation: A verbal response analysis. *Journal of Social and Clinical Psychology, 5,* 34-50.

Leary, M. R., Rogers, P. A., Canfield, R. W., & Coe, C. (1986). Boredom in interpersonal encounters: Antecedents and social implications. *Journal of Personality and Social Psychology, 51,* 968-975.

Markman, H. J., Notarius, C. I., Stephen T., & Smith, R. J. (1981). Behavioral observation systems for couples: The current status. In E. E. Filsinger & R. A. Lewis (Eds.), *Assessing marriage: New behavioral approaches* (pp. 234-262). Beverly Hills, CA: Sage.

McDaniel, S. H., Stiles, W. B., & McGaughey, K. J. (1981). Correlations of male college students' verbal response mode use in psychotherapy with measures of psychological disturbance and psychotherapy outcome. *Journal of Consulting and Clinical Psychology, 49,* 571-582.

McGaughey, K. J., & Stiles, W. B. (1983). Courtroom interrogation of rape victims: Verbal response mode use by attorneys and witnesses during direct examination vs. cross-examination. *Journal of Applied Social Psychology, 13,* 78-87.

McLaughlin, M. L., & Cody, M. J. (1982). Awkward silences: Behavioral antecedents and consequences of the conversational lapse. *Human Communication Research, 8,* 299-316.

McMullen, L. M. (1987, June). *Speech styles of females in mixed-sex versus same-sex dyadic interactions.* Paper presented at the Canadian Psychological Association Convention, Vancouver, British Columbia.

McMullen, L. M., & Krahn, E. E. (1985). Effects of status and solidarity of familiarity in written communication. *Language and Speech, 28,* 391-402.

McMullen, L. M., & Murray, W. A. (1986). Effects of status and solidarity on familiarity in verbal behaviour. *Journal of Language and Social Psychology, 5,* 49-52.

Meeuwesen, L. (Ed. and trans.). (1984). *Handleiding voor een taxonomie van verbale antwoordwijzen: Een beschrijving en bewerking van Stiles "Verbal Response Modes (V.R.M.)."* Vakgroep Klinische Psychologie, University of Nijmegen, Nijmegen, The Netherlands.

Meeuwesen, L. (1988). *Spreekuur of zwijguur: Somatische fixatie en sekse-asymmetrie tijdens het medisch consult.* Den Haag: Cip-Gegevens Koninklijke Bibliotheek.

Meeuwesen, L., Schaap, C., & van der Staak, C. (1991). Verbal analysis of doctor-patient communication. *Social Science & Medicine, 32,* 1143-1150.

Millar, F. E., & Rogers, L. E. (1976). A relational approach to interpersonal communication. In G. R. Miller (Ed.), *Explorations in interpersonal communication* (pp. 87-103). Beverly Hills, CA: Sage.

Miller, N. L., & Stiles, W. B. (1986). Verbal familiarity in American presidential nomination acceptance speeches and inaugural addresses (1920-1981). *Social Psychology Quarterly, 49,* 72-81.

Morley, I. E., & Stephenson, G. M. (1977). *The social psychology of bargaining.* London: Allen & Unwin.

Notarius, C. I., & Markman, H. J. (1981). The couples' interaction coding system. In E. E. Filsinger & R. A. Lewis (Eds.), *Assessing marriage: New behavioral approaches* (pp. 112-127). Beverly Hills, CA: Sage.

Ohmann, R. (1972). Instrumental style: Notes on the theory of speech as action. In B. B. Kachru & H. F. W. Stahlke (Eds.), *Current trends in stylistics.* Edmonton, Alberta: Linguistics Research, Inc.

Orlinsky, D. E., & Howard, K. I. (1986). Process and outcome in psychotherapy. In S. L. Garfield & A. E. Bergin (Eds.), *Handbook of psychotherapy and behavior change* (3rd ed., pp. 311-381). New York: John Wiley.

Orth, J. E., Stiles, W. B., Scherwitz, L., Hennrikus, D., & Vallbona, C. (1987). Patient exposition and provider explanation in routine interviews and hypertensive patients' blood pressure control. *Health Psychology, 6,* 29-42.

Packer, M. J., & Addison, R. B. (Eds.). (1989). *Entering the circle: Hermeneutic investigation in psychology.* Albany: State University of New York Press.

Perls, F. S. (1969). *Gestalt therapy verbatim.* Lafayette, CA: Real People Press.

Perls, F. S., Hefferline, R. F., & Goodman, P. (1951). *Gestalt therapy.* New York: Julian.

Pinsof, W. M. (1986). The process of family therapy: The development of the family therapist coding system. In L. S. Greenberg & W. M. Pinsof (Eds.), *The psychotherapeutic process: A research handbook* (pp. 201-284). New York: Guilford.

Porter, E. H., Jr. (1942a). The development and evaluation of a measure of counseling interview procedures: I. The development. *Educational and Psychological Measurement, 3,* 105-126.

Porter, E. H., Jr. (1942b). The development and evaluation of a measure of counseling interview procedures: II. The evaluation. *Educational and Psychological Measurement, 3,* 215-238.

Potter, J., & Wetherell, M. (1987). *Discourse and social psychology: Beyond attitudes and behaviour.* London: Sage.

Premo, B. E., & Stiles, W. B. (1983). Familiarity in verbal interactions of married couples versus strangers. *Journal of Social and Clinical Psychology, 1,* 209-230.

Putnam, S. M., & Stiles, W. B. (1991). *Verbal exchanges in medical interviews: Implications and innovations.* Manuscript submitted for publication.

Putnam, S. M., Stiles, W. B., Jacob, M. C., & James, S. A. (1985). Patient exposition and physician explanation in initial medical interviews and outcomes of clinic visits. *Medical Care, 23,* 74-83.

Putnam, S. M., Stiles, W. B., Jacob, M. C., & James, S. A. (1988). Teaching the medical interview: An intervention study. *Journal of General Internal Medicine, 3,* 38-47.

Rak, D. S., & McMullen, L. M. (1987). Sex-role stereotyping in television commercials: A verbal response mode and content analysis. *Canadian Journal of Behavioral Science, 19,* 25-39.

Robin, A. L., & Weiss, J. G. (1980). Criterion-related validity of behavioral and self-report measures of problem-solving communication skills in distressed and non-distressed parent-adolescent dyads. *Behavioral Assessment, 2,* 339-352.

Rogers, C. R. (1951). *Client-centered therapy. Boston: Houghton Mifflin.*

Rogers, L. E., Courtright, J. A., & Millar, F. E. (1980). Message control intensity: rationale and preliminary findings. *Communication Monographs, 47,* 201-219.

Rogers, L. E., & Farace, R. V. (1975). Analysis of relational communication in dyads: New measurement procedures. *Human Communication Research, 1,* 222-239.

Roter, D. L. (1977). Patient participation in the patient-provider interaction. *Health Education Monographs, 5,* 281-315.

Russell, R. L. (1986). Verbal response modes as species of speech acts?: An unhappy case of an interdisciplinary merger. *Explorations in Knowledge, 3,* 14-24.

Russell, R. L. (Ed.). (1987). *Language in psychotherapy: Strategies of discovery.* New York: Plenum.

Russell, R. L. (1988). A new classification scheme for studies of verbal behavior in psychotherapy. *Psychotherapy, 25,* 51-58.

Russell, R. L., & Stiles, W. B. (1979). Categories for classifying language in psychotherapy. *Psychological Bulletin, 86,* 404-419.

Sackett, G. P. (1979). The lag sequential analysis of contingency and cyclicity in behavioral interaction research. In J. Osofsky (Ed.), *Handbook of infant development* (pp. 623-649). New York: John Wiley.

Sackett, G. P. (1987). Analysis of sequential social interaction data: Some issues, recent developments, and a causal inference model. In J. Osofsky (Ed.), *Handbook of infant development* (2nd ed., pp. 855-878). New York: John Wiley.

Sacks, H., Schegloff, E. A., & Jefferson, G. A. (1974). A simplest systematics for the organization of turn-taking in dyadic conversation. *Language, 50,* 697-735.

Sarbin, T. R. (Ed.). (1986). *Narrative psychology: The storied nature of human conduct.* New York: Praeger.

Schegloff, E. A. (1987). Analyzing single episodes of interaction: An exercise in conversation analysis. *Social Psychology Quarterly, 50,* 101-114.

Searle, J. R. (1969). *Speech acts: An essay in philosophy of language.* Cambridge, UK: Cambridge University Press.

Searle, J. R. (1975). Indirect speech acts. In P. Cole & J. L. Morgan (Eds.), *Syntax and semantics, vol. 3: Speech acts.* New York: Academic Press.

Searle, J. R. (1976). A classification of illocutionary acts. *Language in Society, 5,* 1-23.

Shrout, P. E., & Fleiss, J. L. (1979). Intraclass correlations: Uses in assessing rater reliability. *Psychological Bulletin, 86,* 420-428.

Sloan, W. W., Jr., & Solano, C. H. (1984). The conversational styles of lonely males with strangers and roommates. *Personality and Social Psychology Bulletin, 10,* 293-301.

Snyder, W. U. (1945). An investigation of the nature of non-directive psychotherapy. *Journal of General Psychology, 33,* 193-223.

Snyder, W. U. (1987). Snyder's classification system for therapeutic interviews. In R. L. Russell (Ed.), *Language in psychotherapy: Strategies of discovery* (pp. 109-129). New York: Plenum.

Solomon, M. R. (1981). *Dress for success: Clothing appropriateness and the efficacy of role behavior.* Ph.D. thesis, University of North Carolina at Chapel Hill, 1981. *Dissertation Abstracts International, 42,* 2026B. (University Microfilms No. 8125621)

Stewart, M. A. (1983). Patient characteristics which are related to the doctor-patient interaction. *Family Practice, 1,* 30-36.

Stewart, M. A. (1984). What is a successful doctor-patient interview? A study of interactions and outcome. *Social Science & Medicine, 19,* 167-175.

Stiles, W. B. (1975). *Listener response modes rating manual.* Unpublished manuscript, University of North Carolina, Chapel Hill.

Stiles, W. B. (1978a). *Manual for a taxonomy of verbal response modes.* Chapel Hill: Institute for Research in Social Science, University of North Carolina at Chapel Hill.

Stiles, W. B. (1978b). Verbal response modes and dimensions of interpersonal roles: A method of discourse analysis. *Journal of Personality and Social Psychology, 36,* 693-703.

Stiles, W. B. (1978-1979). Discourse analysis and the doctor-patient relationship. *International Journal of Psychiatry in Medicine, 9,* 263-274.

Stiles, W. B. (1979). Verbal response modes and psychotherapeutic technique. *Psychiatry, 42,* 49-62.

Stiles, W. B. (1980). Comparison of dimensions derived from rating versus coding of dialogue. *Journal of Personality and Social Psychology, 38,* 359-374.

Stiles, W. B. (1981). Classification of intersubjective illocutionary acts. *Language in Society, 10,* 227-249.

Stiles, W. B. (1982). Psychotherapeutic process: Is there a common core? In L. E. Abt & I. R. Stuart (Eds.), *The newer therapies: A sourcebook* (pp. 4-17). New York: Van Nostrand Reinhold.

Stiles, W. B. (1984a). Client disclosure and psychotherapy session evaluations. *British Journal of Clinical Psychology, 23,* 311-312.

Stiles, W. B. (1984b, June). *Familiarity and felt importance.* Paper presented at the Fourth Invitational Conference on Natural Interaction, Kill Devil Hills, North Carolina.

Stiles, W. B. (1985). Measuring roles in service encounters: The verbal exchange structure. In J. A. Czepiel, M. R. Solomon, & C. Surprenant (Eds.), *The service encounter* (pp. 213-223). New York: Lexington.

Stiles, W. B. (1986a). Development of taxonomy of verbal response modes. In L. S. Greenberg & W. M. Pinsof (Eds.), *The psychotherapeutic process: A research handbook* (pp. 161-199). New York: Guilford.

Stiles, W. B. (1986b). Levels of intended meaning of utterances. *British Journal of Clinical Psychology, 25,* 213-222.

Stiles, W. B. (1987a). "I have to talk to somebody." A fever model of disclosure. In V. J. Derlega & J. H. Berg (Eds.), *Self-disclosure: Theory, research, and therapy* (pp. 257-282). New York: Plenum.

Stiles, W. B. (1987b). Some intentions are observable. *Journal of Counseling Psychology,* *34,* 236-239.

Stiles, W. B. (1987c). Verbal response modes as intersubjective categories. In R. L. Russell (Ed.), *Language in psychotherapy: Strategies of discovery* (pp. 131-170). New York: Plenum.

Stiles, W. B. (1988). Psychotherapy process-outcome correlations may be misleading. *Psychotherapy, 25,* 27-35.

Stiles, W. B. (1989). Evaluating medical interview process components: Null correlations with outcomes may be misleading. *Medical Care, 27,* 212-220.

Stiles, W. B. (1990). *Narrative in psychological research.* (Occasional Papers in Psychology: Visiting Fellowship Series No. 1. ISSN 0110-6961). Palmerston North, New Zealand: Department of Psychology, Massey University.

Stiles, W. B. (1991). *Quality control in qualitative research.* Manuscript submitted for publication.

Stiles, W. B., Au, M. L., Martello, M. A., & Perlmutter, J. A. (1983). American campaign oratory: Verbal response mode use by candidates in the 1980 American presidential primaries. *Social Behavior and Personality, 11,* 39-43.

Stiles, W. B., McDaniel, S. H., & McGaughey, K. (1979). Verbal response mode correlates of experiencing. *Journal of Consulting and Clinical Psychology, 47,* 795-797.

Stiles, W. B., Orth, J. E., Scherwitz, L., Hennrikus, D., & Vallbona, C. (1984). Role behaviors in routine medical interviews with hypertensive patients: A repertoire of verbal exchanges. *Social Psychology Quarterly, 47,* 244-254.

Stiles, W. B., & Putnam, S. M. (1989). Analysis of verbal and nonverbal behavior in doctor-patient encounters. In M. Stewart & D. Roter (Eds.), *Communicating with medical patients* (pp. 211-222). Newbury Park, CA: Sage.

Stiles, W. B., & Putnam, S. M. (in press[a]). Categories for coding medical interviews: A metaclassification. In M. Lipkin, Jr., S. M. Putnam, & A. Lazare (Eds.), *The medical interview.* New York: Springer-Verlag.

Stiles, W. B., & Putnam, S. M. (in press[b]). Verbal exchanges in medical interviews: Concepts and measurement. *Social Science & Medicine.*

Stiles, W. B., Putnam, S. M., & Jacob, M. C. (1982). Verbal exchange structure of initial medical interviews. *Health Psychology, 1,* 315-336.

Stiles, W. B., Putnam, S. M., & Jacob, M. C. (1984, May). *Question-asking by patients in initial medical interviews: Sequential analysis of verbal antecedents and consequences.* Paper presented at the Midwestern Psychological Association Convention, Chicago.

Stiles, W. B., Putnam, S. M., & Jacob, M. C. (1986). Understanding patient-physician communication. In R. J. Brook, G. C. Arnold, T. H. Hassard, & R. M. Pringle (Eds.), *The fascination of statistics* (pp. 123-137). New York: Marcel Dekker.

Stiles, W. B., Putnam, S. M., James, S. A., & Wolf, M. H. (1979). Dimensions of patient and physician roles in medical screening interviews. *Social Science & Medicine, 13A,* 335-341.

Stiles, W. B., Putnam, S. M., Wolf, M. H., & James, S. A. (1979a). Interaction exchange structure and patient satisfaction with medical interviews. *Medical Care, 17,* 667-681.

Stiles, W. B., Putnam, S. M., Wolf, M. H., & James, S. A. (1979b). Verbal response mode profiles of patients and physicians in medical screening interviews. *Journal of Medical Education, 54,* 81-89.

Stiles, W. B., & Shapiro, D. A. (1989). Abuse of the drug metaphor in psychotherapy process-outcome research. *Clinical Psychology Review, 9,* 521-543.

Stiles, W. B., & Shapiro, D. A. (in press). Disabuse of the drug metaphor: Psychotherapy process-outcome correlations. *Journal of Consulting and Clinical Psychology.*

Stiles, W. B., Shapiro, D. A., & Elliott, R. (1986). Are all psychotherapies equivalent? *American Psychologist, 41,* 165-180.

Stiles, W. B., Shapiro, D. A., & Firth-Cozens, J. A. (1988). Verbal response mode use in contrasting psychotherapies: A within-subjects comparison. *Journal of Consulting and Clinical Psychology, 56,* 727-733.

Stiles, W. B., Shapiro, D. A., & Firth-Cozens, J. A. (1989). Therapist differences in the use of verbal response mode forms and intents. *Psychotherapy, 26,* 314-322.

Stiles, W. B., Shuster, P. L., Barth, M. G., Joseph, C., Kappus, B., Mason, L., Zimmerman, K. J., Lucic, K. S., & Harrigan, J. A. (1989, August). Verbal response mode use during anxiety induction. In R. Rosenthal (Chairperson), *Verbal and nonverbal analysis of anxiety.* Symposium presented at the American Psychological Association Convention, New Orleans, LA.

Stiles, W. B., Shuster, P. L., & Harrigan, J. A. (1989, May). *Disclosure and anxiety: A test of the fever model.* Paper presented at the Midwestern Psychological Association Convention, Chicago.

Stiles, W. B., & Sultan, F. E. (1979). Verbal response mode use by clients in psychotherapy. *Journal of Consulting and Clinical Psychology, 47,* 611-613.

Stiles, W. B., Waszak, C. S., & Barton, L. R. (1979). Professorial presumptuousness in verbal interactions with university students. *Journal of Experimental Social Psychology, 15,* 158-169.

Stiles, W. B., & White, M. L. (1981). Parent-child interaction in the laboratory: Effects of role, task, and child behavior pathology on verbal response mode use. *Journal of Abnormal Child Psychology, 9,* 229-241.

Strupp, H. H. (1955). An objective comparison of Rogerian and psychoanalytic techniques. *Journal of Consulting Psychology, 19,* 1-7.

Strupp, H. H. (1957a). A multidimensional system for analyzing psychotherapeutic techniques. *Psychiatry, 20,* 293-306.

Strupp, H. H. (1957b). A multidimensional analysis of techniques in brief psychotherapy. *Psychiatry, 20,* 387-397.

Strupp, H. H. (1957c). A multidimensional comparison of therapists in analytic and client-centered therapy. *Journal of Consulting Psychology, 21,* 301-308.

Suh, C. S., Strupp, H. H., & O'Malley, S. S. (1986). The Vanderbilt process measures: The Vanderbilt Psychotherapy Process Scale (VPPS) and the Vanderbilt Negative Indicators Scale (VNIS). In L. S. Greenberg & W. M. Pinsof (Eds.), *The psychotherapeutic process: A research handbook* (pp. 285-324). New York: Guilford.

Tinsley, H.E.A, & Weiss, D. J. (1975). Interrater reliability and agreement of subjective judgments. *Journal of Counseling Psychology, 22,* 358-376.

Vendler, Z. (1972). *Res Cogitans: An essay in rational psychology.* Ithaca, NY: Cornell University Press.

Verschueren, J. (1983). Review of *Speech act classification: A study in the lexical analysis of English speech activity verbs* by Thomas Ballmer and Waltraud Brennstuhl. *Language, 59,* 168-175.

Viney, L. L. (1983). The assessment of psychological states through content analysis of verbal communications. *Psychological Bulletin, 94,* 542-563.

Walcott, C., & Hopmann, P. T. (1975). Interaction analysis and bargaining behavior. *Experimental Study of Politics, 4,* 1-19.

Waung, M. P., Knight, D. P., Lowry, C., & Stiles, W. B. (1987, July). *Gender and the use of presumptuous verbal response modes.* Poster session, Third International Conference on Social Psychology and Language, Bristol, UK.

Wigutoff, D. H. (1988). *The language of change: A sequential analysis of matched mode utterances of therapists and clients as a test of the effect of congruence and responsibility in the process of psychotherapy.* Ph.D. thesis, University of Nevada, Reno.

Winefield, H. R., Bassett, D. L., Chandler, M. A., & Proske, I. (1987). Process in psychotherapy as decreasing asymmetry between patient and therapist: Evidence from the verbal interaction. *American Journal of Psychotherapy, 41*, 117-126.

Index of Coded Examples

General Index

227

About the Author

William B. Stiles is a Professor of Clinical Psychology at Miami University in Oxford, Ohio. After he received his Ph.D. in psychology from UCLA in 1972, he was on the Psychology faculty at the University of North Carolina at Chapel Hill. He has also held visiting positions in the Psychology Department at Massy University in Palmerston North, New Zealand, and in the MRC/ESRC Social and Applied Psychology Unit at the University of Sheffield in the United Kingdom. His research interests include verbal interaction processes in psychotherapy, medical interviews, and a variety of other kinds of conversation.